Communications
in Computer and Information Science 126

Stefan De Wannemacker   Geraldine Clarebout
Patrick De Causmaecker (Eds.)

Interdisciplinary Approaches to Adaptive Learning

A Look at the Neighbours

First International Conference
on Interdisciplinary Research on Technology,
Education and Communication, ITEC 2010
Kortrijk, Belgium, May 25-27, 2010
Revised Selected Papers

 Springer

Volume Editors

Stefan De Wannemacker
Katholieke Universiteit Leuven, Kortrijk, Belgium
E-mail: stefan.dewannemacker@kuleuven-kortrijk.be

Geraldine Clarebout
Katholieke Universiteit Leuven, Kortrijk, Belgium
E-mail: geraldine.clarebout@kuleuven-kortrijk.be

Patrick De Causmaecker
Katholieke Universiteit Leuven, Kortrijk, Belgium
E-mail: patrick.decausmaecker@kuleuven-kortrijk.be

ISSN 1865-0929   e-ISSN 1865-0937
ISBN 978-3-642-20073-1   e-ISBN 978-3-642-20074-8
DOI 10.1007/978-3-642-20074-8
Springer Heidelberg Dordrecht London New York

Library of Congress Control Number: 2011925897

CR Subject Classification (1998): K.3, I.2.6, I.2, H.5, J.1, K.4, J.3

Typesetting: Camera-ready by author, data conversion by Scientific Publishing Services, Chennai, India

Printed on acid-free paper

Springer is part of Springer Science+Business Media (www.springer.com)

Preface

ITEC 2010, the First International Conference on Interdisciplinary Research on Technology, Education and Communication, was held during May 25–27, 2010 in Kortrijk, Belgium. This meeting, organized by the interdiscplinary research group itec, was the first in a series of conferences that will serve as a forum for an international communitiy of researchers. We brought together researchers that interacted and exchanged ideas within the fields of computer sciences, applied linguistics, methodology and educational technology.

In this first conference, we received an excellent number of 38 submissions. After a thorough reviewing phase we accepted 21 contributions. The authors of the accepted papers were invited to present their work at the conference and to submit an extended paper. From these extended papers, 11 were accepted for publication in the conference proceedings.

The conference program was enriched significantly by keynote presentations of renowned experts in their respective domains. Peter Brusilovsky from the University of Pittsburgh spoke about "Addicitive links: Adaptive Navigation Support in College-Level Courses," Theo Eggen and Bernard Veldkamp from the University of Twente gave a presentation on "The Merits of Computerized Adaptive Testing for Computer-assisted Learning" and Fridolin Wild from the Open University UK spoke about "Science 2.0: The Open Orchestration of Knowledge Creation." These different perspectives were a real value to the interdisciplinary nature of the conference.

We believe this first edition to have been a successful event that stimulated collaborative work in this field and we would like to express our thanks to the authors for submitting their work to ITEC 2010, to the invited speakers for their broader enrichment which stimulated the discussion significantly, and to all the members of the Program Committee for their help in the reviewing process. Last but not least, we thank the local organization for all the technical and non-technical support. The organization of such an event, especially for the first time, would not have been possible without this mostly voluntary work.

December 2010

Stefan De Wannemacker
Geraldine Clarebout
Patrick De Causmaecker

Organization

Organizing Committee

Geraldine Clarebout	itec K.U. Leuven, Belgium
Patrick De Causmaecker	itec K.U. Leuven, Belgium
Piet Desmet	itec K.U. Leuven, Belgium
Rik Van de Walle	Multimedia Lab UGent, Belgium
Wim Van Den Noortgate	itec K.U. Leuven, Belgium

Advisory Committee

Yolande Berbers	K.U. Leuven, Belgium
Geraldine Clarebout	itec K.U. Leuven, Belgium
Patrick De Causmaecker	itec K.U. Leuven, Belgium
Stefan De Wannemacker	itec K.U. Leuven, Belgium
Piet Desmet	itec K.U. Leuven, Belgium
Erik Duval	K.U. Leuven, Belgium
Jan Elen	K.U. Leuven, Belgium
Rianne Janssen	K.U. Leuven, Belgium
Sien Moens	K.U. Leuven, Belgium
Hans Paulussen	itec K.U. Leuven, Belgium
Fred Truyen	K.U. Leuven, Belgium
Rik Van de Walle	Multimedia Lab UGent, Belgium
Wim Van Den Noortgate	itec K.U. Leuven, Belgium

Program Committee and Referees

Yolande Berbers	K.U. Leuven, Belgium
Peter Brusilovsky	University of Pittsburgh, USA
Iona Ciuciu	Vrije Universiteit Brussel, Belgium
Geraldine Clarebout	itec K.U. Leuven, Belgium
Wilfried Cools	itec K.U. Leuven, Belgium
Frederik Cornillie	itec K.U. Leuven, Belgium
Patrick De Causmaecker	itec K.U. Leuven, Belgium
Stefan De Wannemacker	itec K.U. Leuven, Belgium
Piet Desmet	itec K.U. Leuven, Belgium
Erik Duval	K.U. Leuven, Belgium
Theo Eggen	University of Twente, The Netherlands

Table of Contents

Adaptive Corrective Feedback in Second Language Learning

Bart Penning de Vries, Catia Cucchiarini, Helmer Strik, and Roeland van Hout

Centre for Language and Speech Technology, Radboud University Nijmegen, The Netherlands
{b.penningdevries,c.cucchiarini,w.strik,r.vanhout}@let.ru.nl

Abstract. The role of corrective feedback (CF) in second language acquisition has received much attention, and it is still a topical issue. Studies on the effectiveness of CF have produced mixed results. An essential problem seems to be that most studies on CF do not take account of individual differences, even though there are clear indications that individual characteristics influence the effectiveness of CF. This points to the necessity of developing research paradigms for CF that can take account of individual learner variation and that can adapt to the learner's needs and preferences. In this paper we suggest using a CALL system that exploits automatic speech recognition (ASR) and that is designed to adapt to individual learner differences.

Keywords: Second language acquisition (SLA), language learning, corrective feedback, individual differences, automatic speech recognition (ASR), computer assisted language learning (CALL).

1 Introduction

The term corrective feedback (CF) has been used in the literature on second language acquisition (SLA) to refer to "any indication to the learners that their use of the target language is incorrect" [1]. As these authors explain: "This includes various responses that the learners receive. When a language learner says, 'He go to school everyday', corrective feedback can be explicit, for example, 'no, you should say goes, not go' or implicit 'yes he goes to school every day', and may or may not include metalinguistic information, for example, 'Don't forget to make the verb agree with the subject'" [1]. Further examples of different types of CF are provided in section 2.1 below. Although intuitively one might think that correcting errors will help improve language performance, so far this has not unequivocally demonstrated in the literature. Proponents of nativist theories claim that second language (L2) learning is driven by exposure to positive evidence and comprehensible input, without any need for CF [2, 3], with Truscott [4] taking the extreme position that CF can even be harmful.

Nevertheless, there are numerous examples of L2 learners immersed in L2 surroundings, whose language proficiency stopped developing well before they fully acquired the target L2, despite ample (positive) language input [5]. This suggests that exposure and input alone are not sufficient for high-level L2 learning (e.g., [6]). This seems to apply particularly to adult L2 learners[1], who are already committed to their first language (L1) [7].

---

[1] Throughout this paper, L2 learning and acquisition refers to adult L2 learning and acquisition.

S. De Wannemacker, G. Clarebout, P. De Causmaecker (Eds.): ITEC 2010, CCIS 126, pp. 1–14, 2011.
© Springer-Verlag Berlin Heidelberg 2011

Empirical studies on the effectiveness of CF have produced mixed results. This has to do in part with the fact that teachers' CF turns out to be inconsistent (within and between studies), especially in oral (classroom) sessions of L2 learning [8, 9, 10]. For instance, teachers may correct a specific error by a learner the first time, but not react at other instances. Relevant conclusions are that CF, to be effective, should be unambiguous, consistent [11], intensive [12], and should provide opportunities for self-repair and modified output [13, 14, 15]. Such conditions cannot easily be met, if at all, in natural interactions or classroom situations.

Another essential conclusion is that most studies on CF do not take account of individual differences, but discuss CF effects on groups as a whole, thus assuming that all learners use CF similarly, whereas there are indications that the effectiveness of CF is dependent on individual characteristics (see section 3.3). The motivation for focusing on group settings and specifically on classroom settings is that these are informative about the overall educational value of CF [16]. However, this view seems particularly tied to traditional approaches to L2 learning and ignores recent developments in CALL and language and speech technology that offer new opportunities for studying the effectiveness of CF and for implementing CF in more individualized, adaptive settings.

Can we develop a research paradigm for CF that can take account of individual characteristics and relates CF effects to those characteristics? To meet the learner's needs and preferences, adaptive learning conditions are required to maximize CF effectiveness. In this paper we propose an adaptive approach that uses a CALL system based on speech technology. In section 2 we provide background information on the notion of corrective feedback in second language acquisition. In section 3 we review relevant literature on CF and indicate issues that could not be properly addressed so far. In section 4 we explain how a CALL system with integrated speech technology can be employed to assess the role of CF in L2 learning in relation to individual learner variables. Section 5 summarizes the main conclusions.

2   CF in Second Language Learning

Nativist theories of L2 acquisition claim that language learning requires only language input, and that L2 acquisition is similar to first language (L1) acquisition (e.g., [2]). The main arguments that CF cannot be effective according to these theories are (a) that language acquisition is an unconscious process, where CF requires conscious processing, and (b) that CF is negative evidence, whereas language acquisition is based on positive evidence, i.e. language input. Theories in favor of CF call either of these arguments into question. Though L1 acquisition can be assumed to be largely an unconscious process as infants lack the cognitive development required [17], it is not conclusively shown that CF (which is consciously processed) is irrelevant for L1 acquisition (e.g., [18]). Moreover, even if conscious learning does not benefit L1 acquisition, the further developed cognitive abilities of adults may still enable consciously processed CF to benefit L2 acquisition. Even more importantly, empirical evidence abundantly shows that adult L2 learners often do not reach a high level of L2 proficiency. That means that there are essential differences in acquiring a L1 and a L2. Even if CF is not effective at all in L1 acquisition, it may be effective in L2 acquisition.

2.1 Types of Corrective Feedback

Lyster and Ranta [19] distinguish six types of feedback in their often-cited classroom observation study:

1. *Explicit feedback*: teacher provides the correct form and clearly indicates that what the student said was incorrect.
2. *Recasts*: teacher reformulates all or part of a student's utterance, minus the error.
3. *Clarification request*: teacher formulates a question indicating that the utterance has been unclear or ill-formed and that a repetition or reformulation is required.
4. *Metalinguistic feedback:* the teacher response contains either comments, information, or questions related to the well-formedness of the student's utterance, without explicitly providing the correct form.
5. *Elicitation*: teachers try to elicit the correct form by asking for completion of a sentence, or asking questions, or asking for a reformulation.
6. *Repetition*: teacher repeats the erroneous utterance in isolation.

Types (2) and (6) provide implicit feedback: it is up to the learner to notice that an error was made. The other types are explicit in indicating that an error occurred. The categories are not as clear cut as may seem, since there may be degrees of explicitness or implicitness. Additionally, CF may be accompanied by visual cues or intonation. Moreover, the interpretation of the distinction relates to the setting of the feedback, e.g., implicit recasts may be argued to be explicit in formal classroom settings [20]. The exact definition of what CF type is studied is often lacking in studies (see [21] for a discussion), which complicates comparing and synthesizing results [22].

2.2 Explicit and Implicit Knowledge and Learning

Two types of language knowledge are distinguished in the literature: explicit knowledge and implicit knowledge. Explicit knowledge refers to knowing rules, while implicit knowledge involves using a rule without being aware of the rule. Explicit knowledge is open to conscious inspection, whereas implicit knowledge is not. The distinction is related to the one between declarative knowledge and procedural knowledge in cognitive psychology [23]. The acquisition of cognitive skills has a declarative and a procedural stage. Processing in the declarative stage is slow and controlled, whereas processing in the procedural stage is fast and beyond active control. Through frequent use, the facts and rules acquired in the declarative stage become automatic procedures.

As explained by DeKeyser [24] "automatized knowledge is not exactly the same as implicit knowledge. While implicit knowledge or implicit memory is always defined with reference to lack of consciousness or awareness ... absence of awareness is not a requirement for automaticity". He further explains how it is possible to have knowledge that is implicit but not automatic, for instance when learners make many errors and fluency is low, and to have knowledge that is automatic but not implicit, in the case of fluent learners that make few errors but are still conscious of rules, for instance language teachers or linguists. Although declarative and procedural knowledge are not exactly the same as explicit and implicit knowledge, they are highly similar and in this paper they will be treated as such for practical purposes.

Closely related, but also clearly different, is the distinction between explicit and implicit learning. Where explicit learning involves conscious intention to find out whether the input information contains regularities or specific elements, implicit learning is input processing on an unconscious level without such an intention [17]. Krashen [2] argues that language proficiency is based on implicit knowledge of the language, and that only implicit learning can increase the learner's proficiency. Implicit learning takes place, he writes, when a learner is exposed to comprehensible language input. Since CF appeals to explicit learning, it is assumed to have no effect on L2 development.

Though there is agreement among SLA researchers that language proficiency is based on implicit knowledge, there is disagreement on whether and how explicit knowledge can contribute to language proficiency. The core issue is whether explicit knowledge stays separate from implicit knowledge, or whether there is an interface and some kind of exchange.

2.3 Interface

Krashen [2] argues that there is no interface between implicit and explicit knowledge. Proponents of the weak interface position [25] argue that conscious learning can, under specific conditions, further the acquisition of implicit knowledge. If the learner's attention is explicitly directed to features of the L2, this knowledge will first be stored as explicit knowledge, but it may under specific circumstances become implicit, for instance by (repetitively) applying explicit knowledge in production [26]. Proponents of the strong interface position argue that implicit knowledge can gradually be formed from explicit knowledge, without any further constraints [27].

2.4 Noticing

Schmidt's Noticing Hypothesis [28] claims that, for learning to take place, a learner must be consciously aware of the difference between his/her rendering of the L2 and the target L2. However, some features of the target language may be difficult to perceive in native speech (e.g. phonetically reduced, or semantically redundant morphology) [29], causing learners not to hear and notice them in their input. In interaction, for example, the conversation partner may only break the flow of conversation to correct an error if the meaning of the speaker is not understood. While the level of conscious awareness for noticing is debated (e.g., [25]), the assumption that noticing a feature in the input is a first step in language acquisition is shared by several researchers (see [30]) for an overview). This suggests a potentially important role for CF to facilitate noticing and focusing learner attention on errors and correct L2 forms. Since exposure to L2 will not automatically guarantee this kind of awareness, CF must come into play to bring learners to focus on language-specific and individual problems and (indirectly) stimulate them to attempt self-improvement [31, 14].

2.5 Learner Differences

The outcome of L2 learning may vary among learners and can result both in high proficiency and low proficiency speakers. Other than L1 acquisition that leads to uniform success, it seems that contextual factors and individual differences have a greater influence in L2 learning [32] than in L1 learning.

In an overview of individual differences in L2 acquisition, [35] identifies five main concepts that predict L2 learning success: motivation, personality, aptitude, learning style, and language learning strategies. Additional variables such as anxiety, creativity, learner beliefs, self-esteem, and willingness to communicate are mentioned but are said to fall under the aspects of personality (anxiety and creativity under motivation or personality), or are in need of more research to determine their exact role and nature. On another level, age and gender are also found to influence L2 learning [16]. Though clearly age and gender are learner differences, they are separate because they interact with each of the five psychological factors. Learner differences are good predictors of L2 success according to [35], but at the same time the characteristics are difficult to pin down in an exact definition. This complicates the theoretical discussion of these variables, but in (educational) practice these factors have been found to influence learning. The importance of individual differences is currently widely recognized in educational contexts and "a great deal of research has been conducted in educational psychology on how to adapt instruction to the strengths weaknesses and preferences of the learners" [35]. In light of the influence of learner differences on L2 learning, CF, and the type and manner in which CF is provided, is likely to affect each learner differently (see for a discussion of CF types, 3.3.). Therefore, it seems that L2 learning could be improved if the learner received optimal CF, i.e. CF adapted to the learner characteristics.

What should be noted, however, is that since many learner characteristics have an influence on language learning, it also becomes necessary to take into account the context of language learning. The setting and situation of language learning will interact with the learner characteristics [35, 20] and should be considered.

3 Research on Corrective Feedback

As explained above, theories of L2 learning make different predictions about the role of CF in language acquisition. The theories have had their influence on language pedagogy (e.g., Krashen's influential comprehensible input theory caused many language teachers to focus mainly on communication), but in turn, pedagogical practices inform theories on the effect of instruction on L2 learning (e.g., [37]). Despite many empirical findings with respect to CF effectiveness, these findings are difficult to combine to support one particular view on the role of CF. In this section we look at CF research so far, and the reasons why CF research has not yet provided conclusive results.

3.1 Overview of CF Research

In a meta-analysis of 49 studies on CF (classroom, laboratory, interaction studies), Norris and Ortega [22] found that these studies collectively suggest that CF has a positive effect on L2 learning. However, in their discussion, they raise several issues with respect to research methodology, one important issue being that several experiments were found to test for explicit knowledge, yet made claims about implicit knowledge. They make several recommendations for improving research practice, such as to reduce the number of variables and to design experiments with replication in mind.

Several meta-analyses of CF studies [22, 38, 39, 16] suggest that CF is effective, and that explicit CF is more effective that implicit CF (types of CF are discussed below). However, caution should be taken when interpreting these results due to different definitions, different operationalizations, and different measures of CF effectiveness adopted in CF studies [21, 16]. Additionally, determining which type of knowledge (i.e. explicit or implicit) is responsible for a learner's performance on pre- and posttests, remains problematic [40] as well as establishing to what extent learning effects are durable beyond the post-test period [41].

Another problem for CF research is variation between individual learners and teachers. For instance, in classroom settings, teachers may have difficulty delivering CF following specific linguistic targets in a consistent manner [21]. Arguably, therefore, studies of CF produce varying results, because "in real classrooms, students rarely get much, if any, individualized attention, and corrective feedback, if provided, is usually given ad hoc, covering a wide range of interlanguage constructions" [12].

Overall, then, research suggests that CF is potentially effective for L2 learning. However, the studies fail to be conclusive due to variability between studies, the variables under study, and uncertainty of outcome measures. Studies on CF should therefore aim to deliver CF in a controlled manner, and be rigorously defined so that replication of the study is possible, to enable cross-comparison and synthesis across experiments.

3.2   Effects of Different Types of Corrective Feedback

The exact definition of what type of CF is studied is often lacking in studies (see [21] for discussion), which complicates comparing and synthesizing results [22]. In observation studies of CF in the classroom, recasts turned out to be by far the most frequent technique for error correction [14, 19, 20]. Compared to the more explicit ways of giving CF that halt the conversation to point to language form (e.g., L: 'the man *goed* to the market', T: 'No, that is incorrect. The man went'), the recast causes less learner anxiety and does not disrupt the flow of communication (L: 'the man *goed* to the market', T: 'The man went to the market'). However, precisely the quality of being so discrete, causes recasts to be often unnoticed as CF [21]. As a result, though most frequently used in the classroom, a recast may not be the most effective type of CF.

Clarification requests, metalinguistic clues and elicitation (types 3, 4, 5 from section 2.1), are so-called negotiation of form techniques, collectively called prompts. They indicate that an error was made without providing the correct form. These feedback moves are considered to be effective because they induce learners to reprocess their output, and to produce "pushed output" [6, 26], but have been criticized because they would contribute to explicit linguistic knowledge and not to competence.

An important factor that turns out to mediate the effectiveness of the various CF types is research setting. In general, laboratory studies indicate greater effectiveness of CF than classroom studies, probably because important variables such as intensity and consistency are better controlled for in laboratory studies [16]. Furthermore, there are important learner characteristics that may be connected to the relative effectiveness of different feedback moves and that so far have received little attention in CF studies [42, 16], as will be discussed in the next section.

3.3 CF and Individual Differences

Very few studies in CF research address learners individually. Classroom observation studies such as Lyster and Ranta's [19] are very informative about the type of CF that is most used in pedagogical settings (see above), but do not provide information about the specific input and output of an individual learner, and how the individual differences interact with CF [33]. Experimental studies also often use groups that receive a particular CF treatment (e.g., [34]). However, individual and contextual factors are likely to play a larger role in L2 acquisition than in L1 acquisition. It seems necessary, therefore, to pay more attention to individual differences [32]. In an individual setting, it is easier to adapt CF to the learner. An example that individualized CF can be more effective is found in [36]. Here a learner was seen to consistently misinterpret written CF from a tutor. Only after specific CF that was adapted to this learner's developmental readiness and L1 background did the learner effectively correct her grammar. Additionally, there are indications that while some learners may require very explicit and immediate forms of CF, others do not appreciate being interrupted during conversation, thus preferring more implicit and delayed feedback moves (see, e.g., [43]).

This general neglect of individual differences and preferences may be related to an equally general feeling that L2 learning research should first of all provide guidelines for educational approaches, which up to now, have been mainly classroom oriented. Recent technological developments provide new opportunities for more individualized, tailor-made approaches to L2 learning in which adaptation can play a prominent role, as will be explained in the next section.

4 New Opportunities for Implementing and Investigating CF in L2 Learning

Although it is difficult to draw firm conclusions on the role of CF in SLA, several requirements stand out in the findings discussed above that are necessary to establish effective CF. For each learner, CF must be unambiguous, understandable, detectable, and short. These criteria can only be met when individual learner differences are taken into account. What is needed is individualized attention, a consistent focus over a longer period on one type of error only, intensive treatment, and, finally, consideration of the learners' developmental readiness and learning style.

These demands are hard to realize in classroom settings where teachers have to distribute their attention over a group of learners and where there is no direct control over what a learner is paying attention to. CALL systems with integrated speech technology may create settings where individual learner variation can be taken into account. How can we use the new technological opportunities to create the settings where learners receive CF adapted to their needs and preferences, and are provided with sufficient opportunities for self-repair and modified output [44]?

4.1 CALL Systems

More optimal learning conditions can be created by resorting to a CALL environment where CF is provided individually. To date, different CALL systems have been used for experimental research on second language acquisition (see, e.g., [45]), in particular to study the role of CF (e.g., [46, 47]). CALL systems offer several advantages for research on CF. Learners interact one-on-one with the system which provides immediate, clearly defined, consistent feedback on all learner utterances. The CALL system engages learners more intensively, and can motivate them to practice until they achieve a 'perfect score' [48]. Additionally, scores on tasks and developmental progress can be logged by the computer. This gives the possibility of optimizing the CF and adapting the program to individual characteristics, e.g., developmental readiness. For research purposes, all data, such as learner output, and reaction times in response to tasks can be logged and analyzed.

The CALL systems used so far use written input, even when investigating oral skills [49, 50]. However, writing is assumed to employ explicit L2 knowledge [51] while to study the role of CF it is necessary to target implicit knowledge through online performance as in speaking. This could be achieved by employing CALL systems that make use of Automatic Speech Recognition (ASR), a specific application of speech technology, intended to parse the incoming speech signal into words. This parsing task is not trivial, especially in the case of non-native speech [52]. Developing high-quality ASR-based CALL systems that can properly handle L2 speech requires the combination of different types of expertise. This might explain why this approach has not been adopted earlier.

4.2 An ASR-Based CALL System for Studying the Effect of CF on Oral Proficiency

In the project FASOP (Feedback on Acquisition of Syntax in Oral Proficiency) we aim to develop a learning setting that copes with individual variation, is replicable, and targets on-line processing by recognizing and analyzing spoken output. To this end we will use a CALL system that employs ASR to analyze the spoken output of learners of Dutch as L2 and to provide systematic, clear, consistent, and adaptive CF on syntax in oral Dutch L2 performance. In this section we motivate and describe the setup of our system for studying CF.

4.2.1 Advantages of ASR Implementation in a CALL System

Developing the proper adaptive ASR-based CALL system requires an interdisciplinary approach. We need to combine and integrate knowledge from the fields of pedagogy, teaching Dutch as a second language, research methodology, and speech technology, in order to increase our understanding of the role of CF in L2 learning and of the effectiveness of adaptive CALL systems.

In this system learners engage individually in dialogues with a virtual language tutor, receive CF on incorrect utterances, and are stimulated to produce modified output. Learners will provide spoken answers. By using an ASR system that is trained on non-native speech, and by constraining learner output, L2 utterances can be recognized with high precision. The FASOP project employs the technology developed in the project 'Development and Integration of Speech technology into Courseware for language learning' (DISCO) [43].

CF is individualized in the sense that it builds on the errors made by a specific learner. The CF targets particular linguistic items or address various related linguistic features at the same time. Moreover, learners can practice as long as they want, at their own pace. This provides additional opportunities for studying the effect of CF on L2 learning, by varying focus, intensity and length of treatment. The crucial advantage for CF research is that all these factors can be handled with a degree of control and systematicity that is not achievable in traditional classroom situations. The effect of different feedback types can be studied by providing CF through various feedback moves and comparing their effectiveness (see 4.2.2.).

A further innovative feature of the FASOP project is that the CALL system will adapt CF on the basis of learner responses and successes. In particular, it adapts to the learner by providing the type of feedback that appears to be more effective. Only a very few studies have investigated the impact of adapting feedback moves in relation to learner characteristics and achievements.

An obvious advantage of applying an ASR-based CALL system is that all learner-system interactions can be logged, to enable a thorough analysis of language input, corresponding learner's spoken output, the system's feedback and the learner's response to the feedback. In the FASOP project these different data sources provide together the basis for the systematic investigation of the role of CF in L2 learning. These sources will be complemented with data derived from pre- and posttests in which more traditional proficiency tests are administered, supplemented by expert judgments on learners' performance. In this way, a comprehensive picture of the impact of CF and its long-term, generalizing effects can be obtained.

A final advantage of this approach to CF research is that it can provide guidelines for improving L2 teaching. Just as traditional, group oriented research was considered to be informative for traditional classroom-oriented L2 education, individualized, adaptive research on L2 learning can provide useful insights and guidelines to develop L2 teaching methods that are individualized and adaptive. In other words, this type of research also has educational value and the experimental conditions are ecologically valid because if the system developed in laboratory conditions appears to be effective, it can also be applied in real learning situations, as a supplement to traditional lessons.

4.2.2 Measuring the Effect of CF

One of the problems in CF research is measuring effectiveness. As mentioned in section 3.1, [22] observed that several of the studies they examined used a pre- and posttests that could be said to target explicit language knowledge. Since the FASOP project specifically focuses on progress in language proficiency, it is necessary to target implicit knowledge. During treatment, this will be done mostly by having learners produce spoken language output (and possibly implementing some form of time pressure, which is another effective way of minimizing the influence of explicit knowledge on production [40]). Crucially, the pre- and posttests must test the level of implicit knowledge, to determine whether the treatment in which CF was provided had an effect. For this reason, we use a timed grammaticality judgment task (GJT) and an elicited imitation (EI) task (see [53, 54] on EI tests; see [55] for an overview of GJT). In the EI test, a learner attempts to verbally repeat specific sentences of the L2. The goal of the test is that the sentences exceed the capacity of the learners' working memory, so that they cannot repeat the sentences verbatim. In restructuring the sentence, the test is able to show where problem areas of the learner's grammar lie. The GJT is a test in which learners have to decide whether a sentence is grammatical or not in the L2. To target implicit knowledge it is essential that this test includes time pressure, so that the learner does not have time to reflect on the sentence but must respond intuitively. These tests were found to be most indicative of implicit language knowledge in a study by Ellis [40], in which he compared test results of native and non-native speakers on various types of proficiency tests.

In FASOP, we will look at the performance and acquisition of learners on one particular grammatical structure, namely verb placement in Dutch. This increases the level of control that we have on the experiment (effectiveness of CF type is also seen to interact with grammatical structure in [56]). Additionally, the effect of the treatment can easily be examined in the pre- and posttests as performance on the target structure.

Information on learner characteristics will be collected through a questionnaire. The data from the questionnaire can then be compared with effectiveness of types of CF. Both performance data during the treatment of the experiment (rate of speech, reaction times, self-correction after CF) and performance of the learner on the pre- and posttests will be examined for correlations.

4.2.3 Design of Planned ASR Based CALL Experiment

The FASOP experiments will use an ASR-based CALL system that engages the learners in a dialogue with a virtual tutor. After watching a short film clip, the learner receives questions about the video, to which the learner must respond by recording a spoken response. Due to the high level of precision we require of the ASR and because the ASR must analyze non-native speech, it is necessary to constrain the dialogue [52]. The responses of the learner must be predictable. As a result, we have decided to provide the learner with 'blocks' with which they must construct the sentence, e.g.:

> Q: 'Waar gaat dit filmpje over?' (what's this film about?)
> Block 1: 'dit filmpje' (this film)
> Block 2. 'gaat' (is)
> Block 3. 'over twee jonge mannen' (about two young men)
> Block 4. 'die verhuizen' (moving house)

This form of constraining the spoken output by the learner enhances the possibility that the produced utterance is correctly identified by the speech recognizer. The feedback that the system gives will be either, a) implicit recast, b) explicit recast, or c) prompt. These are operationalized as follows:

a. Implicit recast: neutral background color plus the correct form of the learner's utterance
b. Explicit recast: red background color, the statement 'no, that is incorrect' and the correct form of the learner's utterance
c. Prompt: red background color, the statement 'no that is incorrect. Try again'. The learner then can re-record the utterance. If the learner again makes an error, the system fills in one block and asks for a learner repetition, until the learner produces a correct utterance.

In this fashion, we can examine two characteristics of CF: implicit (implicit recasts) versus explicit CF (explicit recasts, prompts), and CF that provides the correct form (implicit and explicit recasts) versus CF that stimulate self-correction by the learner (prompts). However, recasts can hardly be said to be implicit in a computer system that is specifically designed to practice L2. Learners using the system are likely to be focused on language form, and not on meaning. To counter this problem, we also include some multiple choice questions about content of the film. For instance, if the man in the film buys apples at the market, the system may ask 'what did the man buy?' and the learner must respond by constructing a sentence, e.g., 'the man bought two apples/pears at the market'. A CF move by the system may then be interpreted by the learner as feedback on content, and not on form. Additionally, the system will also randomly repeat correct sentences to further ensure that the implicit feedback is implicit to the learner (see also section 2.1).

In this manner, it is possible to systematically provide CF on spoken learner utterances using ASR. By comparing the performance of a control group that works with the system but does not receive CF from the system, with the experimental groups, we can determine in a highly controlled experimental environment whether CF is effective for learning a specific grammatical structure of Dutch. Additionally, by examining the effectiveness of CF types, and relating that to learner characteristics, it is possible to adapt the CF according to learner requirements.

5 Conclusions

We have argued that a new research paradigm is needed to study CF in second language acquisition in which clear, systematic, consistent, intensive and adaptive CF can be delivered to language learners. ASR-based CALL systems can provide such a paradigm. Further experiments are required to support our approach and to provide evidence for the role of CF in second language acquisition.

References

1. Lightbown, P.M., Spada, N.: How Languages are Learned, pp. 171–172. Oxford University Press, Oxford (1999)
2. Krashen, S.D.: The input hypothesis: issues and implications. Longman, New York (1985)
3. Schwartz, B.: On explicit and negative data effecting and affecting competence and linguistic behaviour. Studies in Second Language Acquisition 15, 147–163 (1993)
4. Truscott, J.: Noticing in second language acquisition: a critical review. Second Language Research 14(2), 103–135 (1998)
5. Han, Z.: Fossilization in adult second language acquisition. Multilingual Matters, Clevedon (2004)
6. Swain, M.: Communicative competence: some roles of comprehensible input and comprehensible output in its development. In: Gass, M.A., Madden, C.G. (eds.) Input in Second Language Acquisition, pp. 235–253. Newbury House, Rowley (1985)
7. Rohde, D., Plaut, D.: Language acquisition in the absence of explicit negative evidence: how important is starting small? Cognition 72, 67–109 (1999)
8. Carroll, S., Swain, M.: Explicit and implicit negative feedback: An empirical study of the learning of linguistic generalizations. Studies in Second Language Acquisition 15, 357–386 (1993)

9. Iwashita, N.: Negative feedback and positive evidence in task-based interaction: Differential, effects on L2 development. Studies in Second Language Acquisition 25, 1–36 (2003)
10. Sheen, Y.: Corrective feedback and learner uptake in communicative classrooms across instructional settings. Language Teaching Research 8, 263–300 (2004)
11. Chaudron, C.: Second language classrooms. Cambridge University Press, New York (1988)
12. Han, Z.: A study of the impact of recasts on tense consistency in L2 output. TESOL Quarterly 36, 542–572 (2002)
13. Panova, I., Lyster, R.: Patterns of corrective feedback and uptake. TESOL Quarterly 36, 573–595 (2002)
14. Havranek, G.: When is corrective feedback most likely to succeed? International Journal of Educational Research 37, 255–270 (2002)
15. Lyster, R.: Differential effects of prompts and recasts in form-focused instruction. Studies in Second Language Acquisition 26, 399–432 (2004)
16. Lyster, R., Saito, K.: Oral Feedback in Classroom SLA: A Meta-Analysis. Studies in Second Language Acquisition 32, 265–302 (2010)
17. Hulstijn, J.: Theoretical and Empirical Issues in the Study of Implicit and Explicit Second-Language Learning. Studies in Second Language Acquisition 27, 129–140 (2005)
18. Saxton, M.: The Contrast theory of negative input. Journal of Child Language 24, 139–161 (1997)
19. Lyster, R., Ranta, L.: Corrective feedback and learner uptake: Negotiation of form in communicative classrooms. Studies in Second Language Acquisition 20, 37–66 (1997)
20. Lochtman, K.: Oral corrective feedback in the foreign language classroom: how it affects interaction in analytic foreign language teaching. International Journal of Educational Research 3, 271–283 (2002)
21. Nicholas, H., Lightbown, P.M., Spada, N.: Recasts as feedback to language learners. Language Learning 51, 719–758 (2001)
22. Norris, J.M., Ortega, L.: Effectiveness of L2 instruction: a research synthesis and quantitative meta-analysis. Language Learning 50, 417–528 (2000)
23. Anderson, J.R., Fincham, J.M.: Acquisition of procedural skills from examples. Journal of Experimental Psychology: Learning, Memory, and Cognition 20, 1322–1340 (1994)
24. DeKeyser, R.: Introduction: Situating the Concept of Practice. In: DeKeyser, R. (ed.) Practice in a Second Language. Cambridge University Press, New York (2007)
25. Ellis, N.C.: At the Interface: Dynamic interactions of explicit and implicit language knowledge. Studies in Second Language Acquisition 27, 305–352 (2005)
26. De Bot, K.: The Psycholinguistics of the Output Hypothesis. Language Learning 46, 529–555 (1996)
27. DeKeyser, R.: Implicit and Explicit learning. In: Doughty, C., Long, M. (eds.) Handbook of Second Language Acquisition, pp. 313–348. Blackwell Publishing, Oxford (2003)
28. Schmidt, R.W.: The role of consciousness in second language learning. Applied Linguistics 11, 129–158 (1990)
29. Ellis, N.C.: Frequency Effects in Language Processing. SSLA 24, 143–188 (2002)
30. Cross, J.: 'Noticing' in SLA: Is it a valid concept? TESL-EJ Teaching English as a Second or Foreign Language, 6 (2002),
   http://writing.berkeley.edu/TESL-EJ/ej23/a2.html
   (accessed online July 25, 2010)

31. Long, M.: The role of linguistic environment in second language instruction. In: Ritchie, W., Bhatia, T. (eds.) Handbook of second language Acquisition. Second Language Acquisition, vol. 2, pp. 413–468. Academic Press, New York (1996)
32. Ellis, R.: Epilogue: A Framework for Investigating Oral and Written Corrective Feedback. Studies in Second Language Acquisition 32, 335–349 (2010)
33. DeKeyser, R.: The effect of error correction on L2 grammar knowledge and oral proficiency. The Modern Language Journal 77, 501–514 (1993)
34. Mackey, A., Philp, J.: Conversational interaction and second language development: Recasts, responses, and red herrings. Modern Language Journal 82, 338–356 (1998)
35. Dörnyei, Z.: The Psychology of the language learner: Individual differences in second language acquisition. Lawrence Erlbaum Associates, New Jersey (2005)
36. Han, Z.: Fine-tuning corrective feedback. Foreign Language Annals 34, 582–599 (2001)
37. Long, M.: Does second language instruction make a difference? A review of research. TESOL Quarterly 17, 359–382 (1983)
38. Russel, J., Spada, N.: The effectiveness of corrective feedback for second language acquisition: A meta-analysis of the research. In: Norris, J., Ortega, L. (eds.) Synthesizing Research on Language Learning and Teaching, pp. 131–164. John Benjamins, Amsterdam (2006)
39. Mackey, A., Goo, J.: Interaction in SLA: a meta-analysis and research synthesis. In: Mackey, A. (ed.) Conversational Interaction in Second Language Aquisition, pp. 407–452. Oxford UP, Oxford (2007)
40. Ellis, R.: Measuring implicit and explicit knowledge of a second language: A psychometric study. Studies in Second Language Acquisition 27, 141–172 (2005)
41. Doughty, C.: Instructed SLA: Constraints, compensation, and enhancement. In: Doughty, C., Long, M. (eds.) The Handbook of Second Language Acquisition, pp. 256–310. Blackwell Publishing, Oxford (2003)
42. Sheen, Y.: The Role of Oral and Written Corrective Feedback in SLA. Studies in Second Language Acquisition 32, 169–179 (2010)
43. Strik, H., Cornillie, F., Colpaert, J., van Doremalen, J., Cucchiarini, C.: Developing a CALL system for practicing oral proficiency: How to design for speech technology, pedagogy and learners. In: Proceedings of SLaTE, United Kingdom (2009)
44. El Tatawi, M.: Corrective feedback in second language acquisition. Working papers in TESOL and Applied Linguistics 2, 1–19 (2002)
45. Hulstijn, J.H.: The use of computer technology in experimental studies on second language acquisition: A survey of some techniques and some ongoing studies. Language Learning & Technology 3(2), 32–43 (2000)
46. Bull, S.: Focusing on feedback. In: Broady, E. (ed.) Second Language Writing in a Computer Environment, pp. 157–175. CILT, UK (2000)
47. Sachs, R., Suh, B.: Textually enhanced recasts, learner awareness, and L2 outcomes in synchronous computer-mediated interaction. In: Mackey, A. (ed.) Conversational Interaction in Second Language Acquisition, pp. 197–227. Oxford UP, Oxford (2007)
48. Wachowicz, K., Scott, B.: Software that listens: It's not a question of whether, it's a question of how. CALICO Journal 16, 253–276 (1999)
49. Scott Payne, J., Whitney, P.J.: Developing L2 Oral Proficiency through Synchronous CMC: Output, Working Memory, and Interlanguage Development. CALICO 20, 7–32 (2002)
50. Sagarra, N.: From CALL to face-to-face interaction: The effect of computer-delivered recasts and working memory on L2 development. In: Mackey, A. (ed.) Conversational Interaction in Second Language Acquisition: A Series of Empirical Studies. Oxford University Press, Oxford (2007)

51. Bialystok, E.: The role of linguistic knowledge in second language Use. Studies in Second Language Acquisition 4, 31–45 (1981)
52. van Doremalen, J., Cucchiarini, C., Strik, H.: Optimizing Automatic Speech Recognition for Low-proficient Non-Native Speakers. Eurasip Journal on Audio, Speech, and Music Processing, 1–13 (2009)
53. Vinther, T.: Elicited imitation: a brief overview. International Journal of Applied Linguisitics 12, 54–73 (2002)
54. Erlam, R.: Elicited imitation as a measure of L2 Implicit knowledge: an empirical validation study. Applied linguistics 27, 464–491 (2006)
55. Tremblay, A.: Theoretical and Methodological Perspectives on the Use of Grammaticality Judgment Tasks in Linguistic Theory. Second Language Studies 24, 129–167 (2005)
56. Ellis, R.: The differential effects of corrective feedback on two different grammatical structures. In: Mackey, A. (ed.) Conversational Interaction in Second Language Acquisition, pp. 339–360. Oxford UP, Oxford (2007)

Mobile Vocabulary Learning: Activities Allowing for Interaction through Input Enhancement

Maribel Montero Perez, Frederik Cornillie, Marie-Paule Senecaut,
Stefan De Wannemacker, and Piet Desmet

Itec - Interdisciplinary research on Technology, Education and Communication
K.U. Leuven Campus Kortrijk, Etienne Sabbelaan 53, 8500 Kortrijk, Belgium
{maribel.monteroperez,frederik.cornillie,marie-paule.senecaut,
stefan.dewannemacker,piet.desmet}@kuleuven-kortrijk.be
http://www.kuleuven-kortrijk.be/itec

Abstract. One of the major challenges of mobile (language) learning consists in designing content that is based on sound pedagogical (theoretical) frameworks and empirical findings. At the same time, content should be adapted to the technological constraints of mobile devices (e.g. screen size, keyboard, etc.). Based on a literature review of existing mobile language learning applications and insights from an interactionist perspective in the SLA literature, we propose a design for mobile vocabulary learning. The design is centered around the idea of providing learners with rich input (multimedia material) and opportunities for receiving input enhancement through interaction. We justify the design choices that were made and illustrate the vocabulary activity by means of some screenshots of a prototype model.

Keywords: mobile language learning, vocabulary, second language acquisition, interaction, input enhancement, multimedia material.

1 Introduction

When consulting literature on mobile (language) learning[1][2] [3], one can conclude rather quickly that a stable and univocal definition of this concept does not exist. Indeed, defining what distinguishes mobile learning from other learning contexts can be based on different angles. Early definitions were often given purely in terms of technology (PDA, cell phone, MP3, etc.) (cf. Traxler[4]), putting the broader learning context aside. Other definitions stress the place and time independence of learning. In this case, the term is used to refer to situations in which the learner is on the go and mobile technologies provide an "anytime and anywhere" (cf. Maag[5] and Motiwalla[6]) access for learning (cf. Price [7]). It is not the aim of our paper to put forward a definition of mobile learning but rather to look at mobile learning in terms of the specific added value that can be realized, what contributes indirectly to a more precise definition. Based on our literature review, we identified four general recurring topics: (1) adaptation and adaptivity of content, (2) pervasiveness of mobile technologies, (3) localization of content and (4) collaborative learning.

S. De Wannemacker, G. Clarebout, P. De Causmaecker (Eds.): ITEC 2010, CCIS 126, pp. 15–27, 2011.

(1) Adaptation and adaptivity of learning materials
Both concepts of adaptation and adaptivity refer to the idea of adapting content. However, the source, or "to what" activities should be adapted, is not the same in the case of mobile learning. Adaptation of learning activities refers to the fact that learning materials and activities presented on a mobile device have to be adapted to the mobile technologies and its constraints (e.g. screen size, keyboard, connection, etc.), while retaining their pedagogical value. On the other hand, adapting content from an instructional point of view, or realizing "adaptivity", is done in function of the learners' individual differences, such as their proficiency level (cf. infra). Learners also have different interests, prior knowledge, background, motivation, etc. which are precisely elements of the sources [8] or "to what" the (mobile) system can adapt.

(2) The pervasiveness of mobile technologies in everyday life has taken the learning process out of the classroom, making it part of informal settings. In her 2009 paper entitled "Will mobile learning change language learning?", Kukulska-Hulme [9] offers some interesting perspectives on how mobile learning changes ways of teaching and learning foreign languages. She points out that mobile learning has brought forth a "rethinking" of some pedagogical aspects, leading to more personalized, situated, authentic, spontaneous, informal learning and therefore more learner-led approach.

(3) The central role of the learner in the learning process can also be noticed in the number of applications that allow for localization of content. Localization of content consists precisely in providing learners with a more contextualized form of learning by adapting materials to a learner's location. In a study published by Ogata & Yano[10], CLUE is presented, a context-sensitive learning environment for Japanese learners that can be accessed on a PDA. By interacting with sensors in the environment, the system provides the learners with appropriate learning materials (expressions) for the context they are in.

(4) Mobile learning has also stimulated different forms of collaborative learning, encouraging social interactions between learners on mobile platforms, wikis, blogs, etc. Different studies on collaborative mobile learning applications find a theoretical framework in sociocultural theory (cf. Lantolf[11]). A study published by Nah, White & Sussex[12] indicates for example that the use of mobile technologies for listening comprehension is more effective than using desktop applications for collaborative learning, just because of the mobility of learners.

This paper focuses mainly on the first aspect, i.e. content adaptation, whereby the design of learning materials and activities need to be adapted to a broadband-ready mobile smartphone with a tactile interface, which is capable of handling multimedia content. From a pedagogical perspective, we can argue that one of the major challenges of mobile learning consists in designing content that is based on sound (theoretical) frameworks and empirical findings. Before we address this theoretical issue in the third part of this paper, we propose a review of some language learning applications in function of the language area they address. We go more into detail on mobile vocabulary learning applications and identify some frequently used techniques. Based on our Mobile-assisted Language

Learning (MALL) review on the one hand and the theoretical concepts identified in the SLA literature on the other, we present a design proposal for a mobile vocabulary learning activity.

2   MALL Applications for Different Language Areas: A Review

The potential of mobile phones for language learning is reflected in the diversity of existing applications, each addressing one or more language components. First of all, the use of mobile phones with internet connection makes it relatively easy to get access to authentic material. This can be particularly interesting for the development of learners' listening skills with authentic material. In their study, Nah et al. [12] used a WAP site for training listening and found that this can indeed be an effective mean. Additionaly, the availability of podcasts creates opportunities for learners to develop their listening skills, anytime and anywhere. However, some "best practices" could make podcasting more effective for learning, for a detailed review see Rosell-Aguilar [13]. Other applications focus on more grammar-related topics such as the TenseITS system developed by Cui & Bull [14]. Their application consists of exercises on grammar tenses for Chinese learners of English and can adapt its content to the learners' knowledge level and current situation. Also the pronunciation component can be trained thanks to mobile applications. A concrete example is given in the MAC project: Mobile Adaptive CALL [15]. This application aims at supporting Japanese speakers of English to distinguish two sounds: /r/ and /l/, causing a lot of problems for native Japanese speakers.

Apart from the isolated examples given above, MALL has proven it may also be beneficial for other language components. One of the components that is most commonly the target of new applications is vocabulary. Different vocabulary learning techniques can be identified each aiming at developing or maintaining learners' vocabulary knowledge outside the classroom. One of the first techniques for explicit vocabulary learning consists in using SMS or short text messages to send learners words or expressions in a foreign language. A concrete example of using SMS for vocabulary was given by the study of Kennedy & Levy [16] in which beginning learners of Italian received vocabulary by means of text messages. A similar initiative was undertaken by Thornton and Houser who provided learners with vocabulary on their e-mail, accessed via mobile phones. They found that "students studying vocabulary by e-mail on their mobile phone learn significantly more than students studying from paper". Moreover, they also indicated that "the students who were frequently sent e-mail were prodded to study more often than students encouraged only once a week to study the paper-based materials and that this more frequent study led to better learning" (cf. Thornton & Houser p. 223 [17]). The use of flash cards on mobile devices was studied by Browne and Culligan [18] who created a vocabulary environment for both Desktop PC and mobile device. Learners start by completing vocabulary exercises on the e-learning platform and can access flash cards on their mobile device after their e-learning session. The system offers personalized content on the learner's mobile device in that the flash cards learners receive are supposed to be the items they need to train more. The aspect of adapting content to learner's individual differences (cf. supra) can also be found in Stockwell's VocabTutor [19] [20] which provides the learners with vocabulary activities, adapted to their given answers (correct or incorrect). The system is accessible both on Desktop PC and mobile phone. Thanks to the ITS (Intelligent Tutoring Systems) system, a learner profile is created for each user, which makes it possible to deliver adapted content. Besides, the system also calculates a competency score based on the learners responses. The system starts with passive vocabulary recognition tasks and ends with active word production activities. Nevertheless, learners seemed to prefer Desktop PC, which could be due to some technological constraints of the mobile device, such as the keyboard.

3   Designing for MALL

3.1   Insights from SLA Theory

Since second and foreign language learning is the central focus of our mobile environment, we propose to study to what extent MALL can benefit from Second Language Acquistion theories. Up till now, studies presenting (design of) MALL applications can generally not be situated within a SLA theoretical perspective, although their main focus is language learning. However, as pointed out by Levy and Stockwell [21]in the context of Computer-assisted Language Learning (CALL), SLA theory might offer a valuable starting point for formulating design principles. One of the frequently used theories in that context is the interactionist perspective. Although CALL and MALL differ on some crucial aspects (such as the technology used, the context of learning, etc.), it might be useful to study to what extent the design of MALL activities can be embedded in interactionist SLA literature.

Interactionist Theory in CALL. In her work, Chapelle[22][23] underlines the benefits of an interactionist theory of second language acquisition for CALL. This cognition-focused theory of language learning is centered around the concepts of input, output and interaction. Input is crucial and is said to be the "sine qua non" as for acquisition to take place (cf. Gass & Mackey[24]). However, chances for acquisition are significantly higher if learners' attention is directed towards particular elements. Noticing[25] consists precisely in drawing learners' attention to features that are more salient than others and thus more likely to be noticed. One technique to encourage noticing is "input enhancement". In her research, Chapelle[22] argues that it is precisely on the level of input that CALL, or more in general, technology, presents major benefits in that it allows "significant new options for input enhancements". Sharwood Smith[26] gives an elaborate definition of input enhancement which boils down to the fact that input can be manipulated without knowing what the effect will be on the learner. Chapelle[22][23] recuperates this concept of input enhancement, applies it to

Table 1. Forms of input enhancement (cf. Chapelle[22])

Input Enhancement	Description
Salience	Marking a grammatical form on the screen or phonologically through stress
Modification	Making the input understandable to the learner through any means that gets at the meaning (e.g., images, L1 translation, L2 dictionary definitions, simplification)
Elaboration	Increasing the potential for understanding the input through addition of plausible, grammatical L2 elaboration to the original text (e.g. defining relative clauses)

the CALL context and distinguishes three main input enhancements: salience, modification and elaboration (see Table 1).

The second central concept that Chapelle uses in her framework for CALL is interaction. The interaction she describes is based on a distinction made by Ellis[27] as proposed in Table 2. Chapelle[22] however showed that the concept of interpersonal interaction, does not only take place between people but can also imply human-computer interaction. The interaction between the learner and the computer consists then in obtaining input enhancement, giving the computer the role of a native speaker (NS) or teacher with whom the learner interacts. These actual interactions are then supposed to lead to more comprehensible input, facilitating acquisition.

Interactionist Theory in MALL. Following Chapelle and her use of interaction for CALL, we propose a similar way of defining interaction in a mobile environment. As is the case in CALL activities, mobile language learners can also have the possibility to interact with the environment in order to receive input enhancement. The fact of obtaining enhanced input takes place in an interactive process, as a result of an interaction between the system and the learner. A negotiation of meaning occurs, thanks to the interaction between the learner and the enhancements he obtained.

The concept of interaction, as defined in SLA theories, has close links with interactivity. In her 2005 article, Chapelle[23] also refers to interactivity, a concept central to human-computer interaction (HCI). Despite nearly three decades of CALL research and practice, Chapelle states that CALL researchers and practitioners still struggle with the term interactivity. She suggests to consider interaction and interactivity as two distinct but related terms. However, she does not further explore the relationship between both constructs. In human-computer

Table 2. Interaction for CALL (cf. Chapelle[22])

Types of interaction based on Ellis[27] and Chapelle[22]		Benefits according to the Interaction Hypothesis
Interpersonal	Between people	Negotiation of meaning
	Between person and computer	Obtaining input enhancement
Intrapersonal	Within the person's mind	Directing attention to linguistic form in the input

interaction (HCI), interactivity is defined as a function of [machine] input required by the learner while responding to the computer, the analysis of those responses by the computer and the nature of the action by the computer (cf. Sims[28] p.159).

In our conceptualization, we propose to consider interactivity as any exchange between the language input provided by the computer and the learner, quite similar to how interactivity is defined from HCI perspective. This exchange does not coincide with interaction as defined in SLA (i.e. interactivity with the purpose of obtaining comprehensible input), but it may cause such interaction. This is why we propose to give interactivity a generic meaning and present the concept of interaction as a specific realization of interactivity, one that involves a two-way exchange which leads to input that is comprehensible for the learner.

Although interactivity does not have a clear definition in many contexts, we think it is essential in our framework for MALL. The specificities of the mobile learning context (i.e. anytime, anywhere, freedom, higher frequency of interruption, learning on the go, etc.), demand a higher level of involvement from the learner than other learning contexts. Interactive exercises that require learners to react immediately on the input they are presented with may involve learners more actively in the learning process, which may positively influence their experience and perseverance to learn in the environment.

The interactivity and interaction between the learner and the mobile device can be represented as in Fig. 1.

In this schema, the learner, interacts with the mobile environment on the device and starts by requesting from the application a new (learning) activity. The system provides the learner with an activity, which may be adapted to the learners profile (e.g. motivation, knowledge level, interests, etc.) or more general context parameters (e.g. location, movement, etc.). The learner starts

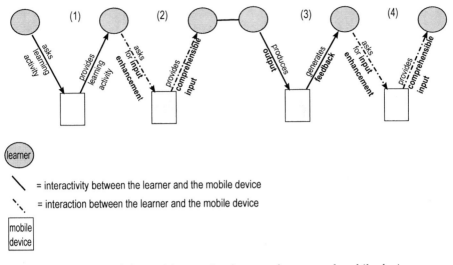

Fig. 1. Interactivity and interaction between learner and mobile device

the activity and interacts with the input, which allows the system to interact with the output produced by the learner. During the activity, a learner may ask the environment for input enhancement that is provided by the environment. The learner continues producing output and receives feedback during and after the exercise. The feedback generated by the mobile environment contains options for activating input enhancements. It is however the learner who decides whether or not he wants to engage in a real interaction.

3.2 Design Proposal: Mobile Vocabulary Learning

As stated rightly by Stockwell [29], "design will always be paramount in any environment where technology plays a role, and carefully thought out design has the capacity to overcome a number of barriers"(cf. mobile phone technological barriers, etc.). Taking into account findings of our MALL literature review and the SLA literature, we propose a concrete activity designed for vocabulary learning on a broadband-ready mobile device with a tactile interface. The central question guiding this design runs as follows: how can we realize adaptation of learning materials to a mobile device, while providing them with rich input and creating opportunities for interactivity and interaction? Three parameters in this question seem crucial: (1) rich input, (2) interactivity and interaction, and (3) content adaptation, each of these described and illustrated by means of screenshots of our mobile vocabulary activity. The numbers between brackets, e.g. (1), refer to the numbers in Fig. 1.

(1) Rich input as a crucial starting point
As shown in our MALL review, the largest group of applications for language learning addressed the vocabulary component. It is generally accepted that vocabulary knowledge is vital for a learner's L2 development. Thanks to mobile technologies, exposure to L2 learning content can be increased enormously.

Studies indicate for example that using SMS or web-based platforms accessible on a wide range of mobile devices, allow learners to train and enhance their vocabulary knowledge in any setting. However, the input in those applications still remains rather limited. Based on existing studies, we can state that multimedia material (e.g. video, photo, etc.) is barely exploited actively (i.e. multimedia is the core around which the activity is built) in current mobile vocabulary learning activities. Three arguments to include multimedia material in language (vocabulary) learning activities can be found in literature. A first one was given by the cognitive theory of multimedia learning [30], which shows that, according to the "multimedia principle", "students learn better from words and pictures than from words alone". A second element can be found in the interactionist SLA literature, stating that rich input is a crucial starting point as for acquisition to take place. A third argument is given by literature on vocabulary learning, arguing that (semi-)contextualized techniques to learn new words, such as visual imagery and keywords, can be a useful aid [31].

The activity starts as follows: Upon launching the exercise, the learner asks and receives a language learning activity (1), which subsequently shows a number of words on buttons (cf. keywords) and a video fragment (Fig. 2). Both the video (audio and images) and the keywords are forms of language input, which may or may not be comprehensible for the learner. The video can be considered as a means to create contextualized vocabulary since audio and images of selected audiovisual material are strongly supportive. The main objective of the exercise, click on the word and identify it when it appears in the video by tapping the screen, can be considered as an explicit vocabulary learning activity. As a concrete example: when the learner sees a picture of a living room in the video fragment, he or she touches the button with the corresponding French word la salle de séjour. Another exploitation of this activity could be that the learner clicks when he sees and hears the keyword in the fragment. A correct answer requires two actions from the learner: 1. Click on the button corresponding to a word that is depicted at any time in the video, 2. Click on the correct word within the restricted amount of time. When the living room appears on the screen for e.g. 3 seconds, the learner only has three seconds and some headroom to click on the button. A number of distractors (i.e. words that are not shown in the video fragment) may also be included in order to make the exercise harder (depending on the learners proficiency level).

(2) Realizing interaction and interactivity

In the third section of this paper, we argued that interactivity might be a way to involve the learner more actively in the course of the exercise. This interactivity can be and has been realized in different ways. First, the exercise in question requires immediate responses of the learner on the input by tapping the screen when he identifies a word. Secondly, the exercise type contains immediate corrective feedback, as a direct response to the learner's given answer. In case of a correct answer, the button turns green immediately after clicking on it, the button changes to a red color in case of an incorrect answer. Thirdly, when a learner taps a word, a new word may fill its slot on the screen. So the system

Fig. 2. Starting the exercise

Fig. 3. Check the answers or try again

Fig. 4. List with correct and wrong answers

Fig. 5. More information

interacts with the output of the learner, showing whether or not the given answer is correct and by replacing a word by a new one during the exercise.

After the video fragment has stopped and the learner chooses to check his answers and receive more feedback, he enters the zone where interaction between the learner and the environment is possible (4). By clicking on check (Fig. 3), the learner receives a list with correct and wrong answers (Fig. 4). The symbol (>) in Fig. 4 invites the learner to click in order to receive more information (cf. input enhancement) on a particular word. In our example (Fig. 5), we ask more information on the French word la salle de séjour. The system gives us a number of input enhancements, i.e. a translation, a picture, a definition, a link to the wiktionary and a possibility to receive more contextualized examples. After consulting the enhancements, the learner can continue and proceed to the next activity. Within the activity, step (2) (cf. Fig. 1)has been omitted and can only take place at the end of the activity (4). Providing input enhancements during the video fragment seems inappropriate and would hamper the course of the activity. We could therefore say that requests for input enhancement can, in this particular activity, be called requests for feedback enhancement as this activity situates all possibilities for enhancement at the end of the exercise, after the learner submitted his answers. As shown by Nation [32], using pictures, etc. which help learners to derive the meaning may help them to better remember the word. Another, more effective, technique is to combine this with verbal support, such as a definition (in light of Paivio's dual encoding [33]), both linguistic and visual elements contribute to word recall). The availability of input enhancements such as definitions, translations, contextualized examples, etc. allow precisely to combine visual elements and linguistic information (cf. L2 keywords and definitions). This may all contribute to the mapping of form and meaning which is crucial during vocabulary practice.

(3) Content adaptation Gay et al. [34] argued correctly that not all learning activities are appropriate for mobile technologies. Content should e.g. be adapted to a number of technological aspects such as the screen size, the keyboard, etc of mobile devices. On the other hand, also the context the learner is in determines the learning process in a definite way. An activity can e.g. become easier or harder, depending on the context. Although this design has not yet been tested by means of an experimental study, we believe that the following elements contribute to its suitability for mobile devices (with tactile interface):

- By providing learners with rich multimedia material and keywords and by requiring tapping on the screen as a unique action, keyboard problems are reduced to a minimum.
- The length of the video fragment is relatively short making it possible to complete an activity in a very limited amount of time.
- Connection problems that could be at the basis of bad quality video fragments, can be avoided by providing learners with audio alone or pictures alone, adapting thus content to technological constraints.

4 Conclusion and Future Work

We started this paper by identifying some general topics in literature on mobile (language) learning. We focused on the issue of content adaptation whereby learning activities have to be adapted to a broadband-ready mobile device with tactile interface. One of the main challenges of this adaptation of content consists in designing activities that are based on a sound pedagogical framework while overcoming technological limitations of mobile devices. In this perspective, we studied the interactionist SLA theory and argued that this is a useful starting point for developing mobile language learning activities. Rich input, interaction and output are crucial concepts in this SLA perspective and are integrated in the framework, substantiating our design. We defined and described the possibilities for interaction and interactivity between learner and input in the context of mobile language learning. By means of some screenshots of the activity, we presented a concrete use case for mobile vocabulary learning and described each step of the activity in light of our theoretical framework. We also argued that adapting content to mobile devices does not necessarily imply a limitation of the amount or quality of (authentic) language input. When analyzing currently used techniques in mobile vocabulary learning, we found that multimedia material is generally not exploited actively, in the sense that the vocabulary activity is in most cases not set up around the use of multimedia. The activity we developed starts with a video and requires immediate reactions of the learner on the video fragment by clicking on keywords. Besides, the environment also contains input enhancements which makes it possible for the learner to engage in a human-mobile interaction, giving him more comprehensible input and augmenting chances to acquire vocabulary.

It is obvious that this design has to be tested by means of some experimentally focused studies. One study should research the effect of the exercise type on vocabulary learning and whether or not the possibilities for interaction augment vocabulary knowledge. Research on the learner behavior will learn us more about the use and frequency of interaction and its effect on learning. Another study should focus on the effect of multimedia material on vocabulary learning. Given the results of previous multimedia learning experiments, we argue that the inclusion of audiovisual elements augments chances for vocabulary learning (cf. contextualized vocabulary). Does video indeed contribute to a better vocabulary learning effect? Is it effective to use pictures, and under what circumstances? Empirical studies will help us to answer these questions and to validate our design proposal.

Acknowledgments. The research activities that have been described in this paper were funded by the Institute for Broadband Technology (IBBT) and are realized within the MAPLE-project (Mobile and Adaptive Personalized Learning Experience).

References

1. Sharples, M., Milrad, M., Sanchez, I.A., Vavoula, G.: Mobile Learning Small devices, Big issues, ch. 14, pp. 233–249. Springer, Heidelberg (2009) (technology edition)
2. Kukulska-Hulme, A., Shield, L.: An overview of mobile assisted language learning: From content delivery to supported collaboration and interaction. ReCALL 20(3), 271–289 (2008)
3. Pachler, N., Bachmair, B., Cook, J.: Mobile Learning Structures, Agency, Practices. Springer, New York (2010)
4. Traxler, J.: Defining, discussing, and evaluating mobile learning: The moving finger writes and having writ...

5. Maag, M.: iPod, uPod? An emerging mobile learning tool in nursing education and students' satisfaction, pp. 483–492. Sydney University Press, Sydney (2006)
6. Motiwalla, L.F.: Mobile learning: A framework and evaluation. Computers and Education 49, 581–596 (2007)
7. Price, S.: Ubiquitous computing: digital augmentation and learning, pp. 33–54. WLE Centre, IoE, London (2007)
8. Wauters, K., Desmet, P., Van Den Noortgate, W.: Adaptive Item-Based Learning Environments Based on the Item Response Theory: Possibilities and Challenges. Journal of Computer Assisted Learning
9. Kukulska-Hulme, A.: Will Mobile Learning Change Language Learning? Re-CALL 21(2), 157–165 (2009)
10. Ogata, H., Yano, Y.: How Ubiquitous Computing can support Language Learning
11. Lantolf, J.P.: Sociocultural theory and second language learning. Oxford University Press, New York (2000)
12. Nah, K.C., White, P., Sussex, R.: The potential of using a mobile phone to access the Internet for learning EFL listening skills within a Korean context. Re-CALL 20(03), 331–347 (2008)
13. Rosell-Aguilar, F.: Top of the Pods - In Search of a Podcasting "Podagogy" for Language Learning. Computer Assisted Language Learning 20(5), 471–492 (2007)
14. Cui, Y., Bull, S.: Context and learner modelling for the mobile foreign language learner. System 33(2), 353–367 (2005)
15. Uther, M., Zipitria, I., Uther, J., Singh, P.: Mobile Adaptive CALL (MAC): A case-study in developing mobile learning application for speech/audio language training. In: Proceedings of the 2005 IEEE International Workshop on Wireless and Mobile Technologies in Education, WMTE 2005 (2005)
16. Kennedy, C., Levy, M.: L'italiano al telefonino: Using SMS to support beginners' language learning. ReCALL 20(03), 315–330 (2008)
17. Thornton, P., Houser, C.: Using mobile phones in English education in Japan. Journal of Computer Assisted Learning 21, 217–228 (2005)
18. Browne, C., Culligan, B.: Combining technology and IRT testing to build student knowledge of high frequency vocabulary. The JALT CALL Journal 42(2), 3–16 (2008)
19. Stockwell, G.: Vocabulary on the move: investigating an intelligent mobile phone-based vocabulary tutor. Computer Assisted Language Learning 20(4), 365–383 (2007)
20. Stockwell, G.: Using mobile phones for vocabulary activities examining the effect of the platform. Language Learning & Technology 14(2), 95–110 (2010)
21. Levy, M., Stockwell, G.: CALL Dimensions Options and Issues in Computer-Assisted Language Learning. Lawrence Erlbaum Associates, New Jersey (2006)
22. Chapelle, C.A.: English Language Learning and Technology. John Benjamins Publishing Company, Amsterdam (2003)
23. Chapelle, C.A.: Interactionist SLA Theory in CALL Research, ch. 5, pp. 53–64. Lawrence Erlbaum Associates, Mahwah (2005)
24. Gass, S.M., Mackey, A.: Input, Interaction, and Ouput in Second Language Acquisition, pp. 175–199. Lawrence Erlbaum Associates, New Jersey (2007)
25. Schmidt, R.W.: The Role of Consciousness in Second Language Learning. Applied Linguistics 11, 129–158 (1990)
26. Sharwood Smith, M.: Input enhancement in instructed SLA: Theoretical bases. Studies in Second Language Acquisition 15, 165–179 (1993)
27. Ellis, R.: Learning a second language through interaction. John Benjamins Publishing Company, Philadelphia (1999)

28. Sims, R.: Interactivity: A forgotten art? Computers in Human Behavior 13(2), 157–180 (1997)
29. Stockwell, G.: Investigating learner preparedness for and usage patterns of mobile learning. ReCALL 20(3), 253–270 (2008)
30. Mayer, R.E.: Multimedia Learning. Cambridge University Press, New York (2001)
31. Oxford, R., Crookall, D.: Vocabulary Learning: A Critical Analysis of Techniques. Tesl Canada Journal/Revue Tsl Du Canada, 7(2) (1990)
32. Nation, I.S.P.: Learning vocabulary in another language. University Press, Cambridge (2001)
33. Paivio, A.: Mental representations: A dual coding approach. OUP, New York (1986)
34. Gay, G., Stefanone, M., Grace-Martin, M., Hembrooke, H.: The effects of wireless computing in collaborative learning environments. International Journal of Human-Computer Interaction 13(2), 257–276 (2001)

Computerized Adaptive Testing in Computer Assisted Learning?

Bernard P. Veldkamp[1], Mariagiulia Matteucci[2], and Theo J.H.M. Eggen[3]

[1] RCEC/University of Twente, P.O. Box 217, 7500 AE Enschede, The Netherlands
[2] University of Bologna, via Belle Arti 41, 40126 Bologna, Italy
[3] RCEC/CITO, P.O. Box 1034, 6801 MG Arnhem, The Netherlands

Abstract. A major goal in computerized learning systems is to optimize learning, while in computerized adaptive tests (CAT) efficient measurement of the proficiency of students is the main focus. There seems to be a common interest to integrate computerized adaptive item selection in learning systems and testing. Item selection is a well founded building block of CAT. However, there are a number of problems that prevent the application of a standard approach, based on item response theory, of computerized adaptive item selection to learning systems. In this work attention will be paid to three unresolved points: item banking, item selection, and choice of IRT model. All problems will be discussed, and an approach to automated item bank generation is presented. Finally some recommendations are given.

Keywords: item-based computer assisted learning, computer adaptive testing, item banking, item response theory, item selection.

1 Introduction

In computerized adaptive testing (CAT) the difficulty of the items is adapted to the ability level of the candidate in order to measure this ability efficiently. This individualized procedure for test administration does have some major advantages above traditional paper-and-pencil (P&P) testing, where all candidates have to answer the same set of items. CAT provides some psychometric advantages. Items that are too easy or too hard do not provide that much information about the candidate. For example, items that are missed or answered correctly by all candidates do not discriminate within the population at all. By offering candidates items at their ability level, most information is gained and the length of the test can be reduced by half of the items in comparison with a P&P test [29]. This implies huge savings in time and money.

Computerized test administration makes it possible to gain full profits of adaptive testing. After the candidate answered the first few questions, the computer can generate an estimate of the candidate's ability level. This estimate still is rather rough, but items can be selected that are most informative at this estimated ability level. After every administered item, the estimate can be update and items can even be selected more on target. Various automated item selection

S. De Wannemacker, G. Clarebout, P. De Causmaecker (Eds.): ITEC 2010, CCIS 126, pp. 28–39, 2011.

rules and ability estimation procedures have been proposed in the literature and their impact on testing outcomes has been the topic of many papers [8,21,27,23]. A lot of methodology for CAT has been developed, but until now, it has been mainly, or maybe even only, applied in high stakes testing programs.

The wide scale availability of computers not only facilitated new testing procedures, it also enabled new learning procedures. Many different computer assisted learning environments have been developed in the past two decades [30]. Some of these environments focus on item-based computer assisted learning, where students are confronted with items and receive feedback on their performance. Feedback varies from hints to solve the item, via knowledge of correct response, to elaborated feedback. Besides, a distinction can be made between immediate and delayed types of feedback, and between different levels of feedback at process-, task- or self level [18,7].

In some item-based computer assisted learning (CAL) applications, students can select the difficulty level of their items themselves, in others fully automated item selection rules, or blended (both computer and candidate) item selection rules have been implemented. However, the impact of different automated item selection rules on learning is still a topic of further research.

CAT and item-based CAL seem to have a lot in common. In both procedures items are offered to candidates, and (automated) item selection rules play an important role. But CAT on the one hand is based on item response theory, and involves a lot of advanced psychometric modeling, where item-based CAL has been developed with a solid foundation in learning theory. Because of this, the question arose whether the methodology of CAT might be applicable to item-based CAL in order to optimize the learning process further.

2   Computerized Adaptive Testing

To answer the question whether CAT methodology can be transferred to item-based CAL, the methodology of CAT will be introduced first. The main idea underlying CAT is that the difficulty of the item is adapted to the estimated ability level of the candidate. However, at the beginning of a CAT, the ability of the candidate is unknown. To adapt the difficulty of the first item to unknown ability, several strategies can be applied [22,13]. Prior information about the candidate could be used to predict the ability, information about the population could be applied to initialize the ability estimate at the mode or at the mean of the distribution, or a random value might be assigned to the ability estimate. In many operational CATs, candidates first answer a few randomly selected items from a subset of the itembank to obtain the initial ability estimate. After initialization of the ability estimate, an item is selected from the item bank that matches the ability level. This item is administered and the ability of the candidate is estimated again, based on the whether the response was correct. Either a maximum likelihood estimator (MLE) or an expected a posterior (EAP) estimator can be applied in this step. Finally, before the next item is selected, it is checked whether the stopping criterion has been met. This stopping criterion might be a fixed test length or a maximum value for the error that is allowed in the ability estimate. The following pseudo algorithm describes these different steps in CAT:

1. Initialize ability estimate.
2. Select the next item from the item bank.
3. Administer the item.
4. Update ability estimate based on the correctness of the most recent response.
5. If stopping criterion has not been met go to Step 2.

Before the steps of item selection (Step 2) and ability estimation (Step 4) will be described more into detail, the measurement theory underlying CAT will be introduced first.

2.1 Item Response Theory (IRT)

The main feature underlying all IRT models is that a distinction is made between item and person parameters in the model. For a dichotomous test, the response behavior of candidates can be described by, for example, the 3-parameter logistic model (3PLM). In this model, the probability of correct answer to item i by candidate j equals:

$$P_i(\theta_j) = c_i + (1 - c_i)\frac{e^{a_i(\theta_j - b_i)}}{1 + e^{a_i(\theta_j - b_i)}}, \tag{1}$$

where θ_j denotes the ability parameter, and a_i, b_i, and c_i denote the discrimination, the difficulty and the pseudo-guessing parameter. The 2PLM and 1PLM are special cases of the 3PLM where respectively all pseudo-guessing parameters are assumed to be equal to zero (2PLM), or all discrimination parameters are assumed to be equal on top of that (1PLM or Rasch model). Other, more complex, IRT models are available for polytomous items [15] or items that need to be modeled by multidimensional IRT [16].

2.2 Step 2: Item Selection

In Step 2 of the algorithm, the next item is selected for administration. To optimize measurement precision, items have to be selected that provide most information about the candidate. Several item selection methods have been proposed in the literature and they are generally based on either, Fisher information, Kullback-Leibler information, or on Bayesian models.

Fisher information is defined to be minus the expectation of the second order derivative of the loglikehood function:

$$I_i(\theta) \equiv -E\left\{\frac{d^2}{d\theta^2}lnL(\theta; u)\right\}, \tag{2}$$

where $L(\theta; u)$ is the likelihood associated with the response vector u. From the assumption of local independence it follows that after administration of $(k-1)$ items

$$L(\theta; u_{k-1}) = \prod_{i=1}^{k-1} P_i(\theta)^{u_i} Q_i(\theta)^{1-u_i} \; , \tag{3}$$

where $P_i(\theta)$ is the probability of a correct response on item i, and $Q_i(\theta)$ is the probability of an incorrect response. For the 3PLM the Fisher information function reduces to:

$$I(\theta) = \frac{a_i^2 Q_i(\theta)(P_i(\theta) - c_i)^2}{P_i(\theta)(1-c_i)^2} \; . \tag{4}$$

Maximum Fisher Information (MFI), the most popular item selection rule in CAT, selects the item that maximizes Fisher information at the current ability estimate. It can be easily demonstrated that an item will provide maximum information, when the ability of the candidate equals the difficulty of the item. For the other parameters it holds that the item information is proportional to the discrimination squared and that when the pseudo guessing parameter increases, the information decreases [10].

Unfortunately, the ability estimate is very unstable at the beginning of the test. If the difference between the ability estimate and the true ability is large, MFI may therefore select items that are too easy or too hard to provide much information. The fact that item selection based on maximum Fisher information may favor items with optimal properties at wrong ability levels is generally known as the attenuation paradox in test theory (see [11], Sect. 16.5). To deal with this problem, the Maximum Interval Information (MII) rule that maximizes Fisher information over an interval was developed, where the size of the interval becomes smaller when the uncertainty in the ability estimate reduces [27].

Another way to deal with the attenuation paradox is to apply Kullback-Leibler information instead of Fisher information in the item selection process. Generally, Kullback-Leibler information measures the distance between two likelihoods over the same parameter space (see [9], Sect. 1.7). The purpose of testing is to measure the ability of the candidate. Therefore items have to be selected generating response vectors with a likelihood at the ability level of the candidate (θ_0) differing maximally from those at any other value of the ability parameter (θ). Formally, Kullback-Leibler information is defined as:

$$K_i(\theta, \theta_0) \equiv E\left[ln\frac{L(\theta_0 \mid u)}{L(\theta \mid u)} \right] \; . \tag{5}$$

Unfortunately, someone's true ability level is unknown and θ is unspecified. Therefore, Kullback-Leibler item selection rules are generally based on a Bayesian alternative, the posterior expected Kullback-Leibler information at the current ability estimate [4,25].

A third group of item selection rules can be described as Bayesian item selection rules. For an overview, see [23]. These criteria generally take into account the posterior distribution of the examinee's ability for selecting the next item. The posterior distribution can be calculated using the Bayes theorem

$$f(\theta \mid u) = L(\theta; u)\frac{f(\theta)}{f(u)} \, , \tag{6}$$

where $L(\theta; u)$ is the likelihood associated with response vector u, $f(\theta)$ is a prior distribution for θ, and $f(u)$ is the marginal probability of response vector u that serves as a normalizing constant in (6). From the assumption of local independence it follows that after administration of $(k-1)$ items, the likelihood function is equal to (3). As a prior distribution of θ a normal distribution is assumed. The normalization constant in (6) can be set equal to

$$f(u_{k-1}) = \int L(\theta; u_{k-1})f(\theta)d\theta \, . \tag{7}$$

Substitution of (3) and (7) in (6) gives an expression for the posterior distribution after $(k-1)$ items have been administered:

$$f(\theta \mid u_{k-1}) = \frac{\prod_{i=1}^{k-1} P_i(\theta)^{u_i} Q_i(\theta)^{1-u_i} f(\theta)}{\int \prod_{i=1}^{k-1} P_i(\theta)^{u_i} Q_i(\theta)^{1-u_i} f(\theta)d\theta} \, . \tag{8}$$

Based on this posterior distribution, several criteria have been proposed. For example, van der Linden in [21] proposed the Maximum Posterior-Weighted Information criterion, that takes the expectation of Fisher's information measure across the posterior distribution and the Minimum Posterior Variance Criterion, that minimizes the posterior variance.

About the statistical properties of these criteria it can be remarked that when an informative prior is used, "inward bias" of estimators of the ability parameter often occurs for shorter tests. On the other hand, the use of an informative prior usually results in a favorable mean-squared error. Asymptotically, no differences between Bayesian criteria and maximum Fisher information exist. How the actual performance turns out in practice depends on many variables, for example the choice of prior, the test length, and the item bank.

2.3   Step 4: Ability Estimation

The method of maximum likelihood estimation is widely applied in IRT. For CAT the items are selected from an item bank and the item parameters are supposed to be known. Therefore, the only parameters to be estimated are the ability parameters. A rather straightforward implementation of Gauss-Hermite quadrature method to find the maximum of the likelihood function defined in Equation (3) will do the job. Unfortunately, MLE suffers from two small drawbacks. First of all, in case of perfect response patterns (all items correct or all items incorrect), no finite estimator will be found. Besides, MLE tends to suffer from outward bias. To correct for these problems, a Warm estimator might be applied [31]. The Warm estimation procedure weights the likelihood with a function with depends on the test information, which solves the problems.

An alternative procedure for estimating the ability parameters is the Bayesian expected a posteriori (EAP) estimator (see [6]). After $(k-1)$ items, this estimator is found as

$$\hat{\theta}_{k-1} = E(\theta \mid u_{k-1}) = \int \theta f(\theta \mid u_{k-1}) d\theta , \tag{9}$$

where $f(\theta \mid u_{k-1})$ is the posterior distribution for the ability parameter given answer pattern u_{k-1}. The uncertainty about this estimator can be expressed by the posterior variance

$$var(\hat{\theta}_{k-1}) = E^2(\theta \mid u_{k-1}) - E(\theta \mid u_{k-1})^2 = \int \theta^2 f(\theta \mid u_{k-1}) d\theta - E(\theta \mid u_{k-1})^2 . \tag{10}$$

This Bayesian estimation method is extremely flexible in handling many different kinds of IRT models, besides, it does not suffer from the drawbacks of the MLE. For small tests however, the use of an informative prior [12] might have an effect on the score of individual candidates in the sense that two candidates from different groups may obtain different scores although they answered the same questions in the same way. For testing, this effects is certainly unwanted and can be diminished by calculating the final scores based on the response patterns only.

3   Issues in Applying CAT to CAL

The measurement models underlying CAT can be applied in item-based CAL rather straightforwardly. The items can be calibrated with an appropriate IRT model and the item parameters might be used to select the items for learning. For example, if a candidate selects an easy item, an item can be selected with a difficulty parameter that is smaller than the estimated ability level of the candidate. However, in order to apply CAT in item-based CAL, some issues have to be dealt with.

3.1   Item Bank Development

To run an operational CAT, one has to develop an item bank from which the items can be selected first. So, in order to adopt CAT methodology for item-based CAL, an item bank has to be developed first as well. To develop such a bank, items have to be written, pre-tested, and the item parameters have to be estimated. This process is rather expensive, because the number of respondents needed to estimate item parameters runs in the couple of hundreds and the number of items needed for the item bank is large. For CAT, the number of items is advised to be at least 12 times the test length [19]. So for a 30 item CAT, the bank needs around 360 items. When you take into account that only half of the items survive the pretesting process, this implies that more than

700 items need to be written for a 30 item CAT and thousands of candidates will be involved in the pretesting process. Such an investment only pays off in case of large numbers of candidates.

To facilitate the item writing process, and to make sure that the right items are being developed, Veldkamp and van der Linden [24,26] proposed a procedure for developing an item pool blueprint. This blueprint describes what kind of items have to be developed for an optimal item bank. The rationale behind this procedure is that the tests can only be as good as the items in the bank. Besides, the use of a blueprint might increase the efficiency of the item writing process. But even when a blueprint is used, the development of an item bank is still quite a job.

Recently, automated item generation has been proposed to reduce the effort of item bank development. Matteucci, Mignani, and Veldkamp [13] developed a method for predicting the item parameters based on item properties. They first apply Classification and Regression Trees (CART, see [2]) to model relationships between item properties and item parameters. Based on these relationships accurate predictions of the item parameters can be made. So, when a blueprint for an optimal item bank is available, it can be derived from the blueprint what kinds of items have to be generated. The CART model translates the item parameters to item properties and the properties can be used to generate the items.

It needs to be mentioned that the CART model only predicts the item parameters. In order to estimate the item parameters they have to be updated on the fly based on response patterns of the candidates. In the beginning of the procedure, these estimates might fluctuate. For testing, this might be unwanted, but for assessment for learning, like item-based CAL, this is less of a problem. The only drawback is that the candidates face items that turn out to be slightly more or less difficult than expected based on the item parameters. In a learning environment the effectiveness of the learning process will be influenced, but this does not lead to any ethical or legal problems.

3.2   Item Selection in CAL

The item selection rules for CAT presented above do have one thing in common. They all aim to select those items that will result in the best possible ability estimate. Even thought different rules apply different strategies, the aim remains the same. In item-based CAL, the objective is no longer to measure the ability of the candidate as precise as possible, but to optimize the learning process.

Learning can be defined in many ways. A rather straightforward approach would be to formulate learning in terms of increase in ability. A candidate starts at his/her current ability level and the aim of the learning process is to end at a higher ability level. An alternative item selection rule, designed to facilitate learning, would be to apply Kullback-Leibler information. Kullback-Leibler information based item selection rules, select those items that discriminate best between two ability levels. In learning, the first ability would be the true ability of the candidate, the other ability would be the ability level the candidate is aiming at. In the beginning of the item-based CAL, the ability estimate is rather unstable, but during the learning process, the ability estimate will become more precise, and more appropriate items will be selected. To improve the performance of the selection rule, collateral information about candidates can be used to predict the initial ability level. More research is needed on this topic to determine whether this procedure not only estimates learning, but also promotes learning.

Another aspect that might be taken into account is motivation of the learner which is assumed to have quite an impact on the learning process [20]. Kullback-Leibler item selection will select items with a difficulty level higher than the ability of a candidate. As a result, the candidate will miss more than half of the items. For CAT it has been demonstrated that motivation decreases when candidates miss more than half of the items. This might also be the case for item-based CAL.

3.3   Ability Estimation

In CAT, the ability of a candidate is assumed to be a stable identity that can be estimated based on a series of responses to items. For estimating the ability parameter, candidates have to answer at least 10 or 15 items. Otherwise the resulting estimates will turn out to be rather unreliable. Unfortunately, the ability parameter in item-based CAL is assumed to be dynamic. Candidates will learn from feedback, and their ability will grow over time. Verhelst & Glas in [28] presented a family of dynamic IRT models that takes into account the preceding responses and/or the feedback obtained. They even present a marginal maximum likelihood procedure for estimating the ability parameters. Application of this kind of models seems more appropriate.

Other promising approaches are Bayesian Knowledge Tracing models [5], and the Elo rating models [3]. These models come with a price. More information will be needed in the parameter estimation process, which implies that more data have to be collected per item and per candidate or stronger assumptions about the model have to be made. Besides, different item selection rules could be developed for dynamic models that maximize change in the ability parameter.

4   Numerical Example: Item Bank Generation

To illustrate the process of item bank development, a model for automated item bank generation has been developed for a number series test, which is part of a test battery for IQ measurement, the Connector Ability [14], exploited by PiCompany, a Dutch HR company. The Connector Ability consists of a number series test, a figure series test and a Raven matrices test. Items for this battery are generated by an automated item generator [17]. A previous item bank of 391 number series items calibrated with the 2PLM [1] was available. Discrimination parameters varied in the interval [0.17; 4.0], with a mean value around 1.3, while difficulty parameters were included in the range [-5.6; 3.9] with a mean of -0.6.

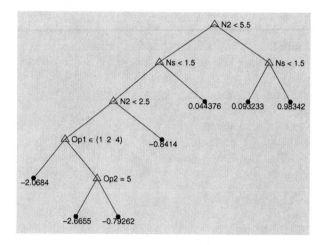

Fig. 1. Tree for predicting the difficulty parameter

Number series items can be described by a starting number, a level 1 operator, and a level 2 operator (an operation on the level 1 operator). An example of a number series item is:

$$1\ 4\ 8\ 13\ ?$$

where the candidate has to select the correct answer out of four alternatives. The starting number in this item equals one, the level 1 operator is plus three, and the level 2 operator (the operation on operator 1) is plus one. The item has been built as 1, 4 (1 + 3), 8 (1 + 3 + 4), and 13 (1 + 3 + 4 + 5). So, the correct answer will be 19 (1 + 3 + 4 + 5 + 6). Both at level 1 and 2 the following operations could be applied: addition, subtraction, multiplication and division. Some items even consisted of two series, for example:

$$1\ 2\ 2\ 4\ 3\ 6\ ?$$

where the item combines the series (1 - 2 - 3 - ?) and (- 2 - 4 - 6 -), and the correct answer would be 4.

Based on the existing item bank, CART techniques were applied to develop models for predicting the item parameters. The classification tree for the difficulty parameter is shown in Fig. 1, and the classification tree for the discrimination parameter in Fig. 2.

For predicting the difficulty parameters the value of the level 2 operator (N2) is the most important predictor, followed by the variable that indicates whether the item consists of one or two series (Ns). The type of operation at level 1 (Op1) and level 2 (Op2) complete the tree. For predicting the discrimination parameter it only matters whether the item consists of one or two series (Ns), where the items that consist of two series discriminate less.

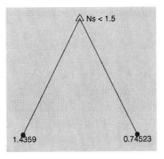

Fig. 2. Tree for predicting the discrimination parameter

In combination with the automated item generator, both trees can be used for automated generation of an item bank that matches a blueprint, without the time consuming and expensive process of item writing, pre-testing and calibration.

5   Conclusion and Discussion

Computer adaptive testing and item-based CAL seem to have a lot in common. Both select items from a bank and adapt the difficulty of the items to the ability of the candidate. However, there also seem to be some differences. CAT is based within a solid framework of psychometric theory, where item-based CAL is based within a learning framework. Therefore the question arose whether item-based CAL could borrow some of the psychometric underpinning of CAT.

Item response theory provides a measurement framework underlying CAT. Person and item parameters are separated, and the item parameters do not depend on the population that was used to estimate them. Because of this, item parameters can be stored in an item bank, and they can be used for future test administrations. IRT can therefore also be applied in item-based CAL. Since the item parameters are supposed to be known, the difficulty level of the new items is known when they are presented to the candidates. In this way, IRT can contribute to the developments in item-based CAL.

Three issues remained. The first one of item bank development might be solved by automated item generation in combination with a model that predicts the item parameters based on item features. The empirical example of a number series test demonstrates the possibilities. On the other hand, the example also provided some remarkable results. In item bank development, a distinction can be made between radicals and incidentals of items. Radicals represent the general principles and incidentals the item specific features. In automated item generation theory, it is assumed that the radicals account for variation in the item parameters, where incidentals do not influence the variation that much. For number series items, the type of level 1 and level 2 operations and the number of series are the radicals. The starting values and the size of the level 1 and 2 parameters are the incidentals. But, unlike our expectations, the size of the level 2 operation turned out to be the most powerful predictor of item difficulty. This might suggest that the size of the level 2 operation functions as a radical rather than an incidental.

Even though both CAT and item-based CAL apply item selection rules for selecting the next item, selection rules from CAT cannot be transferred straightforwardly. The purpose of item selection in CAT is to find those items that measure the ability as precise as possible, where in item-based CAL the purpose is to optimize the learning process. Kullback-Leibler based item selection might be applied in both CAT and item-based CAL, but still a lot of research is needed to validate the proposed rules. The biggest challenge however in transferring methodology from CAT to item-based CAL however, seems to be the dynamic nature of ability in the learning process. In CAT the ability is assumed to be stable during the test, where in item-based CAL the aim is to maximize change in the ability parameter. Dynamic IRT models, like the model proposed in [28], might fit this purpose rather well, but the consequence is that all procedures of item bank development and item selection have to be modified in order to be able to handle the dynamic nature.

Because of this it can be concluded that CAT offers several interesting psychometric features that might be applicable in item-based CAL. Transferring methodology from CAT to item-based CAL turned out to be far from straightforward and a lot of additional research is needed to facilitate this process.

References

1. Birnbaum, A.: Some Latent Trait Models and their Use in Inferring an Examinee's Ability. In: Lord, F.M., Novick, M.R. (eds.) Statistical Theories of Mental Test Scores, pp. 397–479. Addison-Wesley, Reading (1968)
2. Breiman, L., Friedman, J.H., Olshen, R.A., Stone, C.J.: Classification and Regression Trees. Chapman and Hall, Boca Raton (1984)
3. Brinkhuis, M.J.S., Maris, G.: Dynamic Parameter Estimation in Student Monitoring Systems. Measurement and Research Department Report 2009-1, CITO, The Netherlands (2009)
4. Chang, H.-H., Ying, Z.: A Global Information Approach to Computerized Adaptive Testing. Appl. Psych. Meas. 20(3), 213–229 (1996)
5. Corbett, A.T., Anderson, J.R.: Knowledge Tracing: Modeling the Acquisition of Procedural Knowledge. User Model User-Adap. 4, 253–278 (1995)
6. Gelman, A., Carlin, J.B., Stern, H.A., Rubin, D.B.: Bayesian Data Analysis. Chapman and Hall, London (1995)
7. Hattie, J., Timperley, H.: The Power of Feedback. Rev. Educ. Res. 77(1), 81–112 (2007)
8. Kingsbury, G.G., Zara, A.R.: Procedures for selecting items for computerized adaptive tests. Applied Measurement in Education 4, 359–375 (1991)
9. Lehmann, E.L., Casella, G.: Theory of Point Estimation. Springer, New York (1998)
10. Lord, F.M.: Application of Item Response Theory to Practical Testing Problems. Lawrence Erlbaum Associates, Hillsdale (1980)
11. Lord, F.M., Novick, M.R.: Statistical Theories of Mental Test Scores. Addison-Wesley, Reading (1968)

12. Matteucci, M., Veldkamp, B.P.: A Bayesian Approach for Introducing Empirical Information in CAT. Paper presented at the First International IACAT Conference on Computerized Adaptive Testing, Arnhem, The Netherlands, June 8-10 (2010)
13. Matteucci, M., Mignani, S., Veldkamp, B.P.: Prior Distributions for Item Parameters in IRT Models. Paper presented at 45th Scientific Meeting of the Italian Statistical Society, Satellite Conference on Statistics for Complex Problems: the Multivariate Permutation Approach and Related Topics, Padova, Italy, June 14-15 (2010)
14. Maij-de Meij, A.M., Schakel, L., Smid, N., Verstappen, N., Jaganjac, A.: Connector Ability; Professional manual. PiCompany BV, Utrecht (2008)
15. Nering, M.L., Ostini, R.: Handbook of Polytomous Item Response Theory Models. Routledge Academic, London (2010)
16. Reckase, M.D.: Multidimensional Item Response Theory. Springer, New York (2009)
17. Schakel, L., Maij-de Meij, A.M.: Enlarging an Item Pool by Rule-Based Item Generation. Paper presented at the First International IACAT Conference on Computerized Adaptive Testing, Arnhem, The Netherlands, June 8-10 (2010)
18. Shute, V.J.: Focus on Formative Feedback. Rev. Educ. Res. 78(1), 153–189 (2008)
19. Stocking, M.L.: Three practical issues for modern adaptive testing item pools (ETS Research Report No. 93-2). Educational Testing Service, Princeton (1994)
20. Timmers, C.F., Veldkamp, B.P.: Attention Paid to Feedback Provided by a Computer-Based Assessment for Learning on Information Literacy. Computers in Education (in press, 2011)
21. van der Linden, W.J.: Bayesian Item Selection Criteria for Adaptive Testing. Psychometrika 63(2), 201–216 (1998)
22. van der Linden, W.J.: Empirical Initialization of the Trait Estimation in Adaptive Testing. Appl. Psych. Meas. 23(1), 21–29 (1999)
23. Veldkamp, B.P.: Bayesian Item Selection in Constrained Adaptive Testing Using Shadow Tests. Psicologica 31(1), 149–169 (2010)
24. Veldkamp, B.P., van der Linden, W.J.: Designing Item Pools for Computerized Adaptive Tests. In: van der Linden, W.J., Glas, C.A.W. (eds.) Computerized Adaptive Testing: Theory and Practice, pp. 149–162. Kluwer Academic Publishers, Boston (2000)
25. Veldkamp, B.P., van der Linden, W.J.: Multidimensional Adaptive Testing with Constraints on Test Content. Psychometrika 76(4), 575–588 (2002)
26. Veldkamp, B.P., van der Linden, W.J.: Designing Item Pools for Adaptive Tests. In: van der Linden, W.J., Glas, C.A.W. (eds.) Elements of Adaptive Testing, pp. 231–246. Springer, New York (2000)
27. Veerkamp, W.J.J., Berger, M.P.F.: Some New Item Selection Criteria for Adaptive Testing. J. Educ. Behav. Stat. 22(2), 203–226 (1997)
28. Verhelst, N.D., Glas, C.A.W.: A Dynamic Generalization of the Rasch Model. Psychometrika 58(3), 395–415 (1993)
29. Wainer, H., Dorans, N.J., Eignor, D., Flaugher, R., Green, B.F., Mislevy, R.J., Steinberg, L., Thissen, D.: Computerized Adaptive Testing: A primer, 2nd edn. Lawrence Erlbaum Associates, Mahwah (2001)
30. Wang, T.H.: What strategies are effective for formative assessment in an e-learning environment? Journal of Computer Assisted Learning 23(3), 171–186 (2007)
31. Warm, T.A.: Weighted Likelihood Estimation of Ability in Item Response Theory. Psychometrika 54(3), 427–450 (1989)

On-Line vs. Face-to-Face Development of Interactive English Oral Competence: An Empirical Contrastive Study

Timothy Read[2], Elena Bárcena[1], Noa Talaván[1], and María Jordano[1]

[1] Department of Foreign Languages and Linguistics, Faculty of Philology, UNED,
Pº Senda del Rey 7, 28240 Madrid, Spain
{mbarcena,ntalavan,mjordano}@flog.uned.es
[2] Department of Computer Languages and Systems, School of Computer Science, UNED,
C./ Juan de Rosales s/n, 28240 Madrid, Spain
tread@lsi.uned.es

Abstract. This article presents a comparative empirical study of the effectiveness of a traditional face-to-face classroom vs. on-line technology for developing interactive oral English competence. The motivation for this study comes from the Clark – Kozma debate regarding the role and effectiveness of digital media in language learning. This question is updated to reflect the nature of modern technology and the way in which languages are currently taught. The learning scenario used for this experiment is presented, the results of which show that while the on-line group did not improve their oral competence as much as the face-to-face group, this was arguably due to behavioural patterns and the related practical difficulties experienced on-line. The authors conclude that, following Kozma's line of reasoning, ICT-based distance learning of second languages can be as effective as face-to-face learning only when measurements are taken to change the behavioural habits of students and to help them acquire the group discipline that these on-line environments demand.

Keywords: e-learning platforms, medium of instruction, blended learning, second language distance learning, interactive oral competence.

1 Introduction

This article presents a comparative empirical study undertaken in UNED (*Universidad Nacional de Educación a Distancia*; the Spanish national open university) as part of the COPPER (Collaborative Oral and written language adaPtive Production Environment) research project[1] [1] to evaluate the relative advantages and limitations of working on oral English interaction in both the traditional face-to-face (henceforth, F2F) classroom and via the use of on-line technology. With the widespread availability of computers and the Internet, and the educational possibilities they offer, the methodological tendency in UNED nowadays is increasingly to structure teaching

[1] This project has been funded by *Vicerrectorado de Calidad e Innovación Docente, UNED (III Convocatoria de Redes de Investigación para la Innovación Docente).*

S. De Wannemacker, G. Clarebout, P. De Causmaecker (Eds.): ITEC 2010, CCIS 126, pp. 40–55, 2011.

around the university's e-learning platform, aLF/dotLRN [2]. This modality coexists with the traditional text-based self-study supported by optional F2F tutorials at regional study centres, making up what is referred to as a blended learning approach.

The objective of this research is two fold: firstly, to evaluate which of these two modalities is more adequate (as far as is possible to ascertain from a hybrid learning approach like this one; see the analysis section below for more detail) for the development of the students' oral interaction skills in a foreign language. Secondly, this research is part of a larger project, named COPPER (Collaborative Oral and written language adaptive Production EnviRonment) which seeks to establish which learning activities are more appropriate within each modality: F2F or on-line. The COPPER project, therefore, ultimately seeks to achieve an optimal balance of learning activities and corresponding modalities. In this project, the "cognitive strengths" of these two different study modalities, the nature of the methods/ media present in each one, and the types of language communicative competence that can be best developed accordingly are explored.

This research is directly linked to the well known Clark vs. Kozma debate. In his 1983 paper, Clark [3] stated that "studies clearly suggest that media do not influence learning under any conditions" (p. 445), that is to say, that the medium (i.e., printed texts, CD-ROM, etc.) used to deliver the content of instruction is not part of its context and does not affect learning ([3], [4], [5]). In 1991, however, Kozma took the position that media *do* influence learning and, therefore, media selection *is* significant. Kozma [6] reframed Clark's question, which primarily addressed media attributes, and added issues regarding whether cognitively relevant characteristics of technologies, symbol systems, and processing capabilities affect learning outcomes.

The blended learning approach used in UNED has provided the authors with accumulative experience and empirical evidence over the years on the nature of this debate, whereby the differential nature between F2F and on-line study modalities appears to support Kozma's position. That is to say, the different contextual characteristics present in both modalities *do* affect learning. This view is argued by the authors both to support Kozma's position and also to extend it, since the inherent nature and availability of learning resources that the students have today under one or the other learning modality (e.g., the physical proximity of the interlocutor vs. the variety of potential interlocutors, the nature of the resources in the classroom vs. those on-line, the ease of group control vs. the level of learner-centredness, the essentially synchronous vs. asynchronous nature of the study and communication, etc.) have evolved and generally improved in both cases since Kozma wrote his article.

In the rest of this article the authors consider the nature of second language learning in the context of distance education, discuss the blended-learning model used in UNED, and go on to present and analyse a comparative empirical study of F2F and on-line learning, as per the Clark vs. Kozma debate, applied to languages.

2 Second Language Learning in a Distance Learning Environment

In the last few decades, second language distance learning has become increasingly popular, especially among professionals and busy adults in general [7]. The reasons vary in each case to some extent but they are related to autonomy, privacy, and the flexibility of timetables, geographical location and study rhythms [8]. While it is clear why this learning modality is popular with students, it should be considered whether it is appropriate for language learning.

Keegan [9, p.44] presented a characterization of distance learning in terms of five key elements, the first of which being the separation between teacher and student. However, not all disciplines are equally affected by the distance between the learning agents. Knowledge-based learning (e.g., geography, history, mathematics), although it is undoubtedly enriched by expert input, peer discussions, etc., can be undertaken in isolation through the passive study of receptive resources (books, maps, etc.). Language learning, on the contrary, is essentially practical and skill-based. The goal of such learning is to be able to undertake activities with other speakers using the target language (producing meaning, understanding, and interacting; [10]). Thus, the process of achieving such competence should involve an active participation (by the student) within a speaking community, using the same cognitive processes as he would in authentic communicative situations. *A priori*, this appears to be virtually impossible in a distance learning context. The fundamental separation of the student from his teacher and peers appears to be a considerable obstacle, not only in the rudimentary communicative sense of not being able to practice basic linguistic production and interaction, but also for the more fundamental and general way in which language use and learning are undertaken. Should, therefore, distance learning be dismissed as not being a suitable modality for languages? In order to answer this question, two key factors need to be considered: firstly, the type of language syllabus used and the way it is articulated in practice; and secondly, how ICT (Information and Communication Technology) and digital media are used as part of the learning process.

Many foreign language syllabi still rely heavily on the "language = vocabulary + structures" equation. They are known as structural or formal syllabi and their topics are organized according to frequency of occurrence and order of complexity and expected assimilation, particularly for the early learning stages ([11] and O'Neill's [12] well known EFL [English as a Foreign Language] books). In parallel, the Communicative Approach ([13], [14]) has advanced from the 1980s and 90s and evolved into the norm today. Its objective is that students are taught to use the foreign language to express values, judgments, etc. adapted to their own communicative needs. Not only linguistic competence, but also sociolinguistic competence is targeted, together with discourse and strategic competences ([13], [14]). Accordingly, second language teachers try to ensure the use of *authentic* materials and pragmatic, meaningful *tasks* in the classroom, while the organizational aspects of language are seen as subservient in the accomplishment of those purposes [15].

The generalized perspective on language teaching nowadays is that over-emphasis on contrastive analysis, structural accuracy and error correction will not necessarily transform linguistic competence into communicative competence. A future speaker of English, who obviously wants to command the language to put it into use and interact with other speakers of this language, must necessarily undergo a training period of intensive interaction. The Communicative Approach emphasizes interaction as the primary goal and, hence, the means of learning a language [16]. The learning objective of the wide majority of second language students is creating meaning, not necessarily producing perfectly grammatical structures and native-like pronounced utterances, but understanding and being understood: communicating, for which emphasis during the training period needs to be placed on personal involvement in vivid, realistic situations with others, which may even transcend the limits of the classroom.

Another key element used in today's language teaching that is becoming common-place is the *Common European Framework of Reference for Languages: Teaching, Learning and Assessment* (henceforth, CEFR; [17]). The framework presented in this document implied a revolution from earlier approaches to language learning where learners were immersed in a seemingly never-ending struggle to learn increasingly more complex and less common elements of a given language. As Morrow [18, p.5] synthesizes: "its impact on language teaching throughout the world is hard to exag-gerate". The CEFR incorporates many of the current methodological issues underly-ing language use and learning. In the last century there has been biased approach to methodological issues, and the focus has been oscillating between the teacher as the knowledgeable instructor, to the materials as learning stimuli, language as an abstract system of forms, structures and rules, and linguistic competence as a modular mental mechanism. Today, as reflected in the CEFR, the view of language use and learning is all-encompassing and considers the teacher, didactic materials, language forms, etc., as part of an integrative network whose driving force is the learning agent: the learner, who is the protagonist of a process that does not take place in a social and communi-cative vacuum, but in a rich and complex real world context.

From the perspective of learning as a socially mediated process, successful learn-ing occurs when social interaction produces cognitive development, i.e., there is a dynamic internalization of language from the interpsychological to the intrapsy-chological plane. The rise of *collaborative learning* practices in a general sense (including group learning, cooperative learning, etc.), partly as a result of the promi-nence of Social Constructivism, challenges the prevailing detailed and strictly struc-tured learning/teaching methods ([19], [20], [21]). Ohta [22] argued that successful learning occurs because there is cognitive development moment by moment during social interaction, i.e., a dynamic process of internalization of the language from the interpsychological to the intrapsychological plane, which happens in the *zone of proximal development*[2]. ([23], [24]) argue that the emergent processes and outcomes in collaborative learning activities are greatly influenced by the joint activity and interaction of the participants, and as such, cannot be fully designed in advance. However, there is also research demonstrating that completely free, unguided or un-structured collaboration does not necessarily result in productive activity or learning ([25], [26]).

Given the problems of distance learning that have been presented above and the essentially social constructivist nature of second language learning and modern approaches to it, the question remains about what ICT can do both to overcome the problems of distance learning of second languages and to facilitate the types of inter-actional situations needed to develop the necessary competences.

Over the last few decades, a lot has been said about the relevance of ICT and digi-tal media in education. In essence, ICT has two functions: shortening the distance between the different agents (teachers, tutors, students, etc.) who need to communi-cate, and providing access to digital resources or media that would otherwise not be

---

[2] The interactional space within which a learner is enabled to perform a task beyond his or her own current level of competence through assisted performance.

easily available. It is a fact that the use of different computational devices (desktop PCs, laptops, hand held, etc.) to access different digital media is part of the learning process nowadays, but the question arises: to what extent do they affect education? The answer to this question became especially pertinent with the progressive introduction of ICT in education. Since technology is constantly improving and becoming more available to the general public, this question is still today a key one in the pedagogical world.

One of the most well known lines of thought regarding this question comes from the Clark vs. Kozma debate on media versus methods, mentioned in the introduction. Clark noted that: 'studies clearly suggest that media do not influence learning under any conditions' [3, p.445]. In essence, he considered that the medium used to deliver instruction was external to learning per se, in the sense that it had no effect whatsoever on the instructional process. However, it is necessary to think about the state of ICT at the time Clark made this statement: computers were slow, memory was very limited, floppy disks were used to store data, audio was recorded in cassettes and it was rare to see colour monitors. That is basically why it was not until seven years later that another academic, Kozma [27], disagreed with Clark by arguing that not only did media influence learning, but also that the type of media chosen was highly significant in the result of the instructional process. He went on to define three parameters considered to be key when trying to understand media effects on education: technological characteristics (for example, a radio, a CD player, a computer, or a television all possess different features), symbol systems (words, audio, texts, diagrams, etc., provide different cognitive insights as far as the learner is concerned), and processing capabilities (what media do with the information).

In the 1990s, technology started changing very rapidly. Improvements in memory, processor speed, hard drive capability, etc., together with the emergence of the CD-ROM, made multimedia instruction possible in a single application. However, at a time when many people had their attention hooked on computer assisted instruction, Clark [28] was still sceptical about the benefits of digital media and still defended pedagogical methods and strategies as the main factor that influenced learning. Kozma kept defending the opposite stance, and in a special issue of *Educational Technology, Research & Development* in 1994, devoted to the Clark vs. Kozma debate, this very author tried to close the discussion advocating that it was time to move on to other topics [6]. Conclusions derived from this special issue when other authors, such as Ullmer [29] and Reiser [30], also expressed their opinion on this matter, shedding light on the problems related to the research and design of effective instruction at a time when big changes in instruction delivery were taking place due to the fast advance of innovation in ICT.

However, a couple of years later, when Intelligent Tutoring Systems appeared in the discipline of Computer Assisted Learning, the debate re-emerged with new voices and arguments. This time, however, the discussion did not focus on the nature of digital media anymore, but on interactivity, that is, on the interaction among media, content, and learner and the nature of such interactions [31].

What really matters about the media/method effects debate and its continuation as far as forms of interactive learning are concerned, is that it contributed to the foundations of educational technology. The elements discussed therein are still analyzed by new researchers in this field and they promote new lines of experimentation and study. What is more, the debate highlighted the complexities and interrelations present in the various types of instruction (and the different media) and human cognition [32]. Nowadays, it can be claimed without a doubt that the presence of ICT and digital resources *do* affect learning to a great extent. Not only that, they even influence instructional methods in many ways. In fact, today it would be necessary to redefine instructional methods as being supported by media, since the latter establish specific conditions for learning to take place, and thus should be considered as part of the method itself. Furthermore, language learning is, above all, facilitated through interaction ([23], [33]), and environments that support negotiation of meaning are optimal for second language learning. To answer the question posed above regarding the suitability of distance learning for languages, it can be argued that distance learning can be a suitable modality for languages *if* suitable ICT and digital media are used as part of the learning process for a suitable language syllabus. Given this theoretical position, which is implicit in the widespread availability of on-line language courses, the authors wanted to explore and test it by undertaking a contrastive empirical study of two different groups of students undertaking the same experiment, one in a F2F classroom and the other using on-line tools. In the next section, the way in which the considerations presented in this section are materialized in UNED is presented and discussed as a way to establish the context in which the comparative learning experiment is to be undertaken.

3 The UNED Blended-Learning Model

Before virtual on-line courses existed in e-learning platforms, students essentially studied in isolation using printed books and materials like manuals, workbooks (obviously with answer keys), audiocassettes, etc., selected by their teaching teams at the main campus in Madrid. The *tutors* from the support UNED regional study centres constituted a key element for narrowing the distance between the *teaching teams* (in the university's base in Madrid) and the students, which are spread all over Spain and, to a lesser extent, also around the world. However, since tutorials were optional and inevitably spaced in time, this distance teaching methodology was clearly insufficient for disciplines like languages, which are skill-based as well as knowledge-based [2]. Indeed, our nature as social learners is particularly evident in the case of foreign language learning. The development of language-based communicative competences necessarily requires intensive interaction with a community of speakers (ideally native speakers, but also fellow students or course mates). The reality for a long time in UNED was that given the abovementioned resources, little could be done to teach interactive language skills. Firstly, the teacher-student ratio was highly unbalanced (around 1,000 teachers in Madrid and 4,000 tutors distributed in regional study centres for over 200,000 students - in particular there was an introductory zero-level English course with over 14,000 students!). Secondly, as mentioned above, the standard student profile (adults with busy personal and professional lives) meant that their availability to attend F2F tutorials was very scarce. Hence, such tutorials were necessarily optional and, furthermore, the centres only ensured tutorial coverage for the core and most numerous subjects. This situation meant that language students could not be required to work on their oral skills as would have been desirable, and hence they could not be evaluated on such aspects either.

In the year 2000 the UNED started its virtual campus using the commercial platform WebCT. At the same time in-house development started to adapt a community e-learning platform developed at MIT, dotLRN, to the UNED's methodology and educational management systems. This modified platform became aLF. aLF is different to other platforms in that students exist in virtual communities and working groups whether or not they are participating in specific courses. Here courses are established, where contents (documents, audio files, etc.) are organised, stored and shared, and activities are planned and performed with the aid of a calendar. News and notifications are published. Questionnaires and closed activities can be designed and easily implemented, and autoevaluation and heteroevaluation finely integrated. All of these functions, public and private, can be largely customized on demand by any user with given administrative permissions. Statistics show that since the year 2000, aLF/dotLRN usage has increased in terms of users and sessions as the functionalities provided by the tools have grown. It currently hosts more than 350 courses and communities, and provides services to 150,000 students, professors and tutors. The number of users grows every year by 22% average, and the number of sessions increases more significantly, 33%, with an average of 4 million transactions per day.

The development of aLF/dotLRN in the UNED (together with the appearance of the Bologna agreement, with which it coincided in time) brought deep changes in the teacher's roles, the student's level of autonomy and control, and the evaluation process, which were unforeseen at the beginning and only became evident with practice and experience. Furthermore, the supportive role of tutors was also redefined to reflect these changes and a new figure was created to provide methodological and technological guidance to students in the on-line courses, namely the *TAR* (Network Support Tutor). There are over 300 TARs at the moment, who dynamize the forums, relocate students' input where appropriate, answer students' queries regarding the functionality of the platform tools, ensure that the documents are all uploaded correctly and stored where they should go, etc. As in every changing methodology, problems have arisen due to human errors and misconceptions, aLF/dotLRN's early lack of robustness to cope with massive student numbers, etc., but they are definitely receding and all parties involved are reasonably satisfied with the progress made.

We have seen in this and the previous section the suitability of distance learning for languages and how such a learning modality is instantiated in UNED. Hence, in the next section an empirical study is presented that was designed to test the reality of distance learning for languages, and in particular for its most challenging component from both a technological and a linguistic perspective: the development of oral interaction skills.

4   An Empirical Comparative Study of Oral Interaction in Second Language Learning

An empirical study was designed and undertaken during the 2008-09 academic year with a selection of 20 student volunteers from a regional study centre in Madrid (group A; which met once a week for sixty-minute F2F tutorial classes) and another 16 volunteers from the on-line course (from different parts of Spain), with whom all contact was computer mediated (group B; who were expected to connect to the course and work therein on a weekly basis). In both cases taking part in this experiment was optional, and rewarded with up to 1 additional point toward their final course mark. Methodologically speaking, it could be argued that undertaking an empirical study that compares two fundamentally different modalities for learning (namely, F2F and e-learning) is questionable, due to the essential differences between them (and the many experimental variables that would need to be controlled to ensure that the comparison is reasonable). While the authors are fully aware of the limitations of this study (and, therefore, the caution that needs to be taken when drawing any conclusions), it is argued here that this experiment is a reflection of the reality of the two different ways in which our students work (as would be expected in a blended-learning institution) and is, therefore, perfectly valid. However, what has to be clearly emphasised (as will be done in the discussion section of this article), is that any conclusions that are drawn about the empirical results of this study need to be treated qualitatively, and used as a starting point for further "finer grained" experiments (within each learning modality).

The students in each group undertook a level test before being admitted to the experiment to ensure that they had similar oral English competence levels (all students had a lower intermediate level of English (levels A2 – B1). The experiment focused on the performance of an oral activity that would be developed and undertaken by the students over a two-month period (during the second semester of the academic year). The activity consisted of a role-playing scenario, namely a job interview for a receptionist position in a hotel. The roles were the following: the job seeker, the secretary at the Human Resources Department (henceforth, HRD) of the employing company and the interviewer. To undertake the activity, the students were divided into subgroups of five, with one student playing the interviewer, another the secretary, and three more as the potential job candidates. They were encouraged to use the monolingual language resources they had available, namely dictionaries, grammar guides, etc. Both the F2F and the on-line group were advised that they could use word processing tools when preparing their dialogues, although plagiarism would not be permitted. The activity was divided into tasks (so that they integrated into the topics dealt with in the respective modules of the course), specifically the following:

- Task 1 (expected time - one and a half weeks): contact the HRD after having read the job advertisement in a newspaper to express interest to be considered for the post. In this task, the students who would play the job seekers had to prepare a written transcript of what they would expect to say when initiating the contact. The students who played the secretary of the HRD and the interviewer would similarly prepare answers to typical questions that might be posed during the initial contact phase. These transcripts were considered to constitute a reasonable analogy of the preparation that a typical job seeker would undertake in this situation, and of the verbal experience of professional interviewers in this type of specialized discourse. Each student would work independently, and learning would be reinforced by making the group comment on each transcript, regardless of the role-played.

- Task 2 (expected time – two weeks): hand in the CV after showing evidence of being a suitable candidate and hence, arranging an appointment for another day. A simplified CV would have to be prepared individually by the students playing the job seekers (showing some previous experience working in hotels, etc.). Similarly, the secretary and interviewer would prepare a set of evaluation criteria to be used when assessing the CVs. These tasks, although they were neither oral nor interactive, were considered to be a realistic reflection of a similar situation in the real world, and also necessary to work on terminology, etc., prior to the undertaking of the final oral interaction task.

- Task 3 (expected time - one and a half weeks): arrive the day of the interview, announcing his/her arrival and being met by the company staff. Here the group would once again divide into two, with the secretary and interviewer preparing a set of questions for the interview (following on from the evaluation made of each CV) and the job seekers preparing answers to typical potential interview questions that could be made about this job and the experience of each candidate.

- Task 4 (expected time – three weeks): hold a rather extensive job interview. Based upon the work done in the previous tasks, each job seeker would undertake the interview. These sessions were to be recorded for subsequent analysis and use. Finally, the group as a whole would work together to listen to the recordings, comment upon each one, and decide, based upon the CVs and interview performance, who should be given the job.

Both groups A and B had tutor figures to coordinate the activity. Group A had a standard F2F tutor who undertook the activity monitoring at the study centre in the conventional way, and group B had a TAR, who did the same on-line. The former undertook the coordination following seven steps:

1. Presenting the activity in detail (the goals, stages, etc.).
2. Creating the working subgroups and assigning roles to each participant.
3. Dividing the time available for the different stages of the project and providing free working time at the end of the tutorial session.
4. Trying to help the students break down the initial anxiety and other emotional blocks and giving them very occasionally tips to improve their ongoing work.
5. Providing them with feedback on demand.
6. Evaluating the activity output and passing a questionnaire to the participants.
7. Writing a final report.

The latter substituted steps 3 and 4 with the following:

3. Resolve technical problems related to use of the e-learning platform and its related tools.
4. Help the group with practical coordination and communication issues related to the activity.

In both groups the students were evaluated using the rubric presented in table 1, which is based upon the work of Arlington County [34]. The results are presented in table 3.

Table 1. Evaluation rubric used for the student groups

Skill	Component Descriptors
Comprehension 1 2 3 4 5 (circle one) low high	Comprehends speech at a normal rate of speed ___ Always ___ Most of the time ___ Much of the time ___ Sometimes ___ Rarely ___ With non-verbal cues only
Vocabulary 1 2 3 4 5 (circle one) low high	___ Uses varied and descriptive language, possibly including native-like phrasing and/or idiomatic expressions ___ Uses vocabulary sufficient to communicate in most social and academic contexts, with some varied and descriptive language ___ Uses vocabulary sufficient to communicate in most social and academic contexts ___ Uses vocabulary sufficient to express basic needs and feelings; responds to simple questions, with limited or no use of first language ___ Uses only basic vocabulary with possible heavy use of first language ___ Uses isolated words or sentence fragments ___ Uses native language only
Grammar 1 2 3 4 5 (circle one) low high	___ Uses basic grammar ___ Makes some errors which obscure meaning (Check only those areas that need work.) ___ Present tense ___ Past tense ___ Future tense ___ Complex verbal structures ___ Gender agreement ___ Singular/Plural ___ Subject-verb agreement ___ Negations ___ Adjective placement ___ Direct object pronouns ___ Prepositions ___ Articles
Fluency 1 2 3 4 5 (circle one) low high	___ Uses native-like flow of speech ___ Uses fluent connected speech ___ Uses fluent connected speech, occasionally disrupted by search for correct form of expression ___ Speech is connected but frequently disrupted by search for correct form of expression ___ Uses simple sentences ___ Uses phrases and "chunks" ___ Uses one-word/two-word utterances ___ Silence
Interaction 1 2 3 4 5 (circle one) low high	___ Can engage in simple and brief information-based conversations ___ Can engage in simple personal conversations to do with routine topics ___ Can engage into long conversations seeking for and providing subtle information ___ Able to manipulate speech to seek for information with subtle intentions, and provide it in a skilful way

As well as the quantitative evaluation, the students were given a questionnaire[3] (presented in table 2) to answer in order to provide the teaching team with qualitative feedback about the learning process and experience.

---

[3] The on-line version of the questionnaire was implemented using a template at the beginning of the activity with a combined closed-open format to enable a semi-quantitative analysis.

Table 2. Student questionnaire

---

1. What is your overall impression of this project? Are you pleased you took part in it?
2. Would you have liked to do more projects like this throughout the year? What have you missed in it?
3. What do you think about your collaboration with your course mates?
4. What do you think of your monitors' role? Would you have liked more support or less interference from them?
5. What type of competence, skill, topic, etc. would you have liked to work on?
6. What specifically do you think you have improved with this project?
7. Did you find it too much work or would you have liked it to be longer and/or more intensive?
8. What do you think about the topic? Did you find it motivating and entertaining?
9. Did you feel confident throughout the project or did anything at all bother you?
10. Would you be interested in participating in another project like this outside the course, just for the benefit of improving your English?

The majority of the students (in both groups) answered the questions that provided important feedback about the experiment. In general, both sets of students were happy with having taken part in the experiment and, in fact, wished that there had been more activities like this one in the course. However, the students from group B expressed less satisfaction that those from the other group (as discussed below).

Tutors from both groups reported that the volunteers showed great interest at first. At the beginning, the TAR's plan was to hold synchronous chat sessions at least once a week, but since the students connected to the platform at different times, it proved very difficult to coordinate these sessions. It was then decided to try asynchronous sessions with deadlines for the initial design stage of the activity, and even then, the participation was extraordinarily small (25% of the students). It is argued that this behaviour reflects the lack of familiarity that the students had working collaboratively on-line. This does not refer to practical difficulties with the communication tools (since the students had shown that they were reasonably competent users earlier in the course), but more to the problems of forming behavioural habits about when to connect and how to work on-line, both individually and collaboratively. A common problem that occurred in both groups was that of student drop out. In group A, four of the twenty students were unable to undertake the activity, so the group was reorganised into four sub-groups of four people. Similarly, in group B, six people dropped out, leaving ten students who were split into two groups of five.

As time passed, the majority of students at the regional study centre were progressing constantly and steadily with their work. It should be noted that these students (all with generally busy personal and professional lives) made the most of their visits to the study centres and organised informal working sessions following each F2F tutorial class, where they met up in the coffee room to work together on the tasks. From the beginning it was noted that it was much harder to identify problems and coordinate the students in group B. Three members of the teaching team plus the TAR started sending several messages to these students to encourage collaboration using different tools, firstly in the forum at the virtual course, and then via personalised email. A few students reacted to this strategy and confessed to feel alone, lost and not understand what they were supposed to do. Every effort was taken on the part of the monitors (teachers and TAR), which helped only to some extent. In the last four weeks of the experiment, six particularly active students on-line were rearranged to work together and this sub-group was without a doubt the most successful of group B. It is argued that this success reflects the way in which students who are already familiarised with using on-line tools, and motivated to do so, can work effectively. This situation clearly contrasted with the behaviour and performance of the students in group A. Not only did all but two students complete their activity, but the tutor also declared that attendance to the tutorial sessions generally rose by almost 23% during the two-month period of the activity as compared to the rest of the academic year.

Table 3. Results of quantitative evaluation of group work

Skill	F2F group (A) %		On-line group (B) %	
	Mean	SD	Mean	SD
Vocabulary	78.7	3	62.5	4
Grammar	74	4	58.3	4
Comprehension	94.4	2	80	1
Fluency	78.4	2	55.5	3
Interaction	58.2	3	57.6	2

If we take the results presented in table 3 at face value, then they would seem to suggest that group A performed marginally better that group B, and as such, learned better. However, these data need to be analysed alongside the results of the question-naires and the impression gained by the tutors and TAR, in order to obtain a more insightful understanding of the result. Such an analysis gives rise to the following considerations:

1. Both the tutors and students have the perception that the F2F group had an easier overall working experience than the on-line group because the former only had to motivate themselves to go to the study centre. Once there, in their group, the work was easily divided and undertaken. There was a very high level of mutual support and collaboration. The latter (on-line group) found it harder to motivate themselves to actually connect to the e-learning platform, and when on-line, did not perceive the same group support. Furthermore, it is well recognised that when a group of students is initially formed to work col-laboratively in an activity, initially there is considerable negotiation and discussion, a lot of which happens almost without the students' explicit awareness. For group B, this had to happen using the on-line tools, which im-plied slower progress and in some cases caused the students to lose the thread of the activity.

2. Related to the first point, the tutor in group A, even though instructed not to help and support the students (so as to reflect the conditions of the on-line group), still inevitably did so, albeit not directly. When quizzed on his behav-iour, he reported that in a real social context with a clearly defined tutor-students relationship, it was practically impossible not to help, something a lot easier to undertake on-line.

3. Certain parts of the activity actually required the students to be working at the same time, so that coordination and communication could take place. This was no problem for group B (who had already come along to the class at the same given time), but was an added difficulty for this group, since the very asynchronous nature of a lot of the tools used in aLF/dotLRN means that the students connect when it suits them. Hence, getting people together at the same time required an additional effort for the on-line group, which was perceived by its members as a severe additional difficulty.

4. Finally, even though the students in the on-line group had used aLF/dotLRN before, they had not used all the tools they were required to use for this activity, and hence, had an additional difficult to cope with them.

After the analysis of the activity data (recordings, transcripts, tutors' reports and questionnaires, etc.) had been undertaken, it became evident that the difference in the results of the two groups can be argued not to be due to intrinsic methodological differences, but to the practical and psychological difficulties that still need to be solved for on-line distance learning. In the next section, these qualitative results will be further discussed and some conclusions drawn about this experiment.

5 Discussion and Conclusions

As has been noted in the introduction, the popularity of distance learning contexts for English is increasing these days due to the hectic personal and professional lives of adult learners. While such a modality is far from perfect, especially for language learning, it is selected by very large numbers of students because they cannot attend F2F courses. As Holmberg [8, p.24] notes, convenience, flexibility and adaptability to individual circumstances is what makes this mode of study so popular. The UNED teaching methodology is hybrid these days, or rather blended, since the ICT and digital media available in the e-learning platform aLF/dotLRN make it possible.

This paper focused on the analysis of the preparation process undertaken by both groups, and presents an analysis of the results. Group A obtained marginally better results than group B in all five language communicative categories under study. Close inspection of the dynamics of both groups' workflow showed that the on-line group did not improve their oral competence as much as the F2F group, not because of any inherent limitations of the e-learning platform and its tools (i.e., that they had learnt less efficiently by using the tools provided), but due to both their behavioural patterns on-line and the difficulties highlighted in the previous section. The few students that were comfortable on-line had previously made an active use of the on-line tools and had comparable results to group A. It is therefore argued here that, in Kozma's words, media influence learning and, therefore, ICT-based digital-media selection *is* significant. However, it should be noted that more than a decade has passed since Kozma's article was published, during which time Internet access and digital-media access are much more pervasive and accepted. Hence, arguably the results of this experiment, rather than just supporting Kozma's thesis, show that ICT-based distance learning of second languages (both oral and written competences) can be as effective as F2F learning when effort is made to change the behavioural habits of the students to help them acquire the confidence, discipline, and the sense of commitment and responsibility that working in on-line environments requires. It should be noted that given the methodological difficulties of controlling the experimental variables in two fundamentally different approaches to learning, then this conclusion needs to treated with caution. Hence, rather than representing the end of the experimental process, the conclusion presented here should in fact be taken as the starting point for a series of additional experiments that further explore the scenario variables within each learning approach (F2F and on-line). However, it is still argued by the authors that the results of the study are valuable, because they reflect the reality of blended learning, an approach that is used by hundreds of thousands of students each year.

Finally, it has been noted in this article that the demand for on-line second language courses is largely driven by the student themselves, reflecting their lifestyles. However, even if this were not the case, it would be unviable for a university like UNED to provide extensive F2F courses of these characteristics, given the very high numbers of students and the unbalanced teacher-student ratio. The authors finally argue, based upon the work presented in this article, that future research in this area should focus on how to optimally integrate three key aspects of on-line second language distance learning to maximize its effectiveness: the linguistic notional-functional syllabus structure and its communicative competence-based focus (following the CEFR and its forthcoming descendants), the socially oriented methodology implicit in the learning, and the ICT-based digital media used as glue to specify quantitatively and implement computationally the above complex linguistic and didactic interrelationships underlying the learning process.

References

1. Read, T., Bárcena, E., Barros, B., Varela, R., Pancorbo, J.: COPPER: Modeling User Linguistic Production Competence in an Adaptive Collaborative Environment. In: Ardissono, L., Brna, P., Mitrović, A. (eds.) UM 2005. LNCS (LNAI), vol. 3538, pp. 144–153. Springer, Heidelberg (2005)
2. Read, T., Ros, S., Rodrigo, C., Pastor, R., Hernández, R.: The UNED ICT Architecture for 'Virtual Attendance'. In: Proceedings of ICDE 2009 – 25th International Conference on Data Engineering, Shangai, pp. 192–199 (2009)
3. Clark, R.E.: Reconsidering research on learning from media. Review of Educational Research 17(2), 92–101 (1983)
4. Hart: I. ITForum (July 25, 1996a),
   http://itech1.coe.uga.edu/itforum/extra3/ex3-6.html;
   ITForum (1996), http://itech1.coe.uga.edu/itforum/home.html
5. Fleming, M., Levie, W.H.: Instructional message design: Principles from the behavioral and cognitive sciences, 2nd edn. Educational Technology Publications, Englewood Cliffs (1993)
6. Kozma, R.B.: Will media influence learning? Reframing the debate. Educational Technology, Research & Development 42(2), 7–19 (1994)
7. Roe, P.: The case for distance: rethinking the foundations. In: Richards, K., Roe, P. (eds.) Distance Learning in ELT. Modern English Pub. and British Council, pp. 54–76. Macmillan, London (1994)
8. Holmberg, B.: Theory and practice of distance education. Routledge, London (1989)

9. Keegan, D.: Foundations of Distance Education. Routledge, London (1996)
10. Swain, M.: The output hypothesis and beyond: Mediating acquisition through collaborative dialogue. In: Lantolf, J.P. (ed.) Sociocultural theory and second language learning, pp. 97–114. Oxford University Press, Oxford (2000)
11. Alexander, L.G.: Longman English Grammar Practice. Longman, London (1990)
12. O'Neill, R.: English works. Longman, Essex (1993)
13. Canale, M.: From Communicative competence to communicative language pedagogy. In: Richards, J., Schmidt, R. (eds.) Language and Communication, pp. 2–27. Longman, London (1983)
14. Canale, M., Swain, M.: Theoretical Bases of Communicative Approaches to Second Language Teaching and Testing. Applied Linguistics 1(1), 1–47 (1980)
15. Freeman, D.L.: Techniques and Principles in Language Teaching. Oxford University Press, Oxford (2000)
16. Galloway, A.: Communicative Language Teaching: An Introduction and Sample Activities. Center for Applied Linguistics Digest, EDRS No. ED357642 (1993), http://www.cal.org/resources/digest/gallow01.html
17. Council of Europe. Common European Framework of Reference for Languages: Learning, Teaching, Assessment. Cambridge University Press, Cambridge (2001)
18. Morrow, K.: Insights from the Common European Framework. Oxford University Press, Oxford (2004)
19. Gokhale, A.A.: Collaborative learning enhances critical thinking. Journal of Technology Education 7(1), 22–30 (1995)
20. Lowych, J., Pöysä, J.: Design of collaborative learning environments. Computers in Human Behavior 17, 507–516 (2001)
21. Palincsar, A.S., Herrenkohl, L.R.: Designing collaborative contexts. Theory Into Practice 41, 26–32 (2002)
22. Ohta, A.S.: Rethinking interaction in SLA: Developmentally appropriate assistance in the zone of proximal development and the acquisition of L2 grammar. In: Lantolf, J.P. (ed.) Sociocultural Theory and Second Language Learning, pp. 51–78. Oxford University Press, Oxford (2000)
23. Vygotsky, L.S.: Mind in Society. The Development of Higher Psychological Processes. Harvard University Press, Cambridge (1978)
24. Wertsch, J.V.: Vygotsky and the Social Formation of Mind. Harvard University Press, Cambridge (1985)
25. Winn, W.: Current trends in educational technology research: The study of learning environments. Educational Psychology Review 14(3), 331–351 (2002)
26. Kreijns, K., Kirschner, P.A., Jochems, W.: Identifying the pitfalls of social interaction in computer-supported collaborative learning environments: a review of the research. Computers in Human Behavior 19(3), 335–353 (2003)
27. Kozma, R.B.: Learning with Media. Review of Educational Research 61(2), 7–19 (1991)
28. Clark: Media will never influence learning. Educational Technology, Research & Development 42(2), 7–10 (1994)
29. Ullmer, E.J.: Media and learning. Are there two kinds of truth? Educational Technology, Research & Development 42(2), 21–32 (1994)
30. Raiser, R.A.: Clark's invitation to the dance: An instructional designer's response. The media influence debate: Read the fine print, but don't lose sight of the big picture. Educational Technology, Research & Development 42(2), 45–48 (1994)

31. Drapper, S.: ITForum (1996),
    http://itech1.coe.uga.edu/itforum/extra3/ex3-28.html
32. Bastian, M., Zellner, R.: First there was the media and the message, then there was content,
    context, and interactivity: The evolution of the Clark/Kozma media effect debate (2000),
    http://www.coe.tamu.edu/~mbastian/Clark-Kozma/
    CK-Ab-Intro.htm#Introduction
33. Johnson, D.W., Johnson, R.T.: Cooperation and competition: Theory and Research. Inter-
    action Book Company, Edina (1989)
34. Arlington County (1997),
    http://www.sites4teachers.com/links/
    redirect.php?url=http://www.cal.org/twi/rubrics/oral1-5.pdf

Speech Technology in CALL: The Essential Role of Adaptation

Joost van Doremalen, Helmer Strik, and Catia Cucchiarini

Centre for Language and Speech Technology,
Erasmusplein 1, Nijmegen, The Netherlands
j.vandoremalen@let.ru.nl,
h.strik@let.ru.nl,
c.cucchiarini@let.ru.nl

Abstract. In this paper we present general guidelines for designing Computer Assisted Language Learning (CALL) applications that make use of Automatic Speech Recognition (ASR) technology. Designing such systems requires a gradual process of adaptation aimed at reaching the optimal compromise between the pedagogical and personal goals of users and the technological possibilities. We also discuss a specific case study in which we applied these guidelines and show the importance of adaptation for satisfactory system performance.

Keywords: Computer Assisted Language Learning (CALL), Automatic Speech Recognition (ASR), adaptation, pronunciation, error detection, feedback.

1   Introduction

Current theories of second language learning emphasize the importance of usage based learning in the L2: language is learned from participatory experience in which language input is processed and language output is produced in meaningful contexts [1]. In addition, since usage based learning is a necessary, but not sufficient condition for L2 learning, explicit instruction and feedback mechanisms are also required to draw learners' attention to specific problematic areas and gaps in their L2. For speaking proficiency such optimal conditions for learning to take place are almost never achieved in traditional classroom settings where one teacher has to deal with many different learners with different characteristics and requirements.

Research indicates that, in general, one-on-one interactive learning situations in which learners receive optimal corrective feedback are to be preferred. The two sigma benefit demonstrated by [2] has provided further support for the advantages of one-on-one tutoring relative to classroom instruction. In the case of language learning, one-on-one tutoring by trained language instructors is usually not feasible for the majority of language learners, because too costly. Furthermore, the increasing mobility of workers worldwide has led to a growing demand for language classes that often outstrips the supply. As a result, alternatives for

S. De Wannemacker, G. Clarebout, P. De Causmaecker (Eds.): ITEC 2010, CCIS 126, pp. 56–69, 2011.

or supplements to teacher-fronted lessons have received increasing attention in the last decades, in particular Computer Assisted Language Learning (CALL) applications.

CALL systems can offer sufficient and varied language input and the possibility of practicing at any time and in any place, at the learner's pace. In addition, such systems can be designed as to provide individualized feedback on the learner's performance. In the specific case of speaking proficiency, advanced CALL applications that can provide practice and corrective feedback can be realized by employing Automatic Speech Recognition (ASR). However, given the current state of ASR technology and the specific difficulties in processing L2 speech, developing high-quality ASR-based CALL systems is a challenging enterprise.

L2 speech may deviate from native speech at the level of pronunciation, morphology, syntax and the lexicon, thus posing serious problems to the use of ASR in CALL systems. Pronunciation deviations may concern the realization of individual sounds, prosody or both. For instance, L2 learners may use phonemes or stress patterns from their L1 when speaking the target language or they may have difficulties in perceiving and/or realizing phonetic contrasts that are not distinctive in their mother tongue. At the level of morphology, L2 learners may find it difficult to produce correct forms of verbs, nouns, adjectives, articles, and so forth. Irregular verbs and nouns may also pose serious problems, resulting in the production of nonexistent regularized forms. Deviations in syntax may concern the structure of sentences, the ordering of constituents and their omission or insertion. As to vocabulary, L2 learners also tend to have a limited and often deviant lexicon. Finally, L2 speech exhibits more disfluencies and hesitation phenomena than native speech and is characterized by a lower speech rate.

To try and circumvent most of these problems and still develop high-quality ASR-based CALL systems that can be useful for improving speaking performance in an L2, it is necessary to consider a whole series of important factors that vary from the teacher and learner's goals to properties of the speech recognizer and eventually make those choices that lead to the best result. In other words, the whole process of system design and development consists in adapting the technology to the pedagogical requirements and then reconsidering the pedagogical requirements given the affordances of the technology. In addition, adaptation at a more individual level is required, to optimize the system for each individual learner. This may also vary from adaptation at the level of errors addressed and feedback forms employed down to adaptation at the level of models in the speech recognizer. The errors that will be addressed depend on the initial level of the learner. As the learner improves, which can be automatically measured by the system, more difficult errors can be addressed. The system can also adapt the feedback form to the learner, by selecting the feedback move that is more conducive to uptake in that specific learner. This recurring process of adaptation takes place at different levels of system development, as will be explained in the current paper.

In section 2 of this paper, we discuss general problems and requirements in developing ASR-based CALL systems for practicing speaking proficiency such as pedagogical and personal goals [3], technological possibilities and challenges, paying special attention to error detection and feedback. In section 3 of this paper we go on to discuss the specific choices we made in developing a particular prototype application for learners of Dutch as a second language (DL2), the SPRAAKMAKKERS system, within the framework of the DISCO project (Development and Integration of Speech technology into COurseware for language learning) [4]. This application aims at optimizing learning through interaction in realistic communication situations and at providing intelligent feedback on important aspects of DL2 speaking, viz. pronunciation, morphology, and syntax. We briefly discuss goal analysis and courseware design (sections 3.1 and 3.2) and then go on to present the system architecture (3.3) and the system implementation (3.4). Section 3.5 deals with speech recognition, 3.6 with error detection, 3.7 with feedback, while 3.8 is devoted to system errors. Conclusions are presented in section 4.

2   Designing ASR-Based CALL Systems

In designing ASR-based CALL systems we have to deal with two important factors. Firstly, learners and teachers have pedagogical and personal goals they both would like to achieve by using the system. Secondly, there are limitations in ASR and speech technology that we have to take into account. In essence, designing such systems requires a gradual process of adaptation aimed at reaching the optimal compromise between the goals and the technological possibilities. In the next sections we will describe how these factors influence the design process and constitute important research topics on their own.

2.1   Goal-Oriented Design

In a goal-oriented design approach, the starting point of the design is the elicitation and analysis of goals [3]. For a specific learning situation and target group, pedagogical goals are elicited from teachers and learners. Pedagogical goals may include a specific target vocabulary or grammar, or, for example, the enhancement of communicative skills.

Besides pedagogical goals, users always have personal goals, which might conflict with pedagogical goals. These include the avoidance of problems and fears from both learners and teachers. For example, teachers may feel unconfident using technology in and around the classroom, or L2 learners may want to improve their L2 pronunciation so as to sound as native as possible. In addition, users may have goals that cannot possibly be achieved given the state of the technology. These are important issues that have to be taken into consideration in the design process.

Different tools exist to elicit these goals, such as interviews and focus groups [5]. In Section 3, we will come back to the specific goal analysis that was carried out for developing our prototype system.

2.2   Technological Possibilities and Challenges

For an ASR-based CALL system to behave in a pedagogically sound and reliable manner, it has:

1. to correctly recognize what the learner said,
2. to detect errors in the learner's utterance, and
3. to give appropriate feedback to the learner.

These three different tasks are carried out by three different but interacting modules. These modules need to be designed in such a way that in tandem they give the desired feedback given the spoken output of the learner. We will now discuss what kinds of problems each of these modules has to face and how these modules interact.

Speech Recognition. Automatic Speech Recognition is a large area of research, which has existed for over 50 years now [6]. Speaker-dependent systems that can recognize carefully produced speech are already available and their performance is in fact quite good. However, their performance drops tremendously when these systems have to recognize spontaneous speech produced by multiple speakers.

The main reason for this decrease in performance is the enormous amount of variation an ASR system has to deal with in recognizing speech from multiple speakers. When conventional ASR systems are applied in a CALL context, ASR performance is likely to plummet. This is the case because CALL systems often have to deal with atypical speech, such as non-native speech or pathological speech, which generally exhibits even more variation. Dealing with this variation is more difficult when the number of word sequences the system has to consider as hypotheses of the spoken utterance (the search space) is large. In other words, when a learner can utter just about anything to the system, without any constraints, it is very difficult to find out which words were actually uttered in what order.

Basically, one can adopt two different strategies to cope with these difficulties: (1) to constrain the search space or (2) to adapt existing technology to better handle the variation.

If the search space is constrained, the output of the learner should in the same way also be constrained. In some cases, such as practicing grammar, learners need to have the possibility of formulating sentences with a certain degree of freedom in order to show whether they master specific grammatical structures. Therefore, a challenge is to design exercises which are relatively constrained and still induce the desired learning effect.

Adapting existing technology to handle speech variation includes building speaker or language dependent models of phonemes and words. In Section 3.5, we will discuss pilot experiments that were aimed at investigating some of these issues.

Error Detection. Once the system has established a reliable hypothesis of what the learner has said, it has to be able to detect possible errors in this utterance.

Depending on the established goals, an ASR-based CALL system may have to be able to detect errors at different levels of speaking proficiency such as syntax, morphology, phonology and prosody.

Some errors might be very difficult to detect in an automatic way, and giving erroneous feedback on these aspects may do more harm than good to the learner. Therefore, it is very important to carefully investigate how well the system can detect errors. For this purpose, feasibility and accuracy studies need to be carried out. On the basis of these studies, one can conclude on which errors the system can reliably provide feedback.

In order to carry out error detection, the system has:

1. to have a representation of what the learner said,
2. to have a representation of what the learner was supposed to say, and
3. to be able to compute the discrepancy between these two representations.

The representations and analyses that are needed for detecting errors depend on several factors, of which the most important are the error and the feedback type.

For the detection of phonological errors, the best way may be to build probabilistic models of correct realizations and compute how well the realized utterance corresponds to this model. The output of such an analysis is continuous and represents a measure of confidence that the detected error is indeed a real error. Errors may be more effectively detected if we take into account specific error patterns that are observed in data or known from the literature. In Section 3.6, we will discuss an experiment in which this idea was applied in the context of our case study.

For the detection of syntactic and morphological errors, possibly other representations and algorithms may be required such as syntactic parse trees, part-of-speech tags and regular expressions [7]

Feedback. After the errors have been detected, feedback can be provided. Two decisions need to be taken: (1) whether feedback will be given on the error and if so, (2) in what form the feedback will be given.

The first decision can be taken on different grounds. For example, usually we only want to give feedback on the errors that have been detected with sufficient confidence. Probably, we do not want to give feedback on all errors in the utterance, as this may demotivate the learner, but only on the most important or prominent errors. Furthermore, the selection of errors to give feedback on may be dependent on the proficiency level of the learner or on the current learning goals.

If feedback is to be provided, the question remains in what form this should be done. A large number of feedback types can be distinguished that vary along several dimensions. For example, the explicitness of the feedback, whether metalinguistic information is given and whether the correct form is provided or elicited from the learner [8]. The question of which feedback form is more effective has been debated for a long time in a large number of publications and is still a topical issue [9]. In fact, ASR-based CALL systems may prove to be an excellent research vehicle to thoroughly investigate the effectiveness of different feedback moves [10] [11] (this volume).

3   Spraakmakkers: An ASR-Based CALL System for Dutch as a Second Language

The SPRAAKMAKKERS system has been developed in the context of the DISCO project [4]. The aim of the DISCO project is to develop a prototype of an ASR-based CALL application for DL2. The application has to provide intelligent feedback on important aspects of DL2 speaking, such as pronunciation, morphology and syntax. The target group of DL2 learners consists of highly-educated people who are seeking a job in the Netherlands or Flanders and are at the A2 proficiency level of the Common European Framework (CEF).

3.1   Goal Analysis

Exploratory in-depth interviews with DL2 teachers and experts were conducted to elicit pedagogical and personal goals [12]. These teachers identified two types of DL2 learners: those who want immediate corrective feedback on errors, and those who want to proceed with conversation training even if they make mistakes. Teachers also believed that our target group, highly-educated DL2 learners, would probably prefer immediate corrective feedback. To cater for both types of learners, the system could provide two types of feedback strategies and have the learners choose the one that suits them better through parameter setting (see 3.7). Furthermore, the teachers noted that DL2 learners often would like to have more opportunities to practice. A CALL system can provide such opportunities. DL2 learners appeared to feel uneasy at speaking Dutch because they are not completely familiar with the target language and culture. Therefore, it might be a good idea to provide some information about the target culture(s), so that learners can try to achieve intercultural competence.

Besides the pedagogical goals, the personal goals of learners should be taken into account. These goals were elicited using a focus group, which is a qualitative research technique [5]. In this case the focus group consisted of 9 DL2 learners. The main results were that DL2 learners often feel discouraged if they do not have sufficient knowledge of the topic of the conversation (politics, habits, etc.). Furthermore, they want to feel respected for their courage and motivation to integrate in the target culture(s). The conversations should therefore preferably deal with habits and practices of the target culture(s). Also, learners indicated that they feel frustrated if they cannot keep up with the pace of conversations in the target language. Finally, DL2 learners showed a desire to practise in a safe environment which helps them to gradually and repeatedly improve their pronunciation and grammar skills.

3.2   Courseware Overview

On the basis of the goals identified [12] a design concept was made. The overall framework for the concept of SPRAAKMAKKERS is conversation simulation in which virtual agents engage the DL2 learner in casual conversations in order to improve oral proficiency. The agents discuss various general topics concerning

Dutch and Flemish society with the DL2 learner, such as travel, money and education. During the conversations, the application monitors and logs user-machine interaction, gives feedback, and offers the DL2 learner tailor-made remedial exercises upon completion of the conversation. The remedial exercises feature a special agent, who helps the learner with specific pronunciation or grammar problems.

The conversation environment offers reasonably free conversation. It would not be technically feasible to provide exercises that accept free learner input, so we chose for an approach in which the learner produces speech in response to prompts. Each conversational turn has several prompts. The student picks a prompt, which takes him/her down a specific conversation path. The conversations can be different each time the learner visits them, depending on the choices. For each utterance that might appear in the conversation, we provide three different exercises:

1. for pronunciation: a prompt that learners simply have to read aloud
2. or morphology: a prompt that contains the root form of a verb, noun or other part of speech, between brackets, and the prompt has to be spoken with the correct inflection
3. for syntax: a prompt that has several constituents which have to be put in the correct order

Thus, for morphology and syntax exercises, learners not only have to utter the prompts, but they have some freedom in formulating their responses. An example of such a syntax exercise is shown in Figure 1. Of course, the conversation simulation is still fairly limited from a communicative point of view. However, our main goal is not to help DL2 learners improve conversation skills, but to help them improve grammar and pronunciation through conversation.

3.3   System Architecture

The system is comprised of three main components: the client, the courseware server and the speech processing server. One of the advantages of separating client and server is that these components can be developed relatively independently, as long as the communication protocol is clearly defined. In most cases this might be the optimal set-up because different components will typically be developed by different experts, for example interaction designers, language teachers and speech technologists. A diagram of the system architecture is shown in Figure 2.

The client handles all the interaction with the user, such as showing the current dialog turn and feedback through the graphical user interface (GUI) and recording the audio. The courseware engine is a module in the client that handles the dialog and excercise flow. It also keeps a record of all the user-system interactions and the learner's results. These interactions and results, as well as the content of the courseware, are stored in the courseware database, the main component of the courseware server.

Fig. 1. Screenshot of a dialog turn in the application. In this example, the learner has to choose one of the two options at the bottom of the screen and then utter the words in the correct order.

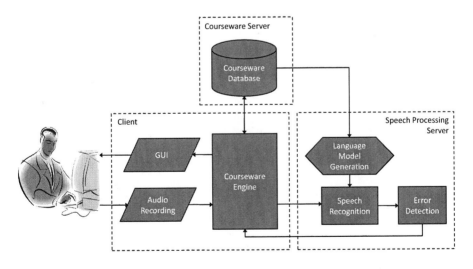

Fig. 2. System Architecture Diagram

The speech processing server is the component which processes the spoken input and detects possible errors. On the basis of the current prompt or remedial exercise, a language model is generated. This language model is used by the speech recognition module to determine the sequence of words uttered by the student. If the speech recognition manages to do this, possible errors in the utterance are detected. Finally, a representation of the utterance, together with the detected errors, is sent back to the client. The client is then responsible for actually providing the feedback to the learner.

3.4   System Implementation

The SPRAAKMAKKERS client is implemented in Java [13]. The speech processing server is implemented in Python [14] and the courseware server is a relational database server which communicates both with the client and the speech processing server.

The speech processing server interfaces with a fixed pool of speech processors. These processors are implemented within the SPRAAK package [15], which is an open source speech recognition package. The low-level modules are wrapped in Python using the `ctypes` module.

At the beginning of the processing chain, the learner's speech is first recorded after he or she has pushed a button. The recorded audio is immediately sent to the speech processing server in several packets through a socket connection. When the learner stops talking this is automatically detected by the client and the recording is stopped. As mentioned before, the audio is processed by the speech processing server, which is able to handle several clients in different threads. When the server is started, a fixed pool of speech processors is initialized in a queue using the `Queue` module. These processors are able to accept jobs from a single client, after which they are put back on the queue. After the speech is processed and the errors are detected, an XML representation is sent back to the client, which contains information on the recognized utterance and detected errors.

A final notable implementational aspect is the lip synchronization of the virtual agents with prerecorded audio. This was done by automatically time-aligning the speech with the canonical phonemic representation of the utterance. This time-to-phoneme mapping was subsequently used to animate the agent's mouth by changing the mouth position and shape at the right time. In order to do this we used drawings of ten mouth shapes, five for consonants, four for vowels and one for silence.

3.5   Speech Recognition

An ASR-based CALL system that has to provide corrective feedback on speech production will first of all have to determine what the learner is trying to say (speech recognition) before proceeding to an analysis of the form of the utterance (error detection). The first step of speech recognition may be very difficult in the case of non-native speakers, in particular those that are still in the process of learning the language. From research we know that non-native speech may differ from native speech with respect to pronunciation, morphology, syntax, and the lexicon. In general, the degree of deviation from native speech will be in inverse relation to the degree of proficiency in the target language. All these deviations make it very difficult to recognize what a person is trying to say.

A common approach to limit the difficulties in non-native speech recognition consists in applying techniques that restrict the search space and make the recognition task easier. In line with this approach, in the SPRAAKMAKKERS system we combine strategies that are essentially aimed at constraining the output of the learner so that the speech becomes more predictable, with techniques that are aimed at improving the automatic recognition of non-native speech. This is achieved by generating possible correct and incorrect responses for each exercise.

For syntax and morphology exercises, this generation is done on the basis of common error patterns in DL2 speech, such as wrong word order, conjugation, declension and the deletion of determiners [7]. The correct and incorrect word sequences are then represented as a finite state transducer. The task of the speech recognizer is to determine which utterance was spoken. In order to do so, the generated finite state transducer is used as a language model, and during recognition the optimal path through this language model is chosen.

Additionally, to adapt the recognizer to the idiosyncrasies of this sort of speech the acoustic models and the lexicon, two main components of a speech recognizer, can be adapted to the speaker or the mother tongue. These forms of adaptation will make the recognizer more tolerant with respect to the incoming speech so that deviant realizations of the intended utterance will more often be recognized as valid attempts to produce a response. In our experiments we obtained significant improvements by optimizing the acoustic models and achieved utterance error rates of about 8-10%. Recognition errors are usually due to confusions with phonetically similar utterances. The occurrences of these errors might be reduced by avoiding phonetically similar utterances during the design of the exercises. More details on these experiments can be found in [16].

After the previous step, which we call utterance selection, the path in the language model is chosen that best matches the acoustic signal. However, the selected utterance does not always correspond exactly to what was actually spoken: the spoken utterance might not be present in the language model, or even if it is present it might not end up as the optimal path. Since giving feedback on the wrong utterance is confusing, we should try to avoid this as much as possible. This is done using an additional step, which is called utterance verification. In order to verify whether the chosen path properly fits the acoustic signal, we have developed an utterance verifier. On the basis of the acoustic fit with the phonemic representation, together with the likelihood of the phoneme durations, we have trained a logistic regression model on a corpus of correctly recognized and misrecognized utterances. The output of this logistic regression model is a confidence measure that indicates the confidence assigned to the recognized utterance. If the confidence is below a certain threshold, the utterance is rejected and the user is prompted to try again. Otherwise the system will proceed to error detection. Experiments conducted using our utterance verifier indicate error rates of about 10% [16].

3.6   Error Detection

In the phase of error detection, different approaches are adopted for pronunciation, morphology and syntax. Syntactic errors can already be addressed after speech recognition. From the output of the speech recognizer we know what kind of error patterns are present in the utterance, because these were used to generate the language model.

For pronunciation it has to be tested whether segments are present or not and whether they are realized correctly. In previous studies we investigated which pronunciation errors are made by learners of Dutch [17], and how these errors can be detected automatically [18]. This can be done by using confidence measures or similar classifiers at the segmental level.

For the well-known goodness of pronunciation (GOP) [19] algorithm we obtained accuracy scores of 82-89% for some consonant pairs which are often confused by DL2 learners [20]. For vowels, the task is often more difficult because errors in these sounds are generally more gradual in nature. In order to improve the performance, we automatically adapted the GOP measure to non-native error patterns found in real, annotated speech data. In recent experiments in which we used this adapted GOP measure called wGOP, we were able to improve the error detection rates significantly from 73% to 78% [18].

Many morphological errors have to do with whether segments are present or not and for these cases error detection is very similar to pronunciation error detection. Other morphological errors are not limited to the presence or absence of a segment, but concern multiple aspects of a word. In other words, the algorithms used for detecting morphological errors are a combination of those used for detecting pronunciation errors and those used for syntactic errors. Achieving sufficient accuracy in the stages of speech recognition and error detection is essential to be able to provide useful corrective feedback. In addition, the results of error detection are used as guidelines to assign remedial exercises to the learner. This is of course an additional form of adaptation that is envisaged in the SPRAAKMAKKERS system and that is highly dependent on the performance achieved by the speech technology modules.

3.7   Feedback

Feedback depends on individual learning preferences: the default feedback strategy is immediate corrective feedback, which is visually implemented through highlighting, and from an interaction perspective by putting the conversation on hold and focusing on the errors. Learners that wish to have more conversational freedom can choose to receive communicative recasts as feedback, which let the conversation go on while highlighting errors for a short period of time. In the final system several parameters are envisaged that can be changed by the learner or teacher. Alternatively, parameters such as error analysis and learner behaviour can be used to have the system behave intelligently so as to adapt itself automatically to the learner.

3.8   System Errors

We have discussed how we designed the SPRAAKMAKKERS system so that it makes as few errors as possible. However, its performance, just like that of real teachers, is not perfect. In this section we discuss the kinds of errors the system can make and how we try to minimize their negative impact.

Since the speech processing is divided in two stages, speech recognition and error detection, there are two possible error sources. In the speech recognition stage two types of errors can be made: false accepts (FAs) and false rejects (FRs). In this case, an FA means that what is recognized is not what was actually spoken: the learner gets feedback on something that was not said. An FR means that an utterance is not recognized even though it is present in the language model: the user will be asked to try again.

In the error detection stage, these two types of errors can also be made. Here, an FA means that 'a form' is accepted although it is incorrect, and a FR means that it is rejected although correct. The modules are not independent. For instance, if during speech recognition an FA occurs, the detected errors can still be correct, e.g. if they concern errors in the correctly recognized part of the utterance.

The influence or weights of the FAs and FRs in the different stages can be changed using different thresholds for utterance verification or error detection. In general, FRs are probably more confusing [21]. This may however differ from person to person, depending on the number and type of errors made. A possibility would be to use adaptive weights. In any case, giving incorrect feedback should be avoided. However, if the thresholds are too high, too conservative, the learner is often prompted to try again, or no feedback will be given on errors. It is clear that a careful balance should be found.

In order to delimit the amount of confusion due to incorrect feedback, there are some other options. One is to show on the screen what is recognized. In this way, the learner can see where the error detection is based on. Another possibility would be to ask for confirmation of every recognized utterance.

4   Conclusions

In this paper we have first presented general guidelines for designing ASR-based CALL systems. We have indicated that there are two main factors driving the design process: learner and teacher goals and technological affordances. Furthermore, we have presented the design and implementation of a case study, the SPRAAKMAKKERS system, in which we have applied these guidelines. We also have shown that using various forms of adaptation, to the task and to the learner, we were able to increase the performance of our system. Finally, we have discussed how to deal with possible system errors.

In the near future we are going to evaluate the system with two groups of learners and teachers in the Netherlands and Flanders. We will carry out a usability test with the learners and measure how well they are able to work with the system and what their own experience is like. The teachers will evaluate the behavior of the system by watching video recordings of the learners working with the system and by analysing user-system interactions.

Acknowledgements

The DISCO project is carried out within the STEVIN programme which is funded by the Dutch and Flemish Governments (http://taalunieversum.org/taal/technologie/stevin/). We are indebted to all other members of the DISCO team for their invaluable contribution to the design and development of the SPRAAKMAKKERS system: Jozef Colpaert, Frederik Cornillie, Margret Oberhofer, Liesbet Melis, Ghislaine Giezenaar and Peter Beinema.

References

1. Ellis, N., Bogart, P.: Speech and language technology in education: the perspective from SLA research and practice. In: Proceedings of SLaTE 2007, pp. 1–8 (2007)
2. Bloom, B.: The 2 Sigma Problem: The Search for Methods of Group Instruction as Effective as One-to-One Tutoring. Educational Researcher 13(6), 4–16 (1984)
3. Colpaert, J.: Elicitation of language learner's personal goals as design concepts. Innovation in Language Learning and Teaching (2010)
4. Strik, H.: DISCO Project Website,
   http://lands.let.ru.nl/~strik/research/DISCO
5. Krueger, R.A., Casey, M.A.: Focus groups: a practical guide for applied research. Thousand Oaks, California (2000)
6. Juang, B.H., Rabiner, L.R.: Automatic Speech Recognition - A Brief History of the Technology. In: Elsevier Encyclopedia of Language and Linguistics, 2nd edn. (2005)
7. Strik, H., van de Loo, J., van Doremalen, J., Cucchiarini, C.: Practicing syntax in spoken interaction: Automatic detection of syntactic errors in non-native speech. In: Proceedings of L2WS, Japan (2010)
8. Lyster, R., Ranta, L.: Corrective feedback and learner uptake: Negotiation of form in communicative classrooms. Studies in Second Language Acquisition 19, 37–66 (1997)
9. Sheen, Y.: The Role of Oral and Written Corrective Feedback in SLA. Studies in Second Language Acquisition 32, 169–179 (2010)
10. Penning de Vries, B., Cucchiarini, C., Strik, H.: The Role of Corrective Feedback in Second Language Learning: New Research Possibilities by Combining CALL and Speech Technology. In: Proceedings of L2WS, Japan (2010)
11. Penning de Vries, B., Cucchiarini, C., Van Hout, R., Strik, H.: Adaptive corrective feedback in second language learning. In: De Wannemacker, S., Clarebout, G., De Causmaecker, P. (eds.) ITEC 2010. CCIS, vol. 126, pp. 1–14. Springer, Heidelberg (2011)
12. Strik, H., Cornillie, F., Colpaert, J., van Doremalen, J., Cucchiarini, C.: Developing a CALL System for Practicing Oral Proficiency: How to Design for Speech Technology, Pedagogy and Learners. In: Proceedings of SLaTE, United Kingdom (2009)

13. Gosling, J., Joy, B., Steele, G., Bracha, G.: The Java language specification, 3rd edn. Addison-Wesley, Reading (2005)
14. Van Rossum, G.: Python Reference Manual. CWI Report CS-R9525 (1995)
15. Demuynck, K., Roelens, J., Van Compernolle, D., Wambacq, P.: SPRAAK: an open source SPeech Recognition and Automatic Annotation Kit. In: Proceedings of ICSLP, p. 495 (2008)
16. Van Doremalen, J., Cucchiarini, C., Strik, H.: Optimizing automatic speech recognition for low-proficient non-native speakers. EURASIP Journal of Audio, Speech and Music Processing (2010)
17. Neri, A., Cucchiarini, C., Strik, H.: Selecting segmental errors in L2 Dutch for optimal pronunciation training. International Review of Applied Linguistics 44, 357–404 (2006)
18. Van Doremalen, J., Cucchiarini, C., Strik, H.: Using Non-Native Error Patterns to Improve Pronunciation Verification. In: Proceedings of Interspeech, Japan (2010)
19. Witt, S.: Use of speech recognition in computer assisted language learning. Ph.D. dissertation, University of Cambridge (1999)
20. Strik, H., Truong, K., de Wet, F., Cucchiarini, C.: Comparing different approaches for automatic pronunciation error detection. Speech Communication 51, 845–852 (2009)
21. Eskenazi, M.: An overview of Spoken Language Technology for Education. Speech Communication 51(10) (2009)

From Multidimensional Needs to Language Training for Mobile Professionals: An Interdisciplinary Approach

Kris Van de Poel and Ine De Rycke

Kris Van de Poel,
Universiteit Antwerpen,
Research Unit for Applied Language Studies,
R. 202, Rodestraat 14, BE 2000 Antwerpen
kris.vandepoel@ua.ac.be

Abstract. In Europe mobility among qualified medical staff is on the increase. The first language and culture of these medical professionals are often different from the country in which they work. Even though the majority of foreign medical professionals is willing to learn a foreign language to its full potential, the reality of medical practice shows that this is not always feasible. Thus, the need for an effective approach to learning and training presents itself. This article reports on the different steps which an international interdisciplinary team took to develop a language training tool that can support medical professionals on the work floor (www.medicsmove.eu). Moreover, it will show how the quality of the tool was and is assured to meet the expectations of stakeholders and beneficiaries, by adopting the stance that needs analysis is never ending and that evaluation of process and product are an integrated component. As such, this paper covers the domains of applied linguistics and educational technology.

Keywords: Language for Specific Purposes, online language training, medical communication, material development, needs analysis, evaluation, educational technology, applied linguistics, medical perform support systems.

1 Introduction: Communication Challenges of Mobile Language Discordant Medical Professionals

1.1 Mobile Medical Professionals

The medical profession in Europe is becoming increasingly heterogeneous because of mobility and the Scandinavian countries are forerunners in this respect: for example, in 2007, more than a quarter (26.2%) of all medical doctors in Sweden was born outside Sweden [1]. Since the language and cultural backgrounds of these mobile medical professionals differ from that of their professional environment, i.e. they engage in language discordant communication, this presents challenges for all involved.

S. De Wannemacker, G. Clarebout, P. De Causmaecker (Eds.): ITEC 2010, CCIS 126, pp. 70–84, 2011.
© Springer-Verlag Berlin Heidelberg 2011

1.2 Effective Medical Communication

Research has shown that there is 'consistent evidence' that race, ethnicity and language have a substantial influence on the quality of the doctor-patient relationship [2]. Moreover, defective doctor-patient interaction can have serious consequences, as there is a correlation between effective physician-patient communication and improved patient health outcomes (e.g. [3], [4]). Therefore, securing good and effective communication between doctors and patients is of the utmost importance. However, even though medical specialists working abroad are motivated to study a foreign language to its full potential, they are often totally immersed in acquiring (and communicating their) professional knowledge and skills, to such an extent that they often do not have the time to focus on systematically learning the new language (see, among others, [5]). Thus, they often face a tension between their professional and communicative functioning. At worst, they risk miscommunication and even communication breakdown, which has negative implications for delicate doctor-patient and doctor-colleague relationships [6], at best they may be difficult to understand, appear indecisive, insensitive, or even rude (cf. [5], [6]). This may result in face-loss and have an adverse effect on the perceived professional status of the medical practitioner, because 'linguistic deficiencies can easily be interpreted as a lack of professional qualifications' ([6]:105).

1.3 Facilitating Interaction

Since medical professionals often do not have time to enrol in traditional contact teaching where general language skills are taught, health administrators have been looking for ways in which to facilitate professional communication and enhance the learning process, like the use of medical interpreters or medical mediators [7] [8] or individualized language training on the workfloor (which is often a pre-condition to an appointment) (see [5], for a description of the Swedish situation). However, as the above authors point out the alternatives to classroom learning are resource- and time-consuming (e.g. individual training is costly and takes time), they require careful planning (e.g. in the case of using interpreters), and they do not always meet the needs when they present themselves in interaction where just-in-time and tailored solutions seem to be the priority. The question thus remains how to adequately respond to the specific communicative needs of language discordant medical professionals, keeping in mind the limitations imposed and opportunities offered by medical practice.

1.4 Medics on the Move: A Response to Multifaceted Communicative Needs

To this end a multinational interdisciplinary project was formulated with the main objective to enhance the intercultural functioning of the mobile medic on a professional, linguistic, and social level. This has crystallized in a multilingual training tool geared towards medical professionals. *Medics on the Move (MoM* 2006-2008 and 2009-2011; [9]) is an online interactive language tool that offers contextualized and individualised language training embedded in the demanding professional life of the medical doctor by making it accessible through traditional computer work stations, but also through web-enabled mobile devices or smartphones, such as IPhone or

Blackberry. In this way, the language discordant medical doctor is offered tailored communication support anywhere and at any time. Thus, *MoM* is a dynamic tool that lends itself for just-in-time or on-demand learning on the work floor.

In this article, we will report on how the quality of the *MoM* tool was assured, by systematically and critically presenting the needs analysis carried out for the project. First, we will present the kind of needs that were identified, and how they were identified (2). Then, we will show how they were translated into learning objectives and materials (3), and how it was ensured that they meet the stakeholders' expectations (4), and finally we will point at ways ahead (5). As such, this paper covers the domains of applied linguistics and educational technology. Even though it will mainly discuss aspects of syllabus design for Specific, i.e. Medical Purposes, based on the communicative needs which were established for an international L2-medical audience, the paper could also be framed in light of performance support systems. Since most of the existing sources deal with native speaker communication, the *MoM*-team has tried to lift out and stress those aspects that make intercultural communication for L2 medical professionals especially challenging, which in turn provides new challenges for the evaluation.

2   A Multi-perspective Needs Analysis

2.1   An Interdisciplinary Approach

The *MoM* development process was fed by a comprehensive needs analysis, which aimed to ensure maximal effectiveness and efficiency for technology-enhanced learning by mobile medical professionals. The needs analysis, which is regarded as a cornerstone in developing course materials for specific purposes [10] [11] [12] [13] was based on findings from the research literature on intercultural and health care communication at the same time drawing on input from different stakeholders: medical professionals working in their first or second language, their colleagues and supervisors, health organisations, language mediators, skills lab trainers, language teachers, etc. Through questionnaires and interviews, not only the institutions' interpretation of the learners' (language) problems was taken into account [14], but also the perceptions of the learners themselves [15] [16] [17]. The *MoM* needs analysts even went one step further and tested professional communicative skills and awareness of the language discordant medics (see [6] for a detailed analysis).

The interdisciplinary project approach was translated into the development of the needs analysis by an international team of researchers and developers, representing the beneficiaries and stakeholders in the field. Stakeholders included hospitals (management, trainers, and career councillors), networks, regional and local medical councils, training institutions and the like. The team of pedagogical consultants and content developers consisted of specialists in curriculum and syllabus design, open and distance learning, material developers for Language for Specific Purposes and intercultural communication consultants[1]. The partnership also included medical and

---

[1] University of Antwerp – Applied Language Studies (Belgium), Videnscenter for Integration (Denmark), Charité (Germany), Immigrant Institute (Sweden), Henco Konsult (Sweden), Training 2000 (Italy).

health associations throughout Europe[2]. Medical consultants and skills labs were integrated in the project, as well as medical mediators and medical language teachers. Different European partners developed and tested the technical framework[3].

In a first instance, the needs analysis was meant to identify the communicative deficiencies and the self-assessed needs of language discordant medical professionals and relate them to some factual information on communication skills training and learning, i.e. previous language learning (type, intensity, duration, …), learning approach and preferences, degree of socio-cultural integration, self-assessment as professional and language discordant communicator, perceived training and learning needs and targets, etc. The findings from the language discordant professionals were then mapped onto the needs as observed by colleagues and/or supervisors. Finally, the *MoM* needs analysis phase also involved gathering technical data on mobile technologies and experiences in a work context (suffice it to say that in 2007 only 50% of the interviewed doctors were familiar with smartphones for work purposes, but with the rapid advancements in technology this situation has dramatically changed, through which the MoM tool has benefited by default).

In the following section we will briefly report on the findings with the intention to show how the different components of the needs analysis work together towards continuous product evaluation and quality control.

2.2 Needs Data

After pilot testing the online questionnaire generated data from medical professionals in Sweden, Denmark, Germany, Italy and Belgium (Flanders) who voluntary participated in the spring of 2007.

The Research Population. The respondents can be characterised as first (L1) or second (L2) language speakers. In order to perform a contrastive analysis data were collected from first language (L1) and foreign language (L2) medical professionals. Questionnaires in Italy, for instance, were filled in by Italian L1-doctors and their colleagues who use Italian as an L2 in their professional context.

The *MoM* research population consisted of 226 medical professionals (N=117 L1 and 143 L2-speakers; the 26 L1 and 28 L2-trainees were left out of the analysis, as well as the 55 incomplete questionnaires) (for more information on the research population, please visit [9]). The L2-professionals differ widely with respect to medical training and experience as well as intensity of language training.

Self-Assessment and Perceived Needs of Language Discordant Doctors. The *MoM* L2 research population was asked to engage in *self-assessment* through a questionnaire that consisted of three parts, i.e. Professional Confidence, Perceptions by Others, and Training Needs.

For the study on *professional confidence* on the work floor a diversity of constellations was taken into consideration: interactants were defined in individual or group

---

[2] Ziekenhuisnetwerk Antwerpen (Belgium), University Hospital Antwerp (Belgium), Charité – Universitätsmedizin Berlin (Germany), Hospitals in South Denmark, Västra Götalandsregionen (Sweden) and different hospital networks in the Marche region (Italy).
[3] TeaM Hutchins AB (Sweden), Henco Konsult (Sweden), Vifin (DK),Training 2000 (Italy), Entente UK (United Kingdom).

encounters with unknown as well as known people, i.e. patients, (superior) colleagues, nursing/administrative/paramedical staff combined with different types of channels used in the interaction, i.e. face-to-face or telephone conversations, as well as different types of topics, i.e. general, medical, or social. These variables generated 26 different speech acts which were presented as statements to be assessed on a four-point Likert scale. The statements were concluded with a possibility for open comments. The results present a clear picture and can be summarised as follows: Matter-of-fact communication, especially with patients, is familiar territory for most L2-doctors in this study. A majority feels confident (74%) when communicating with employers/supervisors, a feeling which increases when communicating with equal colleagues (84% feel positive) or patients (86%). When meeting new colleagues the language discordant medical professionals feel slightly more apprehensive, but still 71% feel confident.

When socialising with colleagues and patients over three quarters of the L2-doctors feel confident (77%). This is less so when socialising with superiors (67%), when a third of the respondents do not feel confident.

Telephone consultations with patients are real stress factors for one third of the respondents as are telephonic interactions with other departments and services. Staff meetings create stress when the foreign doctors have to present a case (i.e. 35% do not feel confident), answer a question (38% are not confident), or give a scientific presentation (40% feel insecure).

Another component of the self-assessment study focused on *perceived professional competence*. L2-doctors feel most often regarded as competent and at ease with equal colleagues (93% responded on the positive side of the scale) and with patients or paramedical staff (90% scored on the positive side of the scale), but slightly less with nursing staff and superior colleagues (where 88% vs. 85% felt perceived as competent). The most negative score goes to superior colleagues by whom a small group (one sixth or 15%) do not really feel regarded competent.

Finally, a self-reported *training needs* inventory was composed on the basis of four open questions regarding the respondents' wishes for formal language training and improvement of their communicative and language skills. Even though the answers do not necessarily correspond to the professionals' real needs (as, for instance, observed by their supervisors - see below), they are indicative of areas worth paying attention to in order to increase the face validity of the envisaged language and communication training. The answers suggested that the L2-doctors' training needs are above all related to various oral communicative situations that they encounter in their work. More than two thirds indicate that they want to improve one or several oral communicative aspects. Furthermore, half want to train or improve their vocabulary, whereas one third mentions grammar. Over one fifth of the doctors states pronunciation as a training need, and slightly less than one fifth writing skills, 14% want to know more about the host country culture, life style and every day life, around 10% either want to improve their listening comprehension and understanding, or want specific medical training, including dealing with emergency situations.

Observed Needs by Supervisors and Heads of Department. The needs analysis was complemented with 54 semi-structured interviews with senior nursing staff and supervisors (heads of departments) of the language discordant doctors and conducted in the project countries.

The following needs were exclusively discerned by the colleagues: communicating non-verbally, understanding dialects, using humour, handling stressful and new situations, and communicating bad news. However, the colleagues also shared concerns with the L2 medical professionals with regard to the following areas: communicating with colleagues and superiors (for administrative purposes), varying (everyday medical) vocabulary, and using the correct pronunciation.

These findings show some discrepancies, as language discordant doctors seem to restrict their needs mainly to linguistically definable and learnable topics, i.e. the register of administration, colloquial medical vocabulary, and pronunciation, whereas their colleagues mainly point at more pervasive and challenging pragmatic areas in which faceloss is a constant threat. In summary, and on a positive note, both groups see room for learning at a professional, linguistic and social level.

Production and Evaluation of Medical Communication. Since effective doctor-patient communication permeates every aspect of medical professional life, many textbooks aim to improve communication skills in training and an increasing number of researchers aim to understand what makes doctor-patient interaction effective and/or defective.

During the *MoM*-needs analysis phase two investigations were performed with a focus on the socio-pragmatic functioning of communication (for a detailed study see [6]). More in particular, it was first studied through discourse completion tasks how doctors use *modification* in their communication with patients, i.e. how they mitigate and consolidate in order to meet the socio-cultural norms that apply to the interaction. Especially in Germanic languages, absence of modification 'may be experienced as (too) direct, impolite, crude, brutal, or even unkind' ([6]: 118). Two examples of modification as a reply to 'How do you put a patient at ease at the beginning of an examination?'

–Don't worry, **tiny** examination. (lexical modification)
–You **shouldn't** worry. (syntactic modification)

In order to investigate whether L1 and L2-doctors use different degrees of modification, comparative statistics were used (Mann-Whitney U Test). Differences were found in L1- and L2-doctors' overall use of modification and use of different types of modification, pointing towards an L2-mechanism of overcompensation to ensure adequate consolidation of the relationship. However, at the same time, certain linguistic and/or communicative traits were underrepresented in the L2-data, which might indicate that they are not entirely assimilated.

Secondly, doctors' *evaluations* of appropriate medical communication was looked into. This investigation studied whether medical doctors have explicit socio-cultural competence and whether it is supported by underlying knowledge. The data collected were analysed in terms of doctors' judgements on appropriateness of the given communication scenarios (on a four-point Likert scale). An example of a scenario:

Scen2: The anaestesiologist enters the patient's room one hour before the operation to get some forms signed. The patient is anxious. The doctor says: 'Hello Sir, I have some more forms for you to sign. Could you please sign here, here, and here?'
In order to investigate whether the L1- or L2-nature of the communicative context

in which the doctor-respondents function results in differences in appropriateness judgements, the L1- and L2-doctors' answers were contrasted by means of comparative statistics. The findings show proof of the L2-doctors' knowledge of medical interactions, but bear witness to some shortcomings in underlying communicative competence. Whereas the L1- doctors report different social and contextual insights and provide vocal and non-verbal contextualisation for communicative encounters, such information is rarely mentioned by the L2-doctors –pointing towards weakness in weighing different communicative components or lack of meta-communicative skills to explain this in writing in an experimental context.

2.3 Needs Analysis as an Ongoing Process

The *MoM* developers' team did not consider the needs analysis as a completed phase, but opted to refine the development process with an ongoing qualitative evaluation by an extended group of developers, researchers, beneficiaries (testees) and stakeholders. Since evaluation may be considered a 'never-ending needs analysis, the goal of which is to constantly refine the ideas gathered in the initial needs analysis such that the program can do an even better job of meeting those needs' (Brown 1995: 233), needs were screened during and at the end of the development process.

3 Syllabus and Material Development

3.1 The Nature of *MoM*

The materials were developed in line with the characteristics of the target audience, i.e. highly trained medical professionals who are totally immersed in their practice, and who have to communicate effectively (accurately and fluently) as soon as possible after joining the work force. Therefore, the *MoM* team choose for a hands-on approach, at the same time offering insights in the intricacies of professional communication. This leads to contextualized materials which focus on the linguistic and communicative needs discerned in the needs analysis.

The main needs identified by both the language discordant doctors and their supervisors involved communication with colleagues, lexical variation, and pronunciation. *MoM* tries to provide an answer to these linguistic needs by embedding the language materials in situations with different interactants (doctor-patient, doctor-colleague, and doctor-other, i.e. relative, administrator, etc.), and supporting them with extensive vocabulary and language tips, including audiofiles and systematic pronunciation advice.

The interviews with colleagues of the language discordant doctors also revealed other language concerns that can jeopardize doctor-patient communication, including non-verbal communication, the use of humour and the communication of bad news. These communication needs are catered for in the communication manual which focuses exclusively on healthcare communication, and initiated in the language and communication tips that complement the language material focusing on challenging interactions.

Moreover, we try to reinforce the medic's self esteem and confidence in handling stressful and new situation by presenting materials that are relevant, i.e. recognisable and identifiable, and can be immediately put to the test. Not only the genuine content, but also the way in which the materials are presented (graphics, navigation, etc.) correspond with the audience's expectations, ensuring a high face validity.

The materials are thus totally focused on covering the perceived and observed needs of language discordant medical professionals.

3.2   From Objectives to Syllabus

The needs analysis data were fed into the *MoM* syllabus, which presents a deductive as well as inductive approach prior to, during, or after a service encounter.

Prior to an encounter the learner may want to consult the language support needed. For example, a scenario on greeting between doctor and patient. The learner can prepare for the encounter by focusing on phrases or particular words, listening to the audios, or by taking note of the language and communication tips.

However, the reality of medical practice does not always allow for interactions to be planned and language discordant medical professional may need immediate linguistic and communicative guidance. *MoM* also allows for inductive use during the encounter, and can be consulted to check on terminology, look for paraphrases, and the like. Afterwards, the learner can reflect on the experience, check on particular aspects, and feed comments back into the system by sharing his experience on the forum, or in a message attached to the page of the encounter. If there is no opportunity to consult *MoM* during the encounter, the learner can follow-up on his unplanned encounter by visiting the platform afterwards, and, for example, look for ways to improve his pronunciation of a particular medical term.

In summary, *Medics on the Move* offers the learner guidance and support before, during and after the encounter, and is therefore a flexible and adaptive platform geared towards the reality of medical practice, but what exactly does it contain?

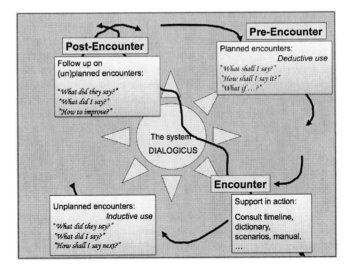

Fig. 1. Graphic Representation of the *Medics on the Move* Syllabus

3.3   From Syllabus to *MoM* Materials

Medics on the Move is developed in the six target languages Danish, Dutch, English, German, Italian, Swedish and is supported by materials in five interface languages, i.e. Arabic, Polish, Romanian, Russian, Turkish.

A first entry point for learners with a basic command of the language is the database of scenarios. The scenarios first and foremost follow the doctor-patient consultation timeline from the Calgary-Cambridge Guide [19] [20], which has been adapted to intercultural communicative settings and has been turned into a performance support system relying on relevant research [21] [22] [23] [24] [25] [26] [27] [28] [29] [30] [31]. However, the database also covers communication with colleagues, supervisors, nursing staff or others, such as patients' relatives and administrators, situations which often cause problems with respect to power relations and the like. Supported with audio, language and communication tips, the scenarios form a searchable database, which is supplemented by a searchable wordlist of everyday medical terms.

Absolute beginners in the language are presented with a systematic and progressive initiation in the language through ten topics also following the above discourse support system. All scenarios and medical wordlists and wordmaps both present the learner text and audio files extended with pronunciation and grammatical advice and point to external links for further follow-up. Communication skills can be further improved by consulting the state-of-the-art communication manual, which focuses on medical communication skills formulated as strategies, background and tips. In addition, *MoM* includes reference tools that include socio-cultural links. Finally, language learning manuals and a technical guide function as a helpline for the learner.

Last but not least, *Medics on the Move* aims to build a community where learners can share experiences and support each other through forum activity or Skype with chat functionality which in the near future will be extended with social forums on Facebook and Twitter.

3.4   MoM's Pedagogical Functionality

The *MoM* materials can be used in various ways. First of all, the beginner is offered a traditional and recognisable learning route that consists of ten different topics (about 50 short scenarios) that build on one another, from greeting at the beginning of a consultation and/or working day through symptom analysis and case presentation to problem solving and apologising for delays. The learning line is gradual (from easy to more complex) and cyclic (linguistically complicated items are repeated in more detail). The training is supported by a library of manuals (Wordmaps and Glossary, Pronunciation, Grammar, Medical and Intercultural Communication) and items to be learned are automatically linked to relevant pages. The user is given pedagogical guidance and assistance while learning through Dr Myriam's help pages and translations. Since authentic language is being used and presented in distinguishable units, the learners can navigate freely and search for relevant materials.

Since *Medics on the Move* contains a database of authentic scenarios in different interactive settings, i.e. between doctor and patient, doctor and colleague, and doctor and other participants in the medical context, it provides the learner with maximal freedom. Medical professionals can select the materials they need, without having to finish modules before being able to access other materials in which they are interested. *MoM* can thus be tailored to anyone's needs, regardless of their language proficiency: the beginner can consult grammar items, whereas the advanced learner, for instance, can study the intricacies of intercultural communication.

Originally, *Medics on the Move* was set up for autonomous learning (2006-2008) and it provided ample assistance for the adult, critical, and professionally qualified learner in the form of technical manuals (How to enter MoM) and pedagogical guides (How to learn with MoM) and different fora (the *MoM*-community), trying to assure user-friendliness in every nook and crany. Even then, usability tests and interviews supported the developers in their convictions that blended learning and coaching would be valuable alternatives for beginners as well as intermediate learners. The second *MoM*-development phase (2009-2011) thus systematically studies the integration of the tool in medical skills labs and medical language programmes.

3.5 Online and Mobile Learning

The online learning platform can be accessed through traditional computer work stations. However, the medical professional's lifestyle and time constraints might limit opportunities to consult the platform. *MoM* is therefore designed in such a way that the platform can be accessed through web-enabled mobile devices such as an IPhone or a Blackberry. The medical doctor is thus offered language support anywhere and at any time; *MoM* is a dynamic tool that lends itself for just-in-time learning on the work floor.

3.6 Technical Framework

The *MoM* technical team opted for a combination of an open public website for general communication and a closed learning management system (moodle). The language material is free of charge, but in a password protected area, and thus requires the reader to log into the system before reaching the language material.

The choice for moodle was motivated by the fact that it can be modified to be an example of the project philosophy of adapting an existing stable platform to give a good web-based learning experience on both a desktop and mobile platform. In addition, moodle's design is strict and sparse, and supports mobile devices by not cluttering the screen.

The innovative aspects of *MoM* represents an iterative approach to innovation, they are small steps that push the envelope of what is possible in a mixed platform environment. In addition, the moodle plugins allow for expanded learning interaction for both the new and experienced language learner.

4 Product Assessment as Ongoing Needs Analysis

The project objective arising from the needs analysis was to enhance the intercultural functioning of the mobile medical professional on a professional, linguistic and social level, at the same time taking advantage of the work environment by supporting the professional functioning on a day-to-day basis and embedding the materials in a context which the professionals recognise. This has crystallized in a communicative contextualised training tool geared towards mature learners who can select their own learning content generated by their own needs and use it in an autonomous, blended, or contact teaching context. The remaining question is of course: Does *MoM* live up to its expectations? To this end different types of evaluation were carried out and are still taking place.

4.1 Evaluation Data

In the first phase, assessment of the *MoM*-tool took into account quantitative and qualitative data collected from testees (potential users) as well as stakeholders (hospitals, regional councils, etc.) along the key evaluation criteria of relevance, added value, efficiency, effectiveness, impact, and sustainability. The data were collected in 2008 and have to be treated with caution, since they represent a first largely narrative and therefore impressionistic and subjective evaluation which will be supplemented with extensive data during the second project phase in early 2011. However, the data are indicative of whether and how *MoM* meets the needs, both linguistic needs as well as well-being, well-feeling, thus ensuring face-validity for the product.

The end-of-project-1 evaluation used a Logic Framework model adapted for use on smaller projects. The complete evaluation process took into consideration management, team working and communication of information as well as the development and implementation of the final product for the Log frame aspects relevance, efficiency, added value, effectiveness impact, and sustainability (cf. [32]). These data were supplemented with results from five semi-structured interviews analysed along the same key evaluation criteria of relevance, added value, efficiency, effectiveness, impact, and sustainability (see 4.4).

4.2 Stakeholder Key Findings

As far as effectiveness is concerned the stakeholders (nine returned completed questionnaires) all agreed that their feedback had been taken into account and resulted in changes to the products; the results that were promised had been delivered; the project results introduces new methodologies and materials for language learning which will be very useful to them and can be used without external support.

As far as impact is concerned the stakeholders agreed that the project results improved their wider understanding of the competence needs of the beneficiaries and improved their awareness of cultural differences. All except two (78%) agreed that the project results had improved their awareness of the needs of minority or under-represented groups.

With respect to potential for sustainability all stakeholders agreed that there is an ongoing need to use the results of this project, which is affordable on a long-term basis, and that there is a process for them to contribute to the future development of the project results.

To conclude, overall, there is tremendous enthusiasm for the *MoM*-language tool from key stakeholders in the project, and the narrative comments seem to only reinforce the very high scores given. As can be expected with any new product, there is some criticism, but it is very constructive, and only points the way to further expansion of the concepts than any really negative perceptions of the potential of the product. In sum, stakeholders are confident of the success of the product, and there is a clear commitment to support further development of the concept.

4.3 Beneficiary Key Findings

All beneficiaries (twelve returned completed questionnaires) agreed that the *MoM*-language tool is accessible with the equipment that they have and that the communication scenarios are appropriate to their needs. All except two (83%) agreed that *MoM* accurately meets the needs of medical personnel for a *translation, interpretation*, and *communication* tool. All except three (75%) agreed that the *MoM*-medical wordlist and the forum are appropriate to their needs.

With respect to efficiency, all respondents agreed that the tutorials and Pedagogical Guide are helpful. *MoM* is fast enough to meet their needs, the layout is clear and text is easy to read, the voice-overs are clear and easy to understand. *MoM* is acceptable for use in professional conversation and acceptable for preparing and debriefing after a day's work. All except one (92%) agreed that *MoM* is easy to navigate and is acceptable for use in patient consultations.

All beneficiaries agree that *MoM* has improved their communication skills in the second language. All except one (92%) agreed that *MoM* can save time in some professional situations. According to most (83%) *MoM* has improved their speaking and listening skills and it can save resources (e.g. using interpreters) (75% agreed).

All the *MoM*-components meet with positive comments with respect to sufficiency. Forum, links and guides are also received well by 75%, but since they belong to the *MoM*-community component they are under constant development.

The tutorials as support resources enabled all to start using *MoM* without any external support and to resolve any difficulties. All except one (92%) agreed that the forum will meet additional needs.

4.4 Semi-structured Interviews

In the course of 2008 five semi-structured interviews were conducted with medical professionals who had thoroughly tested the materials in the different target countries [33]. They delivered valuable qualitative data that correspond largely with the quantitative data gathered for the evaluation.

The *MoM* learning space was positively received by all respondents. They expressed their enthusiasm about the nature of the *MoM* language: the contextualisation of the materials and its exclusive focus on medical professionals was applauded. Respondents emphasised that due to content's focus on the medical lexicon, time was saved. In addition, the quality of the content was considered to be very high, and some of its specific features as the audio file were being evaluated as high quality and useful. The multimedial and interactive aspects of the learning space were also highly appreciated.

Some interviewees volunteered that their oral language skills had improved and all of them agreed that the product could teach or help them find words, medical terms and phrases. The product definitely focuses on the development of oral language skills and one interviewee wished he had only had the tool when he first came to his new working environment; it would have enabled him to communicate better and more correctly with colleagues and patients.

From the interviews, it has become clear that the language tool can serve language learners in a variety of ways and for a variety of needs. Not only can it instruct, it can also support and help language learners become more proficient in a foreign language. It is not so much *MoM's* purpose to teach and correct, rather to support and provide guidance when and where it is needed. The interviews show that the product does exactly that. All the respondents have used the learning space in a flexible way in search for guidance, support and language help rather than systematically study grammar points and vocabulary items.

5 Summary and Conclusion

Since 2006 an international team of developers has tried to answer some of the communicative needs of a growing group of internationally mobile professionals, i.e. language discordant medics. The project members followed the creed that evaluation is an integrated part of a never-ending needs analysis [18]. The second project phase (2009-2011) therefore heavily relies on the findings of the first evaluation and has taken into account the comments and suggestions voiced. It is well underway and will be evaluated in 2011.

In summary, the impressions of the medical professionals can be taken as very considered judgements, and in view of the high marks achieved for all of the criteria the results are remarkable. Without sight of the individual evaluation questionnaires, it is not so clear here that most of the negative markings relating to the 'usability' of the products are made by people who are not so comfortable with the technology, or were in a very specific branch of the medical profession (e.g. accident & emergency; psychology; psychiatry) that the *MoM* tool does not (yet) fully address because of mobile phone functionality or content. What is apparent from the narrative comment is that *MoM* actually challenges the existing mobile phone technology, which is considered by most of the more technically proficient users to be too slow. Clearly, with the rapid advancements that we have come to expect in technology, this situation will change, and the *MoM* tool will benefit by default. Other than this, there seems to be little shortfall in the content and sufficiency of the tool that cannot be realistically addressed in any future development.

The *Medics on the Move* product is the result of joined efforts from partners from different fields, resulting in an interdisciplinary approach to on-the-job language training. The fact that part of the *MoM*-database is based on internationally acknowledged guidelines for the structure of the medical interview in English, but has been applied to intercultural and transcultural communicative settings, has redefined the concept of professional performance support system and its need for evaluation. In following this route the team has tried to address the multidimensional needs of a growing group of mobile medical professionals by translating these needs into a database of culturally supported and professionally adequate language materials which are constantly evaluated and amended in order to address the needs even better.

References

1. Sveriges Kommuner och Landsting (SKL). Utrikes födda anställda i landsting och regioner 2006 [Foreigners employed in counties and regions]. SKL, Sweden (2009), http://www.skl.se/web/Antalet_anstallda_i_kommuner_och_lands ting_fodda_utomlands_okar.aspx
2. Ferguson, W.J., Candib, L.M.: Culture, Language, and Doctor-Patient Relationship. Family Medicine 34(5), 353–361 (2002)

3. Stewart, M.A.: Effective physician-patient communication and health outcomes: a review. Canadian Medical Association Journal 15(9), 1423–1433 (1995)
4. Travaline, J.M., Runchinskas, R., D'Alonzo, G.E.: Patient-Physical Communication: Why and How. The Journal of the American Osteopathic Association. Clinical Practice 105(1), 13–18 (2005)
5. Berbyuk Lindström, N.: Intercultural Communication in Health Care. Non-Swedish physicians in Sweden. Gothenburg Monographs in Linguistics, vol. 36. University of Gothenburg, Dept. of Linguistics Dissertation, Gothenburg (2008)
6. Van de Poel, K., Brunfaut, T.: Medical communication in L1 and L2 contexts: Comparative modification analysis. Intercultural Pragmatics (IPRG) 7(1), 103–130 (2010)
7. Hudelson, P.: Improving patient-provider communication: insights from interpreters. Family Practice 22(3), 311–316 (2005)
8. Rudvin, M., Tomassini, E.: Migration, Ideology and the Interpreter-Mediator. The Role of the Language Mediator in Educational and Medical Settings in Italy. In: Garcés, C.V., Amrtin, A. (eds.) Crossing borders in community interpreting: definitions and dilemmas, pp. 245–266. John Benjamins Publishing Company, Amsterdam (2008)
9. Medics on the Move (2006-2011), http://www.medicsmove.eu
10. Dudley-Evans, T.: Developments in English for Specific Purposes: A multi-disciplinary approach. Cambridge University Press, Cambridge (1998)
11. Dudley-Evans, T., St John, M.J.: Developments in English for Specific Purposes. Cambridge University Press, Cambridge (1998)
12. Flowerdew, J., Peacock, M.: Research Perspectives on English for Academic Purposes. Cambridge University Press, Cambridge (2001)
13. Basturkmen, H., Elder, C.: The Practice of LSP. In: Davies, A., Elder, C. (eds.) The Handbook of Applied Linguistics, pp. 672–694. Blackwell Publishing, Oxford (2006)
14. Nunan, D.: Syllabus Design. Oxford University Press, Oxford (1988)
15. Hutchinson, T., Waters, A.: English for Specific Purposes: A Learning-Centered Approach. Cambridge University Press, Cambridge (1987)
16. Basturkmen, H.: Ideas and Options in English for Specific Purposes. Lawrence Erlbaum Associates Inc., Mahwah (2006)
17. Jasso-Aguilar, R.: Sources, Methods and Triangulation in Needs Analysis: A Critical Perspective in a Case Study of Waikiki Hotel Maids. In: Cook, G., North, S. (eds.) Applied Linguistics: A Reader, pp. 171–194. Routledge, New York (2010)
18. Brown, J.D.: The Elements of Language Curriculum: A Systematic Approach to Program Development. Heinle & Heinle, Boston (1995)
19. Kurtz, S., Silverman, J., Draper, J.: Teaching and Learning Communication Skills in Medicine. Radcliffe Publishing, Oxford (2006)
20. Silverman, J.D., Kurtz, S.M., Draper, J.: Skills for Communicating with Patients. Radcliffe Publishing, Oxford (2006)
21. Bickley, L.S.: Bates' Pocket Guide to Physical Examination and History Taking. Lippincott Williams & Wilkins, Philadelphia (2007)
22. Bickley, L.S., Szilagiy, P.G.: Bates' Guide to Physical Examination and History Taking. Lippincott Williams & Wilkins, Philadelphia (2007)
23. Glendinning, E.H., Holmström, B.A.S.: English in Medicine. A Course in Communication Skills. Cambridge University Press, Cambridge (2002)
24. Glendinning, E.H., Howard, R.: Professional English in Use. Medicine. Cambridge University Press, Cambridge (2007)
25. Iedema, R. (ed.): The Discourse of Hospital Communication. Tracing Complexities in Contemporary Health Care Organizations. Palgrave Macmillan, Houndmills (2007)

26. Parkinson, J.: A Manual of English for the Overseas Doctor. Churchill Livingstone, Edinburgh (1999)
27. Pendleton, D., Schofield, T., Tate, P., Havelock, P.: The New Consultation. Developing Doctor-Patient Communication. Oxford University Press, Oxford (2007)
28. Prabhu, F.R., Bickley, L.S.: Case Studies to Accompany Bates' Guide to Physical Examination and History Taking. Lippincott Williams & Wilkins, Philadelphia (2007)
29. Silverman, J., Kurtz, S., Draper, J., Van Dalen, J.: Vaardig communiceren in de gezondheidszorg. Een evidence-based benadering. Lemma, Utrecht (2000)
30. Tate, P.: The Doctor's Communication Handbook. Radcliffe Publishing, Oxford (2007)
31. Wouda, J., Van de Wiel, H.B.M., Van Vliet, K.P.: Medische communicatie. Gespreksvaardigheden voor de arts. De Tijdstroom, Leusden (2000)
32. Van de Poel, K.: Medics on the Move: The Effect and Effectiveness of On-The-Workfloor Language Training. In: International Council for Open and Distance Education, ICDE 2009 (2009), http://www.ou.nl/eCache/DEF/2/11/523.html
33. Cox, A.: Project and Product Assessment: New insights Through Semi-Structured Interviews. Unpublished Master's Thesis. University of Antwerp, Antwerp (2008)

Science 2.0: The Open Orchestration of Knowledge Creation

Fridolin Wild

Knowledge Media Institute, The Open University
Walton Hall, Milton Keynes, MK7 6AA, UK
f.wild@open.ac.uk
http://kmi.open.ac.uk

Abstract. Science 2.0 focuses on supporting new practices with new tools. In this keynote, an overview on recently emerging open research support environments is given and substantialized with a set of examples of new practices of creating awareness, facilitating networked collaboration, and supporting reflection.

Keywords: Science 2.0, Research Support Environments.

1 Introduction

The notion science 2.0 is a rather young one. Not even old enough to have one single, established definition. Not to speak of an accepted set of schools of thought. Though, this new concept already has a number of advocates who are trying to shape its meaning.

In the words of [1], science 2.0 relates to new practices of scientists who post raw experimental results, nascent theories, claims of discovery and draft papers on the Web for others to see and comment on. The authors of [2] postulate even further that science 2.0 offers more potential than mere efficiency optimization (through improved workflows and better sharing possibilities): participation in research can be broadened beyond existing scientific communities. A science 2.0 is about crowd-sourcing of ideas and the refinement of knowledge in an open debate. It is a logical consequence of the socio-culturalist insight that information is a social concept (cf. [3]). As language underspecifies meaning, the co-construction of a scholarly network apt to perceive and understand is part of the research work itself.

Most obviously, this foreseen potential is only possible due to recent advances in web and information technology from which improved awareness, socialization, collaboration, and orchestration possibilities arise.

From the background of the open network of excellence in technology-enhanced learning STELLAR, this keynote gives an overview on the recent advances in practices and technology supporting academic explorers in their knowledge creation, sharing, and identification endeavors.

S. De Wannemacker, G. Clarebout, P. De Causmaecker (Eds.): ITEC 2010, CCIS 126, pp. 85–86, 2011.
© Springer-Verlag Berlin Heidelberg 2011

Mash-ups [4,5], social proxies [6], distributed feed networks [7], research recommenders [8], enriched with textmining technologies such as meaningful interaction analysis, provide the technological building blocks supporting the emergence of these new practices.

References

1. Waldrop, M.: Science 2.0. Scientific American 298(5), 68–73 (2008)
2. Underwood, J., Luckin, R., Smith, H., Walker, K., Rowland, D., Fitzpatrick, G., Good, J., Benford, S.: Reflections on Participatory Science for TELSci2.0. In: Science2.0 for TEL, Workshop at the 4th European Conference on Technology-Enhanced Learning (ECTEL 2009) Nice, France (2009)
3. Hammwoehner, R.: Information als logischer Abstraktor? Ueberlegungen zum Informationsbegriff. In: Eibl, Wolff, Womser-Hacker (eds.) Designing Information Systems, pp. 13–26. UVK, Konstanz (2005)
4. Wild, F., Kalz, M., Palmr, M.: Proceedings of the 1st Workshop on Mash-Up Personal Learning Environments, CEUR Workshop Proceedings (2008)
5. Wild, F., Kalz, M., Palmr, M., Mueller, D.: Proceedings of the 2nd Workshop on Mash-Up Personal Learning Environments, CEUR Workshop Proceedings (2009)
6. Wild, F., Valentine, C., Scott, P.: Shifting Interests: Changes in the Lexical Semantics of ED-MEDIA. International Journal of e-Learning 9(4) (2010) (to appear)
7. Wild, F., Sigurdarson, S.: Distributed Feed Networks for Learning. Upgrade IX(3) (2008)
8. Wild, F., Ochoa, X., Heinze, N., Crespo, R., Quick, K.: Bringing together what belongs together: A recommender-system to foster academic collaboration. In: Verbert, Duval, Lindstaedt, Gillet, Scott (eds.) Proceedings of the Workshop on Context-aware Recommendation for Learning, Stellar Alpine Rendezvous (2009)

miLexicon: Harnessing Resources for Personal and Collaborative Language Inquiry

Joshua Underwood, Rosemary Luckin, and Niall Winters

London Knowledge Lab, 23-29 Emerald Street, London WC1N 3QS, United Kingdom
{J.Underwood,R.Luckin,N.Winters}@ioe.ac.uk

Abstract. This paper introduces miLexicon, an innovative mobile tool for self-initiated, resource-based language learning. In essence, miLexicon consists of two interacting and extensible collections. One collection contains the language items a learner chooses to investigate, the other references resources (e.g. people, tools, media) useful to this inquiry. We describe this process of personal and collaborative language inquiry and show how we derive it from interviews with language learners. We then indicate how miLexicon is designed to support this process and prompt learners to reflect on their resource use. In describing the development of miLexicon we also provide an exemplar application of a novel framework for designing technology-rich learning contexts.

Keywords: language learning, context, design, ecology of resources, mobile learning, open learner models, personal learning environments.

1 Introduction

This paper introduces miLexicon, an innovative mobile tool for self-initiated, resource-based language learning. In essence, miLexicon consists of two interacting and user extensible collections. One collection contains the words and phrases a language learner encounters and chooses to investigate. The other contains resources (e.g. people, tools, strategies, media) that are useful in this inquiry, and in the construction of personal and cultural meanings. Users can share words, resources and inquiries with collaborators and can import these to their personal collections. Collections can be accessed, added to and edited on handheld devices thus facilitating use of miLexicon in and across varied settings. Ultimately, miLexicon aims to guide learners in the selection and collection of personally and contextually appropriate 'new' language and the resources that help learners understand and use this language.

Here, we describe the design framework [1] that guides development of miLexicon, initial analysis of user study data and the instructional design for personal and collaborative language inquiry that we derive from these studies. We then describe how we aim to support learners through this process of personal and collaborative language inquiry. We also present an initial prototype. Finally, we discuss some limitations and implications of this work and outline our plans for formatively evaluating and evolving miLexicon. First though, we briefly summarise the research in mobile learning and supporting learner autonomy, on which we build, and outline the understanding of context that informs our design approach.

S. De Wannemacker, G. Clarebout, P. De Causmaecker (Eds.): ITEC 2010, CCIS 126, pp. 87–98, 2011.

1.1 Mobile Assisted Language Learning (MALL)

Personal, portable, networked devices can support collaborative inquiry in situ [2], help learners make connections across settings and events [3], facilitate 'on the fly' recording of data and reflections [4], and enable interaction with resources that would not otherwise be available. Recent research explores these opportunities in relation to language learning, using mobiles to: capture and share observations of language in use [5]; provide access to distant human help [6]; support learners in 'noticing' significant language features [7]; share reflections on language and cultural insights gained in situ [8]. However, these processes are not often joined together and it is rare that instructional guidance is designed into the software and technologies used; appropriate instructional design is critical in ensuring that the potential for learning with mobiles is realised [2]. In miLexicon we aim to guide learners through a structured vocabulary learning process that makes use of the affordances described.

While there is very substantial interest in mobile software for vocabulary learning, try a search for language learning on Android Market or iTunes apps, very few of the applications available take advantage of the affordances described above. Many applications for vocabulary learning use flash card techniques (e.g. Tiny Classroom[1]); occasionally these are personalisable (users can add words), can be shared in a community (e.g. Smart.fm Study[2]) and can be annotated with multimedia (e.g. MyWordBook[3]). Such applications exploit the 'anytime anywhere' aspect of mobile learning, helping learners make use of 'dead time' (e.g. while commuting, waiting, etc), but do not exploit the affordances for situated learning or connecting learning across settings. In contrast recent research using mobiles for vocabulary learning often does aim to support collaboration, situated learning and connect learning across settings and time. Cloudbank [5] encourages learners to share annotated observations of language in use in a collaborative repository of new language. Wong and Looi [9] use mobiles both for personal and collaborative vocabulary learning, in activites that connect classroom and out of school learning; learners create personal visual representations of language presented in school, out of school, and then share these online and discuss them back in school. Other research supports the effectiveness of mobiles in promoting temporally spaced vocabulary study, often using SMS [e.g. 10]. Such approaches prompt learners to revisit new language and can be personalised to suit individual learner's linguistic competence and memory cycles [11].

In miLexicon we build on existing work in MALL by helping learners harness the affordances of mobiles described in this section (e.g. 'on the fly' data recording, in situ inquiry activity, ubiquitous collaboration). Like others we aim to enable learners to create, annotate and share personalised multimedia vocabulary records and we intend to prompt learners to revisit these records at suitable intervals. However, miLexicon differs from the work described earlier in that it explicitly aims to prompt learner reflection and promote autonomy. Key differentiating features that support this are: an inspectable interaction history for each language item added, customizable resources to support inquiry into new language, prompts for self-assessment.

---

[1] See http://www.tinyclassroom.com/
[2] See http://linklens.blogspot.com/2010/08/smartfm-android-study-dictionary-v11.html
[3] See http://learnenglish.britishcouncil.org/en/mobile-learning/mywordbook

1.2   Promoting Autonomy with Open Learner Models

Helping learners become autonomous has long been a key objective for Computer Assisted Language Learning [12]. A commonly accepted definition of autonomy is 'the ability to take charge of one's learning'; this requires learner involvement and reflection [13]. Reflection can lead to self-assessment and self-management, which are skills regularly employed by successful language learners [14]. However, learners need help in acquiring these skills [13]. One motivation for Open Learner Models (OLMs) is precisely to help learners acquire these metacognitive skills [15]. OLMs promote these skills by making system models of learner knowledge and activity visible to the learner and sometimes by allowing learners to challenge or adjust these models. In this way OLMs promote reflection and encourage self-assessment and self-management [15]. An example in language learning is Notice [16], an independent inspectable learner model that promotes self-assessment. One way reflection and self-assessment can be promoted is by displaying representations of the learner's target language production and correct uses side-by-side, and using saliency techniques to highlight differences, thus prompting learners to notice these. Independent learner models, not embedded in tutoring systems, can help users recognise problematic issues and prompt learners to resolve these independently using resources available outside the system. In independent OLMs the responsibility for identifying appropriate resources and assistance and undertaking learning activities lies with the learner [15]. However, learners often lack the knowledge and skills to make adequate choices about the resources that can support their learning and how to employ these [17]. Often, teachers and/or peers can help learners make these choices more effectively. Key objectives for miLexicon are to respond to challenges identified in developing personal learning environments: 1) to raise awareness of the range of resources available [18] to learners in any particular setting and 2) to support learners in developing the skills necessary to select and exploit these [19]. We support these by allowing users to customize and share the resources available within miLexicon.

1.3   Understanding Context for Design

Consideration of context is critical in understanding and designing support for any human activity [20], particularly learning [21]. The importance of the interaction between context and learning is highlighted with the arrival of personal, portable, networked, context-aware computing and the accompanying exploration of new opportunities for Technology-Enhanced Learning (TEL) (e.g. [2],[3],[5],[6],[7],[8]). Consequently, in mobile learning there is a particular concern to understand and engage with context, though research has often tended to focus on only physical and location aspects [22], and the need for theoretical frameworks that interpret context more broadly and relate context to learning is widely acknowledged [23], [3].

Ubiquitous and mobile adaptive systems aim to deliver personalized and contextually appropriate content [24]; i.e. the "right" thing, at the "right" time, in the "right" way [25] and in the "right" place. For example activities suited to the learner, her location, the time available and the likelihood of interruption [26]. However, with respect to learning there is a potential conflict when designers and systems take on too much responsibility for deciding what is 'right'. In encouraging learner autonomy, fostering human context-awareness and "proactive" engagement must be at least as important as context-aware "proactive computing" [27]. A key challenge for TEL is then, the development of appropriate models of context with which to inform the design of adaptive context-aware socio-technical systems that maintain the right balance between human and computer initiative.

It is precisely the balance of initiative between teachers and learners that is a key aspect of socio-cultural models of learning. Vygotsky describes learning as driven by activity, enabled through collaboration with a more able partner, which stretches beyond a learner's independent ability but within range of development [28]. This sensitive range is described as the Zone of Proximal Development (ZPD). Scaffolding [29] is a pedagogic technique that aims to provide and fade support so as to promote learner activity within the ZPD. Van Lier [30] emphasises this view of scaffolding as an autonomy building process in which learner and teacher initiative respectively grow and fade, claiming this handover/takeover is the defining feature of scaffolding.

In designing miLexicon, we are employing a new framework for designing technology-rich learning contexts, the Ecology of Resources (EoR) [1]. The EoR conceptualizes context as the learner's interactions with an ecology of human and other resources, is grounded in an interpretation of the Zone of Proximal Development [28], and applies the pedagogic strategy of scaffolding [29] to guide decisions about when and how to provide and fade support for learners in response to their developing skills and independence. Section 2 describes this model of context.

1.4 Summary

In summary, miLexicon builds on research in mobile learning by helping learners make integrated use of the affordances of mobile devices described in section 1.1. We extend current work in MALL by drawing on research in OLMs to promote autonomy described in section 1.2. We hypothesize that by representing to learners the available resources and learner's interactions with these we will prompt learners to reflect on their own resource use and learning and this will lead to greater language learning autonomy. Specific objectives for miLexicon are:

1. To guide learners through a multi-step personal and collaborative language inquiry process, which we derive from our user studies (see section 3).
2. To help learners identify, access and manage the resources they can employ in this process and in developing their own Personal Learning Environments (PLE).
3. To prompt learners to reflect on their resource use and PLEs and consequently help learners to take better control of their own language learning contexts.

2 Design Methodology

In designing miLexicon we employ a novel framework, the EoR, for designing technology-rich learning contexts. In doing so we are providing an exemplar application of the framework, which will be useful to others wishing to evaluate or adopt it. The EoR framework [1] brings designers and learners together in a participatory process that aims to understand and redesign learners' contexts, the resources available and the constraints that apply. This is an iterative process involving cycles of context modelling, design and evaluation. Designers and learners work together to build a description of the resources potentially available to learners. We then design adjustments so as to improve access and scaffold learners using these resources. Implementations of the designs can be considered representations of hypotheses about appropriate support for learning. These are grounded in our developing understanding of users and context. These designs are then evaluated and refined through 'in context' evaluations, analysis of which feeds in to redesign.

2.1 The Ecology of Resources Model of Context

Many aspects of context have been identified as relevant for design [20]. However, there is a danger that as designers we conceive context from the outside and that at 'design time' we misinterpret the personal lived experience of context as created at 'run time' by a user's interactions with and interpretations of our designs in actual social and physical settings [31]. The Ecology of Resources model describes context as "a learner's dynamic lived experience of the world constructed through their interactions with multiple concepts, people, artefacts and environments. These interactions are spatially and historically contingent and are driven by the goals and feelings of those who participate. Partial descriptions of the world are offered to a learner through the resources with which they interact" (p.30) [1].

The EoR extends our previous work in user and context modelling [32] and in designing and evaluating technology to support learning across settings [33] by modelling context as something created by learners' interactions with resources. *Resources* may be characterized as anything that supports learning. Key resource categories for designers to consider are: *knowledge* and *skills*, *people*, *tools* and the *physical environment*. Learners also bring their own resources to any interaction. These include: the individual's prior knowledge and skills, experiences, cognitive and physical capacities, motivations, interests and emotions. Personal, portable, networked technologies enable learners to carry new resources with them and to interact with an increasingly wide range of distant resources and consequently can have a particularly significant impact on learning context. However, learners' interactions with, and access to resources are always constrained in many ways, such as by rules, regulations, the behaviour of others or the learner's expectations. In the EoR model these constraints are referred to as *filters*, and we note that these filters can be both positive, facilitating interactions, and negative preventing or hindering other interactions. For example, my existing knowledge filters the way I interact with new knowledge; the rules and norms in a classroom or other setting may filter my use of a mobile phone; my physical embodiment (e.g. hands and senses) and location filter my perception of the physical world and the possible range of my interactions with resources in the world; and cultural resources, including language and gesture, filter our attempts to construct shared meanings with others.

Applying the EoR involves: first outlining the resources potentially available to learners and the filters that affect interactions with these resources; and second identifying and describing in more detail the subset of these resources that are best suited to a particular learning focus and the relations between these. This subset represents the range of resources that can potentially help learners perform activity towards the current learning focus and beyond their independent competence. However, changes may be required to optimize the learner's interactions with these resources. The third phase of activity involves designing 1) adjustments that remove obstructions and facilitate access to appropriate resources: and 2) identifying or creating resources (people and/or adaptive systems) that can scaffold interactions with these resources. The next step is to test and revise the design and any particular implementation of it, through evaluations. Introducing the designed artefact impacts on the way learners construct context and naturally leads to further iterations through the design framework. In the next section we describe an initial iteration through the first phase of the EoR framework in which we identify resources available to learners.

2.2 Identifying Language Learner Resource Ecologies

We can draw many examples of resources and filters involved in language learning from research [14,18,19,34]. Resources include: people (e.g. teachers, siblings, friends) and tools (e.g. online forums, email, e-dictionaries, grammar books, blogs, YouTube), knowledge and skills (e.g. learning strategies), and environments (e.g. cafes, shop signs, virtual communities, language classes). The primary purpose of the activity surrounding a learner's use of a resource is often a particularly significant filter. For example, e-dictionaries are often preferred for finding meanings rapidly to support primary activities such as reading for pleasure or talking, while paper dictionaries, which can provide greater detail and support annotation but require more time and attention, are often preferred when the user's primary focus is learning [34].

In order to gain further insight into language learners' resource use and particularly the way interactions with resources interleave with learning activity we have been conducting semi-structured interviews with successful adult language learners. In these interviews we prompt learners to reflect on the resources they use to support their language learning and also ask them to describe one or two significant recent language learning experiences in depth. In our ongoing analysis of these interviews we code transcripts in terms of the general categories suggested by the EoR framework (Filters, People, Tools, Skills, Knowledge and Environment) and use open coding and constant comparison [35] in order to identify subcategories of resources and filters and to describe the relationships between these. The resulting codes are used to structure our developing model of language learning contexts. In the following section, for reasons of space and focus, we provide only a small number of examples from our initial analyses of these ongoing interviews.

3 Initial Analysis of Language Learner Resource Ecologies

Here we provide three example scenarios drawn from the many rich narrative accounts of personal learning experiences given by participants in our interviews (see Table 1). These scenarios are illustrative of some of the ways in which resources are used to support language learning. Following the scenarios we indicate some of the resources and filters involved in these scenarios and suggest how these might be used in adaptive systems (Table 2).

Table 1. Language learning scenarios drawn from interviews

An advanced learner of Spanish, with a passion for trees, is on a country walk with her Spanish speaking partner. She takes a photo of a particularly beautiful tree and asks her partner what it is called in Spanish. He is unsure but thinks it's an 'Haya'. Later they consult a Spanish language nature guide and use images of the leaves to identify the tree. Later still, she posts the photo to her blog and describes the tree in Spanish and English in writing.

A learner of English watches CNN every morning for business news. He notices the unfamiliar phrase 'pave the way' in the scrolling text during a news report. He thinks he understands what it means in this context but notes the phrase down to check in a dictionary. Days later, talking to an English-speaking friend on Skype, he tries to use the expression. Initially, the friend is confused and this leads to the friend correcting his pronunciation and some discussion.

A translator is unsure how to translate an unusual combination of words and a place name in a Russian academic text into English. She searches Google and finds references to a treaty in that place. She decides the text probably refers to this treaty and translates it as 'treaty of...'. Later, she checks by email with her Russian editor who confirms this is an appropriate translation.

Common to these scenarios are: an event motivating the acquisition of some linguistic or cultural knowledge, the formation of tentative hypotheses (e.g. about meaning), use of reference and communication tools, collaboration with others to test and refine hypotheses, and learning that is connected across varied times and settings. We described this pattern as *personal and collaborative language inquiry*.

Table 2. Example resources and filters and potential scaffolds and adjustments

Resources	Use & Filters	Scaffolds/Adjustments
Learner Resources: Interests & motivations. Memory. First & foreign language skills & knowledge	Motivates and enables the activity. Supports prosecution of the activity over time and across settings. Existing skills filter interactions with resources.	Make learner aware of opportunities to pursue interests using target language. Support memory using prompts and keeping records of past activity. Match resources to existing knowledge and skills.

Table 2. *(Continued)*

Communication Tools: Skype, e-mail, blog	Support collaboration with others and provide opportunities for authentic language practice. Their use is filtered by location, availability, learners' awareness and knowledge of the tools, their usability, etc.	Make learner aware of available communication tools and their availability in any setting. Prompt use to support inquiry and language practice. Adjust access to and usability of tools.
People: Native speaker, partner, friend, colleague.	Provide help, feedback and opportunities for foreign language communication and hypothesis testing. Relationships and common interests, amongst other factors, filter interactions between people.	Connect learners to potential collaborators. Make collaborators aware of learner interests and language competencies. Prompt learners to communicate with others and to attempt to use new language.
Reference Tools: Dictionary, Google, target language nature guide	Support personal investigation of language, meaning and cultural references. Use is filtered by awareness, familiarity with, access to, location of, etc.	Make learner aware of available and appropriate reference tools, prompt timely use, and provide ubiquitous access. Track usage to support learners in evaluating tool utility.
Language Sources & Prompts: TV, on screen text, physical environment & tree, written text for translation	Provide meaningful setting and examples for new language. Interaction with these resources is strongly filtered by interests, motivation, location, chance, awareness, etc.	Prompt users to engage with language content sources and features of physical world that are matched to interests, competence and possibly location.
Data & Context Capture Tools: Paper & pen, notes, camera & photos	Supports capture of language and setting. Supports recall and reflection and communication with others.	Prompt noticing and recording of language and context, relevant to interests and competence. Prompt usage of media and notes.

4 Supporting Personal and Collaborative Language Inquiry

These scenarios reveal the ways in which resources are used in learning that frequently takes place over disjointed periods of time and in varied settings in which access to, and the appropriateness of resources differs. From these findings we derive two principal requirements for miLexicon: 1) to support memory and users in connecting learning across settings and times (e.g. capture new language and context, prompt users to 'follow up' new language items, represent user interaction history), 2) to help users identify, access and manage their interactions with the resources most appropriate to each stage of a personal and collaborative language inquiry process.

In the socio-cultural approach we adopt, learner agency is central [30]. Consequently, our starting point is personally meaningful self-initiated inquiry, typically sparked by learners' communicative needs and/or encounters with unfamiliar language or culture as evident in the scenarios in table 1. We aim to enhance this kind of inquiry in two ways: 1) by designing the miLexicon user interface so as to provide narrative guidance [36] that suggests a specific but not necessarily linear process through which users record and investigate new language, 2) by facilitating access to helpful resources at each step in this process. We refer to this as guided personal and collaborative language inquiry. This process, which parallels accounts of experience driven language learning [30], involves recording the word or phrase of interest along with supporting media (e.g. photos, sound clips, observations), forming and refining an interpretation using appropriate resources (e.g. dictionaries, collaborators, concordancers), making personally meaningful associations (e.g. using imagination, acting out), preparing to use (e.g. practicing pronunciation, role-playing), and trying out (e.g. using for communication). We suggest these steps build associations between learners' prior and new experiences. In this way each language item added to miLexicon and investigated becomes part of the learner's growing lexicon and indexes into her own personal and shared experiences.

Delivering this design requires two user editable and extensible collections, one for the language items encountered and another for the resources used to assist investigation of new language. We also need to provide an interface that guides users through the process described above. Our initial prototype (figure 1) aims to achieve this by providing a structured record for each language item added to the system. The structure implies learners should add notes and associate media. It also prompts learners to reflect on, and rate their understanding of, and ability to use a language item and displays a history of learner interactions with the item. The item menu provides direct access to resources and aims to prompt learners to use these.

Fig. 1. From right to left: 1) User collated list of language items to investigate. 2) Entry for a language item with image and short note added, showing menu of resource options below. 3) User provided resources for 'looking up' an item. 4) Resources found on the phone suitable for sending an item; e.g. by Bluetooth or SMS to a collaborator, or to a Facebook feed.

5   Discussion and Future Work

Work towards miLexicon is still at a relatively early stage. However, we feel we have outlined a design for a promising and innovative tool for language learning. We build on current research in mobile learning and open learner models with the intention of helping language learners harness the affordances of mobile devices for self-directed learning and supporting learners in reflecting on the way they use resources in their learning. In section 4 we describe the process of *personal and collaborative language inquiry* that we aim to support and show how we derive this process from successful language learners' accounts of their learning (see section 3). Our application of the EoR framework in analysing interview data illustrates how learning contexts can be conceptualized in terms of learner interaction with resources and filters. We also describe how this EoR model of language learning context feeds into our design and how we have implemented the design in an initial prototype. The requirements and scenarios that ground this design are currently drawn from learners' memories and interpretations of how they interact with resources and learn, rather than from direct observations. However, in seeding design we are as interested in plausible accounts of what *might be* as we are in researchers' interpretations of *what is*. Not withstanding, the next phase of our user studies will involve observation and recording of resource use and language learning as it happens using the miLexicon tool. Analysis of these data will compliment interpretive data from interviews and feed into the iterative redesign of miLexicon.

Currently, we are providing early prototypes of miLexicon to a small but growing number of language learners. We are asking these learners to use miLexicon to support their language learning over several months. These early trials are revealing amongst other things, usability issues, interaction patterns, useful resources and new requirements. These initial users are in direct contact with the developer, thus facilitating co-design and agile development. We will be rapidly feeding findings from these studies into further iterations of prototype development. Simultaneously, we are starting to populate both generic and language specific collections of the resources these learners find useful. These collections will be used to provide initial resource suggestions to new users. Once we have developed a stable version of the miLexicon system we will be recruiting a small group of (5 to 15) language learners to participate in formative evaluations. These users will be asked to keep diaries reflecting on their learning and use of the prototype over several months. The prototype also logs use, keeping a record of words added and resources used and this logged data can be triangulated with users' accounts of learning using miLexicon.

Ultimately, we aim to go beyond static guidance embedded in the structure of the interface by dynamically 'scaffolding' learners' progress through the process of personal and collaborative language inquiry. This will involve the system taking more, or less initiative, contingent on a learner's activity. We want to explore how adaptive navigation (e.g. dynamically changing the order and salience of menu items, the structure of language item records, etc) in response to user activity, characteristics and circumstances, may be implemented so as to prompt learners to reflect on their learning and resource use and interact with particular resources. We also plan to make miLexicon adaptive to individual and contextual factors by dynamically filtering the resources offered (e.g. prompting investigation of language related to a learner's interests, suggesting resources appropriate to the learner's current location and physical and social setting, prompting use at appropriate times).

Acknowledgements. I would particularly like to thank all interview participants and the anonymous reviewers for their helpful suggestions. This doctoral research is funded by EPSRC grant EP/E051847/1 SCAffolding Rich Learning Experiences through Technology: SCARLET project.

References

1. Luckin, R.: Re-designing Learning Contexts: Technology-rich, Learner-centred Ecologies. Routledge, London (2010)
2. Rogers, Y., Price, S.: The Role of Mobile Devices in Facilitating Collaborative Inquiry in Situ. Research and Practice in Technology Enhanced Learning 3(3), 209–229 (2008)
3. Looi, C.K., Seow, P., Zhang, B., So, H.-J., Chen, W., Wong, L.H.: Leveraging Mobile Technology for Sustainable Seamless Learning: a Research Agenda. BJET (2009), http://dx.doi.org/10.1111/j.1467-8535.2008.00912.x
4. Li, I., Dey, A., Forlizzi, J.: Graffiter: Leveraging Social Media for Self Reflection. Crossroads 16(2), 12–13 (2009)
5. Pemberton, L., Winter, M., Fallahkhair, S.: A User Created Content Approach to Mobile Knowledge Sharing for Advanced Language Learners. In: Proceedings of mLearn 2009, Orlando, Florida, pp. 184–187 (2009)
6. Ogata, H., Li Hui, G., Yin, C., Ueda, T., Oishi, Y., Yano, Y.: LOCH: Supporting Mobile Language Learning Outside Classrooms. IJMLO 2(3), 271–282 (2008)
7. Kukulska-Hulme, A., Bull, S.: Theory-based Support for Mobile Language Learning: Noticing and Recording. International Journal of Interactive Mobile Technologies 3(2), 12–18 (2009)
8. Comas-Quinn, A., Mardomingo, R., Valentine, C.: Mobile Blogs in Language Learning: Making the Most of Informal and Situated Learning Opportunities. ReCALL 21(1), 96–112 (2009)
9. Wong, L.H., Looi, C.K.: Vocabulary learning by mobile-assisted authentic content creation and social meaning-making: two case studies. Journal of Computer Assisted Learning 26(5), 421–433 (2010)
10. Lu, M.: Effectiveness of vocabulary learning via mobile phone. Journal of Computer Assisted Learning 24(6), 515–525 (2008)
11. Chen, C.M., Chung, C.J.: Personalized mobile English vocabulary learning system based on item response theory and learning memory cycle. Computers & Education 51, 624–645 (2008)
12. Oxford, R.L.: Intelligent Computers for Learning Languages: The View for Language Acquisition and Instructional Methodology. CALL 6(2), 173–188 (1993)
13. Little, D.: Language Learner Autonomy: Some Fundamental Considerations Revisited. Innovation in Language Learning and Teaching 1(1), 14–29 (2001)
14. Rivers, W.P.: Autonomy at All Costs: An Ethnography of Metacognitive Self-Assessment and Self-Management. The Modern Language Journal 85(2), 279–290 (2001)
15. Bull, S., Kay, J.: Metacognition and Open Learner Models. In: Roll, I., Aleven, V. (eds.) Workshop on Metacognition and Self-Regulated Learning, ITS 2008, pp. 7–20 (2008)
16. Shahrour, G., Bull, S.: Does 'Notice' Prompt Noticing? Raising Awareness in Language Learning with an Open Learner Model. In: Nejdl, W., Kay, J., Pu, P., Herder, E. (eds.) AH 2008. LNCS, vol. 5149, pp. 173–182. Springer, Heidelberg (2008)
17. Clarebout, G., Elen, J.: Tool use in computer-based learning environments: towards a research framework. Computers in Human Behavior 22, 389–411 (2006)

18. Palfreyman, D.: Social Context and Resources for Language Learning. System 34(3), 352–370 (2006)
19. Guth, S.: Personal Learning Environments for Language Learning. In: Thomas, M. (ed.) Handbook of Research on Web 2.0 & Second Language Learning, pp. 451–471. IGI, UK (2008)
20. Beyer, H., Holtzblatt, K.: Contextual Design: Defining Customer-Centered Systems. Morgan Kaufmann, San Francisco (1998)
21. Nardi, B.: Context and Consciousness. Activity Theory and Human-Computer Interaction, pp. 69–102. MIT Press, Cambridge (1996)
22. Frohberg, D., Goth, C., Schwabe, G.: Mobile Learning Projects - a Critical Analysis of the State of the Art. Journal of Computer Assisted Learning 25(4), 307–331 (2009)
23. Sharples, M., Taylor, J., Vavoula, G.: A Theory of Learning for the Mobile Age. In: Andrews, R., Haythornthwaite, C. (eds.) The Sage Handbook of E-learning Research, pp. 221–247. Sage, London (2007)
24. Zimmermann, A., Sprecht, M., Lorenz, A.: Personalisation and Context-Management. User Modeling and User-Adapted Interaction 15(3-4), 275–302 (2005)
25. Fischer, G.: User Modeling in Human-Computer Interaction. User Modeling and User-Adapted Interaction 11(1-2), 65–86 (2001)
26. Cui, Y., Bull, S.: Context and Learner Modelling for the Mobile Foreign Language Learner. System 33(2), 353–367 (2005)
27. Rogers, Y.: Moving on from Weiser's Vision of Calm Computing: Engaging UbiComp Experiences. In: Dourish, P., Friday, A. (eds.) UbiComp 2006. LNCS, vol. 4206, pp. 404–421. Springer, Heidelberg (2006)
28. Vygotsky, L.: Thought and Language. MIT Press, Cambridge (1986)
29. Wood, D.: Scaffolding, contingent tutoring and computer-supported learning. IJAIED 12, 280–292 (2001)
30. van Lier, L.: Action-based Teaching, Autonomy and Identity. Innovation in Language Learning and Teaching 1(1), 46–65 (2007)
31. Dourish, P.: What we talk about when we talk about context. Personal and Ubiquitous Computing 8(1), 19–30 (2004)
32. Tunley, H., du Boulay, B., Luckin, R., Holmberg, J., Underwood, J.: Up and Down the Number Line: Modelling Collaboration in Contrasting School and Home Environments. In: Ardissono, L., Brna, P., Mitrović, A. (eds.) UM 2005. LNCS (LNAI), vol. 3538, pp. 424–429. Springer, Heidelberg (2005)
33. Luckin, R., du Boulay, B., Smith, H., Underwood, J., Fitzpatrick, G., Holmberg, J., Kerawalla, L., et al.: Using Mobile Technology to Create Flexible Learning Contexts. In: Jones, A., Kukulska-Hulme, A., Mwanza, D. (eds.) Portable Learning: Experiences with Mobile Devices. JIME, vol. 22 (2007), http://jime.open.ac.uk/2005/22
34. Kobayashi, C.: The use of pocket electronic and printed dictionaries. In: Bradford Watts, K., Muller, T., Swanson, M. (eds.) Proceedings of JALT 2007. JALT, Tokyo (2008)
35. Cohen, L., Manion, L., Morrison, K.: Research Methods in Education, 6th edn. Routledge-Falmer, London (2007)
36. Plowman, L., Luckin, R., Laurillard, D., Stratfold, M., Taylor, J.: Designing Multimedia for Learning: Narrative Guidance and Narrative Construction. In: Proceedings of ACM CHI 1999 Conference on Human Factors in Computing Systems, pp. 310–317 (1999)

Ontology-Driven Adaptive and Pervasive Learning Environments – APLEs: An Interdisciplinary Approach

Ahmet Soylu[1,2], Mieke Vandewaetere[1,3], Kelly Wauters[1,4], Igor Jacques[1,2], Patrick De Causmaecker[1,2], Piet Desmet[1], Geraldine Clarebout[1,3], and Wim Van den Noortgate[1,4]

[1] K.U. Leuven, Interdisciplinary Research on Technology Education & Communication, Kortrijk, Belgium
[2] K.U. Leuven, Department of Computer Science, CODeS Group, Kortrijk, Belgium
[3] K.U. Leuven, Centre for Intructional Psychology and Technology, Leuven, Belgium
[4] K.U. Leuven, Centre for Methodology of Pedagogical Research, Leuven, Belgium
Name.Surname@kuleuven-kortrijk.be

Abstract. This paper reports an interdisciplinary research project on adaptive and pervasive learning environments. Its interdisciplinary nature is built on a firm collaboration between three main research domains, namely, instructional science, methodology, and computer science. In this paper, we first present and discuss mutual, as well as distinctive, vision and goals of each domain from a computer science perspective. Thereafter, we argue for an ontology-driven approach employing ontologies at run-time and development-time where formalized ontologies and rules are considered as main medium of adaptivity, user involvement, and automatic application development. Finally, we introduce a prototype domain context ontology for item-based learning environments and demonstrate its run-time and development-time uses.

Keywords: Adaptive Learning, Pervasive Learning, Learner Control, Item-based Learning Environments, Ontologies, Model Driven Development.

1 Introduction

The new computing vision, i.e. Pervasive Computing (PerCom) [1], and technological advancements, e.g., Semantic Web, re-organize the way people use and interact with the technology. Not surprisingly, learning is one of the domains which closely follows such a fundamental shift. Table 1, extended from [2], reflects the shift and the convergence between the learning and the technology. Ubiquity (i.e. pervasiveness), personalization, and adaptivity within the context of this paper, are of importance.

First of all, computing is not predefined to any time or any location anymore, but it is rather *ubiquitous*. PerCom, in succession to the personal computer and main frame computing era, allows the user to be served by multiple computers anytime anywhere [3]. In this respect, learning is also not limited to predefined times or places since people need to continually enhance their knowledge and abilities [4]. On the one hand, Computer Assisted Learning (CAL) systems using desktop computers are not embedded in the real world and are not mobile, therefore those systems hardly

S. De Wannemacker, G. Clarebout, P. De Causmaecker (Eds.): ITEC 2010, CCIS 126, pp. 99–115, 2011.
© Springer-Verlag Berlin Heidelberg 2011

support anytime and anywhere learning [5]. On the other hand, most of the smart labs simply remediate the physical space to the classroom. Going pervasive means augmenting the physical space rather than re-mediating the physical space to the classroom [6]. However one should not link PerCom only with informal and open learning and ignore the traditional learning environments providing valuable feedback, assessment, etc. mechanisms. It is also needed to enable these systems to be part of pervasive environments through reaching rich contextual information and delivering their content and functionalities to different settings.

Table 1. Shift in technology and the convergence between the learning and the technology [2]

Learning	Technology
Personalized	Personal
Learner Centered	User Centered
Situated	Mobile [Dynamic]
Adaptive	Context-aware
Collaborative	Networked
Ubiquitous	Ubiquitous
Lifelong	Durable

Secondly, PerCom envisions that computing shall seamlessly immerse into the daily life which requires computing systems to be "intelligent" in order to adapt to different settings and users, so that users do not realize or bother about the applications and devices around [3]. On the one hand, absolute focus placed on machine control by PerCom vision ignores the importance of user involvement (e.g., user/learner control etc.) which is crucial for learning as well as computing in general. On the other hand, focus of learning is more on *personalization,* in order to enhance learning and performance [7] by taking into consideration that, learners differ in prior knowledge, skills, and abilities, have different demographic backgrounds, and show different affective states. Emergence of Pervasive Learning led to a complete understanding of *adaptivity* by considering that the learning systems shall not only provide a user-tailored experience through personalization but shall also adapt (to) the setting, in which the learner is engaged, through *context-awareness.*

These critiques introduce important questions: how do we realize such adaptive learning applications and "intelligence", how "intelligent" will they be, who will take the control - learner or system - and how? In order to address aforementioned questions, we conduct an interdisciplinary research project on Adaptive and Pervasive Learning Environments (APLEs). The interdisciplinary nature is built on a firm collaboration between three research domains, namely, instructional science, methodology, and computer science. In this paper mutual, as well as distinctive vision and goals of each domain are presented and discussed from a computer science perspective. Thereafter, we argue for an ontology-driven approach. Our experience with different learning environments shows us that, adaptations and static reasoning logic are embedded in applications in an ad-hoc manner making it difficult to incorporate new adaptation and control mechanisms addressing different educational scenarios and contexts. As a response, in this paper, ontologies are employed at development time in terms of automated code generation by following Model Driven Development (MDD) mantra and at run-time together with rules in terms of reasoning, dynamic adaptations and user involvement. We also introduce a domain context ontology for item-based learning environments in order to demonstrate the anticipated uses of our approach.

The remainder of this paper is structured as follows. In section 2, the three domains and their perspectives on adaptivity are presented. In section 3, a discussion is presented from a computer science point of view. In section 4 and 5, we speculate on the necessity of an ontological approach, introduce a prototype domain context ontology, and demonstrate its run-time and development-time uses. In section 6, we present the related work and finally we conclude the paper in section 7.

2 Research Domains

Considering *instructional science:* Adaptivity is defined as the capability of a system to alter its behavior, according to the learner's needs and other characteristics [8]. Existing research demonstrate that, individualized instruction is superior to the uniform approach of more traditional and one-size-fits-all teaching approaches [9]. The strong empirical support for the superiority of the individualized instruction has led to firm confirmation of the mere value of adapting the learning environment to the specific needs of the learner. Current research on computer based adaptive systems is built upon the research on and the development of Intelligent Tutoring Systems (ITS). ITS make inferences about the learner characteristics in order to dynamically adapt the characteristics of the environment. Traditional ITS include (1) a learner model containing mechanisms to understand what the student knows and does not know [10], (2) an expert or domain model modeling content and knowledge to be taught and relationships between the domain elements, (3) a pedagogical model encompassing an inherent teaching or instructional strategy [11], and (4) the learning environment providing the means for the student to interact with the ITS. Based on the learner model, the domain model and the instructional model are adapted to personalize the interaction between the learner and the environment. Adaptive instruction can be considered as having tripartite nature: (1) the source of adaptive instruction, that is, "to what will be adapted?", (2) the target of adaptive instruction, that is, "what will be adapted?", and (3) pathways of adaptive instruction, that is, "how to translate the source into the target?" Considering the ITS, the typical source can be found within the learner [12]. Three groups of individual characteristics can be placed centrally in learner models; (1) cognition related such as prior knowledge and learning style, (2) affect related such as motivation and confusion, and (3) behavior related characteristics. As a target, typical ITS contain an outer loop and an inner loop, with the outer loop describing which task the learner should be doing next, and with the inner loop representing the support (e.g., hints). A first and most applied dimension of the target of adaptive instruction is the learning material itself [13]. Accompanying support [14] and presentation [15] are the examples of other dimensions. The transition from the source information to the target information occurs by rule based step analysis, containing 'if ...-then...' rules. Adaptive instruction can be offered by changing the degree of control which an instructor or learner can be engaged in; full program or instructor control, full learner control, shared control [16] and adaptive advisement [17]. Adaptive advisement aims at enhancing self regulation skills of the learner while the main goal of the shared control is to enhance motivation of the learner. Accordingly, several research questions arise. Which learner characteristics are worthwhile to include in the user model? What is the impact of learner control and adaptive learner control as an instructional technique?

Considering *methodology*: As pointed out, research has shown that adaptive learning environments have a positive influence on learning effectiveness. Several adaptation techniques, under which adaptive curriculum sequencing, have been implemented in ITS in order to create such a personalized learning environment [18]. The practice of adaptive curriculum sequencing aims at generating a personalized course, by dynamically selecting the most optimal task at any moment, in order to learn certain knowledge in an efficient and effective way. The manner in which it is implemented depends on the type of learning environment. A distinction can be made between task-based learning environments, consisting of main problems that are often tackled by means of scaffolding problems, and item-based learning environments, consisting of simple questions that can be combined with hints and feedback. The focus of the methodology domain, in the context of this project, is on adaptive curriculum sequencing in item-based learning environments by matching the item difficulty level to the learner's knowledge level. From this perspective, it seems obvious to make use of the IRT (Item Response Theory) [19], as it is frequently implemented in CAT (Computerized Adaptive Testing) [20]. IRT is a measurement model that specifies the probability of a discrete outcome, such as a correct response to an item, in terms of person and item parameters. In CAT, IRT is used to generate an item bank of which the item parameters (e.g., item difficulty level) are known and to estimate and update a person's ability, in order to decide on the next item to render. The selection of the most appropriate item for persons based on their knowledge level can potentially shorten testing time, improve measurement precision, and increase motivation [20]. Analogously, applying IRT for adaptive curriculum sequencing in item-based learning environments could enhance learning and motivation, as excessively difficult course materials can frustrate learners, while excessively easy course materials can cause learners to lack all sense of challenge and thus to waste time [21]. However, differences between learning and testing environments entail several challenges for the extrapolation of IRT ideas to item-based learning environments, which are the subjects of our research. First of all, the data gathered in learning environments are not very well structured as in testing environments due to skipped and not reached items, especially if the learner is free to select items. Consequently, one of the challenges is estimating the item difficulty levels and learner's knowledge level properly. Secondly, while the objective of testing environments is to measure the person's knowledge level as precisely as possible, the objective of learning environments is to optimize learning efficiency. This raises several questions: do we select items that maximize the measurement precision or do we select more easy or difficult items? Would allowing learners to select the item difficulty level of the next item from among a number of difficulty levels (i.e. learner control) increase efficiency? If so, how do we keep the learning outcome optimal?

Considering *computer science*: PerCom aims at the creation of "intelligent" digital ecosystems which are seamlessly situated in user's physical environment. Such an ecosystem is defined as a collection of loosely integrated, mobile/stationary and autonomous/non-autonomous devices and applications. Higher mobility and autonomy are crucial. "Intelligence" for such systems is defined as the capability of being able to perceive computing context and to respond collectively, proactively and properly in order to maximize the utility of the user [3]. That being the case, context-awareness is crucial for PerCom environments since such systems need to perceive elements of the changing computing setting and complex relationships between them. Once a concrete perception of the computing setting is acquired, dynamics of the setting can be re-organized through adaptation. This can be formally defined as a process of mediation between the computing setting and the individual/common characteristics, capabilities and requirements of the entities available through the setting (e.g., users, devices etc.). We consider adaptivity as a primary relation between context and computing in context-aware computing settings while the user is the primary reference point [3]. Context is an open concept characterizing the situation of an entity [22]. It can encompass infinite number of characteristics and appropriateness of a context dimension is volatile; characteristics being part of the context in one setting could be irrelevant in another [23]. Context exhibits particular types of properties [3]. First of all, it is a dynamic construct; although some context dimensions are static like name of a user, most of the context dimensions like learner knowledge are highly dynamic. More importantly, it evolves rather than being regenerated. Secondly, it is relational, that is, different types of relationships exist between different context dimensions. In this regard, perception is not just about realizing concepts, but also about understanding relationships between these concepts which are necessary to interpret situations in a given setting. Finally, it is imperfect because of the ambiguity, irrelevance, impreciseness, and incompleteness of context dimensions [24]. Adaptive behaviors of context-aware systems not necessarily need to depend on the current context rather, these systems should be proactive, by making use of both current context and past context to predict the future context of the setting. PerCom matures the computational grounding of the idea of always on education, removes its technological barriers, partially at this stage. It extends existing educational theories such as collaborative learning, constructivism, information rich learning environments, self-organized learning, adaptive learning, multimodal learning, and a myriad of other learning theories [25]. PerCom takes part in an experience of immersion as a mediator between the learner's mental (e.g., prior knowledge), physical (e.g., other learners close by) and virtual (e.g., learning material) contexts [26]. Accordingly, in terms of software development, the general research question is formulated as: how do we effectively realize complex APLEs?

3   Synthesis

Given these road maps, available links between the three research domains can be properly interpreted. The overall research landscape has been extracted and represented in the Fig. 1. The main discussion will be around the common set; adaptivity, learner characteristics, learner control, and mobile computing.

In the first place, a common understanding of *adaptivity*, not necessarily a definition, needs to be constructed. Seemingly the current research in instructional science considers the adaptation in terms of personalization which is a process in between the learner and the application (e.g., ITS). Educational research should primarily be based on sound educational theories rather than technologically complex ones [27]. But, it is also evident that the advancements in the technology should be considered and new sound educational scenarios should be created to exploit new possibilities. In this context, a user-application (i.e., learner - ITS) view of adaptivity reflects a producer-consumer model (i.e., classroom model) of computing and learning where teachers act as content producers and students act as content consumers. However, we argue for a context-computing setting view of adaptivity, depicted in Fig. 2. In this model, the learning process and the setting are adapted to the context while the learner's characteristics remain in the core of the context.

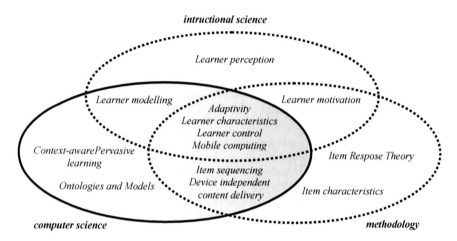

Fig. 1. Research landscape spanning instructional science, methodology and computer science

A learning process should not supposed to be supported by a single application, but through various applications (e.g., Mashups [28]), and the learning environment should not supposed to be accessed solely through browsers or desktop computers, but through any device capable for particular scenarios (i.e., not limited to predefined devices, interfaces, and modalities). Therefore, adaptivity, in APLEs, should not be understood as one-to-one relation between the user and the application, rather as a relation between computing setting and the context (see Fig. 2). Therefore adaptation in PerCom is not limited to the personalization, rather every entity (even the user) in the computing setting needs to be tailored to each other. The learner, that is, the user is the central notion in all the three of these research domains. Computer science is interested in *learner characteristics* in broader perspective, by considering any kind of information describing the state of the user. Possible characteristics of a user are twofold: internal characteristics such as knowledge etc. and external characteristics such as gender, age etc. Internal characteristics are usually harder to sense compared to the external characteristics [29]. Naturally, instructional science is interested in the characteristics of the learner, which are meaningful for the educational process such as prior knowledge, motivation etc. The methodology domain has the most specific focus on this matter. An accurate estimate of the learner's ability level is crucial for adaptively selecting the most appropriate learning items by comparing the learner ability with the item difficulty. Regarding possible categorizations of adaptivity, we propose the following categorization which we described in [3]: (1) context based filtering and recommendation of information and services, (2) context based presentation and access of information and services: e.g., multimodal and dynamic user interfaces etc., (3) context based information and service searching: e.g., query rewriting for a search for available learning items, (4) context adaptive navigation and task sequencing, (5) context based service and application modification/configuration: e.g., disabling particular features depending on the capabilities of the target device, (6) context based actions: manual, semi-automatic, and automatic, (7) context based resource allocation (digital / non-digital).

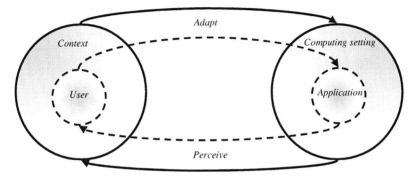

Fig. 2. User-application versus context-computing setting perspective of the adaptation process

Learner control leaves an open room in all the three of these research domains. Instructional science employs shared control, where a learner and a system share the control of learning environment and learning process, in different weights in order to increase the learner motivation. On top of that, instructional science employs adaptive advisement to guide the learner during the educational process and to enhance the self-regulation skills of the learner. The methodology domain employs the learner control, to increase the motivation of the learner, thereby leading to increased efficiency. Computer science domain constructs its perspective on two particular arguments. (1) Smart technologies should not make people dumb and adapt activities and environment to this dumbness [6], and (2) an "intelligent" system cannot take the place of a teacher or a facilitator: it can only keep limited dialogue at the level of actions, and it has no way of exploring student's misunderstandings or helping them to reach a shared understanding [30]. These arguments find their roots in the importance of self-regulation skills and the way by which the current "intelligent" (adaptive) systems are developed. Since it is the responsibility of computer science to provide generic means to realize a variety of different scenarios, a holistic perspective is followed, by considering that the control over the environment and the learning process might totally be held by the system or the user/learner. Alternatively, it can be shared while the final decision is still taken by either the system or the user. In the latter case, informative input is provided by the second party through user mediation [31] or adaptive user guidance/advisement respectively. Considering adaptive advisement, we argue that, adaptive application behaviors do not necessarily need to result in "must"s or "have-to"s, but can also result in "should"s and "might"s, leaving some degree of control to the user, while providing possible directions and the reasoning behind those directions [3]. The system can extend the limits of contextual information (i.e., increased user awareness), perceivable by the user's physical capabilities, by serving the collected contextual information to the user, rather than automatically adapting itself [3], where incorrect actions might be frustrating [32]. Considering user meditation, adaptive behaviors are usually realized by means of hard-coded and predefined mappings of behavior space to the context space. However, context space is usually huge and ambiguous. Therefore, it is not always possible to enumerate all context - behavior mappings and ensure the reliability of the behaviors selected. According to the severity of behaviors, systems should mediate the user to decide on accuracy of the contextual information or the adaptive behavior, while the ideal case is placing less load on the user's side [33].

Increasing ubiquity of the technology definitely opens up new research challenges for instructional science and methodology such as, the investigation of new indoor/outdoor scenarios, or more specifically its effects on psychology and experience of the learner such as, motivation and easiness, for instance, while the test environment is accessed through a small terminal having a small screen size. The *mobile computing* track is mainly driven by the computer science domain. Indeed, it is situated in PerCom vision and constitutes a sub-space of the original problem. However, we believe that within the broader PerCom vision, the notion of mobility should refer to mobility of the user experience, thus to the mobility of the learning process, rather than to the mobility the device, software etc. Since PerCom environments are not yet realized, mobile computing provides ready-to-use infrastructures, without any extra investment, for computer science which aims at providing enabling technologies compliant with the overall PerCom vision. PDAs and other mobile devices should be seen more as extensions, rather than replacement of the existing learning tools, and not all kinds of learning content and activities are appropriate for mobile devices [34]. In this respect, the role of computer science is not only exploring the new technologies upon which instructional science can build new pedagogic scenarios, but also to enable accessibility of available pedagogical scenarios to different context of use. The following vision [35] provides a potential roadmap in this respect. It considers devices as portals, applications as tasks, and physical surroundings as computing environments. Based on this vision, the application life-cycle is divided into three parts: design-time, load time and run time. Criteria and models for each part are defined in [35]. Considering design time, it is suggested that, applications and application frontends should not be written with a specific device in mind. Applications should not have assumptions about available services, therefore abstract user interfaces and abstract services need to be described. The structure of the program needs to be described in terms of tasks and subtasks instead of simply decomposing user interaction. Considering load time, it is suggested that, applications must be defined in terms of requirements and the devices must be described in terms of capabilities. Considering run-time, it is noted that, it must monitor the resources, adapt applications to those resources and respond to changes. This approach is based on higher abstractions of entities, including applications themselves. Indeed, that is how programming evolved from machine code assemblers to data structures etc. to cope with the increasing complexity.

4 Approach

In PerCom and Adaptive Systems literature, ontologies have an increasing impact. PerCom employs ontologies to formalize context and to build reasoning and adaptation mechanisms on top, e.g., [36], in order to provide a context-tailored user experience. Adaptive learning systems follow the same path and use ontologies as a main medium of adaptivity through formalizing user models, domain knowledge etc. (e.g., [37]). On the one hand, adaptive learning systems lack a complete utilization of context, because of their absolute focus on the user, thereby ignoring other contextual information. On the other hand, neither PerCom nor adaptive learning systems sufficiently justify the use of ontologies, and available implementations do not properly explain (even explore) the full potential. Firstly, although it is claimed that, ontologies provide knowledge share and interoperability, which is theoretically true, in practice, it is already known that there might be millions of ways to model the world [38]. Therefore, it is quite difficult to utilize ontologies for global integration purposes, since everyone has her own requirements and perspective. Secondly, ontologies are complex and hard to develop, so why should one use ontologies instead of other less complex mechanisms (e.g., at meta-data level)? In the followings, we present our driving mantra behind the use of ontologies.

Our approach is based on ontologies and higher abstractions and shaped by concrete argumentations, originating from the problem and the solution domains. Ontologies are not right for everything; they are particularly useful for highly logical, knowledge oriented, complex, and domain specific applications, otherwise their presumed benefits might be lesser than the load of the complexity which they introduce. APLEs are highly complex, knowledge-oriented, and logical, therefore ontologies are of greater use for their development, maintainability, and sustainability. This is because, while the traditional applications are designed for a specific and restricted context of use [3], APLEs are based on enumerations of possible contexts of use, through predefined mappings, between situations in contextual space to behaviors in behavior space [39]. Such predefined mappings are built on strong and hard-coded logical assumptions (i.e., reasoning logic) and computational procedures, defined by developers and embedded in the application. Thus, practically, expert knowledge is lost; more accurately, that knowledge is embedded in code ready for architectural archeology by someone who probably would not have done it that way [40]. However, PerCom extends the context space and behavior space to infinity, which makes reasoning logic, adaptations, and application knowledge hard to manage. In other words, adaptive and pervasive systems are presently developed in an ad-hoc way, through encoding adaptive behaviors and static reasoning logic into the application code, which in turn, introduces manageability problems and exhaustive development overheads. It is hard to implement new adaptation mechanisms at run-time and at development-time and there is no real inference and reasoning mechanism. Ontologies are promising in the sense of their use at run time and development-time [39, 41]. Considering run time (i.e., ontology-driven systems [42]), ontologies are of use as external knowledge bases over which a reasoning component can reason. Therefore, the use of ontologies enables separation of application logic from code thereby facilitating the management of reasoning logic and binding between diverse landscapes of contextual space and behavior space [39]. Use of ontologies also provides a unified framework of understanding between computers-computers, users-computers, and users-users, which in turn, facilitates application development, and user involvement both at development and run-time. Considering the development point of view (i.e., ontology-driven development [42]), an ontological approach, following MDD mantra, can be used to automate application development, which is crucial for rapid and sustainable development of long living APLEs. We provide a review of literature and a discussion on context-awareness and adaptivity in relation with ontologies and pervasive environments in [3], and speculate on possible merging of ontologies and MDD in [39].

5 A Domain Ontology and Validation

In [3, 43], we elaborated a context categorization constructing an upper context conceptualization. The proposed categorization mainly aims at representing main entities of a typical PerCom setting and can easily be formalized as an upper context ontology. In this section, we introduce a prototype domain context ontology, based on aforementioned upper conceptualization, for an item-based learning environment to demonstrate how ontologies can be used to both develop and operate an APLE. A simplified view of the ontology is presented in Fig. 3. It spans the main concepts relevant to three domains: (1) *learners*, (2) *devices* and (3) *learning objects (LOs)*.

The idea behind it is adaptive filtering, sequencing and selection of LOs based on the learner characteristics , the hardware the user works on, the properties of the LOs, and the relationships between the LOs. The presented ontology assumes a pool of elemental LOs (i.e., items – subclass of elemental learning object), i.e. representing the smallest LOs in terms of granularity, and compound LOs encapsulating other LOs through *hasChildElementalObject* and *hasChildCompoundObject* properties (sub-properties of transitive *hasSubObject* property). Each LO is assumed to have an associated goal (might also be compound), and dependencies to other LOs represented through *hasPrerequisite* property (sub-property of transitive *hasNecessity* property), e.g., one cannot access LO A before LO B is completed if LO B is prerequisite of LO A. The learner is assumed to have at least one goal connecting her with a set of LOs through *hasAccessTo* property (a LO is accessible to the learner if it is within the scope of the learner's goals) and its role chain axioms (e.g, hasGoalLearner *o* isGoalOfObject -> hasAccessTo) following the hierarchy constructed by the *hasChildCompoundObject, hasChildElementalObject, hasPrerequsite,* and *hasChildGoal* (sub-property of transitive *hasSubGoal* property) properties. A state is maintained for each LO - learner and goal – learner pairs. A state represents the overall situation of a learner – LO/Goal pair such as availability or complete/incomplete status of a particular LO for a particular learner. Different types of criteria can be applied through rules to set the state data properties. Example rules given in Fig. 4 provide a demonstration: the first rule sets the states of all LOs having incomplete child LOs (*isSubObjectOf*) to incomplete, and the second rule sets the states of all the LOs having incomplete prerequisite LOs (*isNecessityOf*) to non-available. Similar rules together with OWL axioms (e.g., transitive, role chains etc.) are employed also for adaptation in terms of gradual filtering, sequencing and selection of items. Ontologies and rules also provide capability of explaining why a particular decision is taken (i.e. feedback) [44], for instance, providing learner with a dependency list or a prerequisite tree when learner wants to access a LO before completing all its prerequisites.

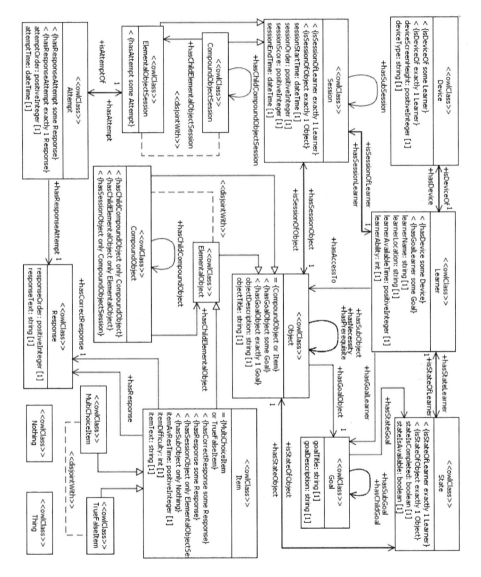

Fig. 3. A prototype domain context ontology visualized with Ontology Definition Meta-model

A session is maintained for each connected LO - learner pair in order to keep track of the learner – LO interaction through the learning cycle. We exemplified two types of elemental and disjoint LOs, namely, multiple choice and true false items. Learner is assumed to have multiple attempts, which might happen in different sessions, for each item through the learning cycle. Therefore each attempt for each learner - LO pair is also maintained.

```
[rule1: (?l type Learner) (?st type State) (?st_any type
State)(?obj type Object) (?p type Object)

(?l hasAccessTo ?obj) (?obj hasSubObject ?p) (?st
isStateOfLearner ?l) (?st isStateOfObject ?obj) (?st_any
isStateOfLearner ?l) (?st_any isStateOfObject ?p)
(?st_any stateIsCompleted 'false')

-> (?st stateIsCompleted 'false')]

[rule2: (?l type Learner)(?st type State) (?st_any type
State) (?obj type Object) (?pr type Object)

(?l hasAccessTo ?obj) (?obj hasNecessity ?pr) (?st
isStateOfLearner ?l) (?st isStateOfObject ?obj) (?st_any
isStateOfLearner ?l) (?st_any isStateOfObject ?pr)
(?st_any stateIsCompleted 'false')

-> (?st stateIsAvailable 'false')]
```

Fig. 4. Two example rules setting the state properties for each connected learner - object pair

The ontology is formalized with OWL 2 Web Ontology Language and visually designed with UML through Ontology Definition Meta Model (ODM) of OMG. We used OWL2UML plug-in of Protégé for ODM.

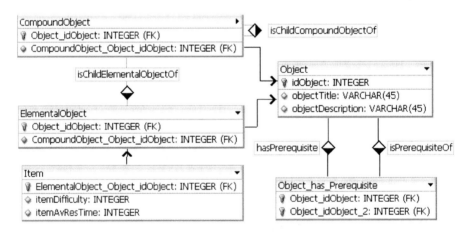

Fig. 5. Example transformation of an OWL ontology to the relational database schema

Pellet reasoner and Jena generic rule engine are used for OWL DL reasoning (e.g., subsumption and realization) and advanced rule based reasoning (Fig. 4) respectively. The transformation of an OWL ontology into its corresponding software artifacts enables rapid development of a fully fledged application and its re-engineering in emergence of structural changes (i.e., requirement adaptability) which cannot be handled through run-time adaptations. The transformation of OWL ontology to a relational database schema is demonstrated in Fig. 5. Cardinality constraints are represented through one-to-one, one-to-many and many-to-many entity relationships. The transformation of ontology to application code is demonstrated in Fig. 6. In this example, Java interfaces and blocker methods are used for representing sub-classes and disjoint classes respectively (since the return types of blocker methods are different, a class cannot implement both, e.g., IntConcept and IntItem, interfaces).

```
interface IntLObject{}
interface IntCompoundObject extends IntLObject {
        IntCompoundObject block_1(); }
interface IntElementalObject extends IntLObject {
        IntElementalObject block_1(); }
interface IntItem extends IntElementalObject {}
interface IntMultiChoiceItem extends IntItem {
        IntMultiChoiceItem block_2(); }
interface IntTrueFalseItem extends IntItem{
        IntTrueFalseItem block_2(); }
class LObject implements IntLObject {}
class CompoundObject extends LObject implements
IntCompoundObject {}
class ElementalObject extends LObject implements
IntElementalObject {}
class Item extends ElementalObject implements IntItem {}
class MultiChoiceItem extends Item implements
IntMultiChoiceItem {}
class TrueFalseItem extends Item implements
IntTrueFalseItem {}
```

Fig. 6. Example code demonstrating OWL ontology to Java code transformation

The domain ontology, and transformations (Java and SQL) are available online, see http://itec.svn.sourceforge.net/ , we refer the reader to section 6 and its references for more elaborate information on mapping rules and transformation algorithms.

6 Related Work and Discussion

In this section, related work and a discussion on logic reasoning and transformation of OWL ontologies into application code and database schema will be presented.

Considering OWL and reasoning: OWL is divided into three sublanguages, OWL Lite, OWL DL, and OWL Full with an increasing expressivity and complexity. OWL DL guarantees computational completeness and decidability, but, OWL Full does not. OWL DL is an optimum choice, however, it has some particular shortcomings. Since, in general, ontologies are limited by the reasoning capabilities, integrated with the form of representation [45], some of which are mentioned in the following [46]. OWL follows Open World Assumption (OWA) and employs monotonic reasoning, while logic programming employs Closed World Assumption (CWA) and employs non-monotonic reasoning. CWA considers statements, which are not known to be true, as false (i.e. negation as failure - NaF) while OWA, in contrast, states that statements, which are not known to be true, should not be considered false. OWA does not allow old facts to be retracted and previous information to be negated because of new information acquired. Furthermore, OWL does not allow use of higher relational expressivity (e.g., composite properties), higher arity relationships, and integrity constraints and exceptions (which are non-monotonic). Therefore, OWL is required to be integrated with logic programming and rules. We have realized higher arity relationships through introducing intermediary concepts. Jena realizes a weak negation (i.e. NaF) through providing an operator only checking the existence of a given statement and provides an operator to remove statements. Although ontology layer of the Semantic Web has reached a sufficient maturity, the logic and rule layer is still under progress, e.g., [46, 47].

Considering transformations of OWL to application artifacts: on the one hand, there exists some fundamental semantic differences between OWL and object oriented systems (OOS), database systems (DBS) etc. [48], implying that, not all ontology constructs can (easily) be mapped into respective artifacts. On the other hand, there exist a compromise between decidability and expressivity during the development of the ontology in terms of reasoning and automated code development. This is because, trying to model every construct related to OOS and DBS might break the decidability of the ontology. However, not every ontology construct is required to be transformed since a part of them will be only required for reasoning purposes. For instance, number restrictions (e.g., cardinality) cannot be defined on non-simple roles (e.g., transitive) [49]. There exists few works demonstrating how OWL constructs can be mapped into respective Java and SQL constructs thereby enabling the transformation of ontologies to Java and SQL [48, 50, 51]. In this respect, use tools and experience in mature MDD field is important. The ODM initiative of OMG (see http://www.omg.org/spec/ODM/1.0/) puts an important step towards integrating these two paradigms by allowing the development of OWL ontologies through UML.

Considering adaptive systems and learning: on the one hand, available adaptive hypermedia applications [52, 53] mostly deals with adaptation techniques and do not present an elaborate methodology for realizing such techniques and applications from a software engineering point of view. On the other hand, existing work employing ontologies in (adaptive) learning domain, e.g., [37, 54, 55], only targets the run-time use of ontologies and do not report the extent they suffer from the immatureness of the logic layer of the Semantic Web. The work presented in this paper addresses these concerns in order to construct a practical methodology for development of APLEs.

7 Conclusion

In this paper we introduced an interdisciplinary project targeting adaptive and pervasive learning environments. PerCom vision manifests an unobtrusive, anytime and anywhere user experience which requires expansion of the personalization era to the context-awareness era. Under this unitive vision, learning process should be immersive and contextualized along with the computing process. Contextualization and immersion of computing require new approaches for software development and management. Therefore, in this paper, we argued for an ontology based approach, employing ontologies at development-time, in terms of automated code generation, and at run-time together with rules, in terms of reasoning, dynamic adaptations, and user involvement. Finally, we presented a demonstration based on a prototype domain ontology. The future work will involve *ontology-driven* development of an *ontology-driven* APLE.

Acknowledgments. This paper is based on research funded by the Industrial Research Fund (IOF) and conducted within the IOF Knowledge platform "Harnessing collective intelligence in order to make e-learning environments adaptive" (IOF KP/07/006).

References

1. Krumm, J.: Ubiquitous Computing Fundamentals. CRC Press, Boca Raton (2009)
2. Sharples, M., Taylor, J., Vavoula, G.: Towards a Theory of Mobile Learning. In: mLearn 2005 Conf., Cape Town, South Africa (2005)
3. Soylu, A., De Causmaecker, P., Desmet, P.: Context and Adaptivity in Pervasive Computing Environments: Links with Software Engineering and Ontological Engineering. J. Softw. 4, I1992–I1013 (2009)
4. Economides, A.A.: Adaptive context-aware pervasive and ubiquitous learning. Intl. J. Technol. Enhanced Learn. 1, 169–192 (2009)
5. Ogata, H., Yano, Y.: How Ubiquitous Computing can Support Language Learning. In: KEST 2003, pp. 1–6 (2003)
6. Hundebøl, J., Helms, N.H.: Pervasive e-learning – In situ learning in changing contexts. In: DREAM 2006 Conf. on Informal Learning and Digital Media (2006)
7. Shute, V.J., Towle, B.: Adaptive E-Learning. Educ. Psychol. 38, 105–114 (2003)
8. Shute, V.J., Zapata-Rivera, D.: Adaptive technologies. In: Spector, J.M., Merril, M.D., van Merriënboer, J.J.G., Driscoll, M. (eds.) Handbook of Research on Educational Communications and Technology, 3rd edn., pp. 277–294 (2008)
9. Kadiyala, M., Crynes, B.L.: Where's the proof? A review of literature on effectiveness of information technology in education. In: 28th Annual Frontiers in Education (1998)
10. Graf, S., Lin, T., Kinshuk: The relationship between learning styles and cognitive characteristics - Getting additional information for improving student modeling. Comput. Hum. Behav. 24, 122–137 (2008)
11. Paramythis, A., Loidl-Reisinger, S.: Adaptive Learning Environments and e-Learning Standards. Electron. J e-Learn. 2, 181–194 (2003)
12. VanLehn, K.: The behavior of tutoring systems. Intl. J. Artif. Intell. Educ. 16, 227–265 (2006)

13. Tseng, J.C.R., Chu, H.-C., Hwang, G.-J., Tsai, C.-C.: Development of an adaptive learning system with two sources of personalization information. Comput. & Educ. 51, 776–786 (2008)
14. Aleven, V., McLaren, B., Roll, R., Koedinger, K.: Toward Meta-cognitive Tutoring: A Model of Help Seeking with a Cognitive Tutor. Intl. J. Artif. Intell. Educ. 16, 101–128 (2006)
15. Jeremic, Z., Jovanovic, J., Gasevic, D.: Evaluating an Intelligent Tutoring System for Design Patterns: the DEPTHS Experience. Educ. Technol. & Soc. 12, 111–130 (2009)
16. Corbalan, G., Kester, L., van Merriënboer, J.J.G.: Selecting learning tasks: Effects of adaptation and shared control on efficiency and task involvement. Contemp. Educ. Psychol. 33, 733–756 (2008)
17. Bell, B.S., Kozlowski, S.W.J.: Adaptive guidance: enhancing self-regulation, knowledge, and performance in technology-based training. Pers. Psychol. 55, 267–306 (2002)
18. Brusilovsky, P., Vassileva, J.: Course Sequencing Techniques for Large-Scale Web-Based Education. Intl. J. Contin. Eng. Educ. Lifelong Learn. 13, 75–94 (2003)
19. Van der Linden, W.J., Hambleton, R.K.: Handbook of Modern Item Response Theory. Springer, New York (1997)
20. Wainer, H.: Computerized Adaptive Testing: a Primer. Erlbaum, London (2000)
21. Chen, C.M., Lee, H.M., Chen, Y.H.: Personalized e-learning system using item response theory. Comput. & Educ. 44, 237–255 (2005)
22. Dey, A.K., Abowd, G.D.: Towards a better understanding of context and context-awareness. Technical Report, Georgia Institute of Technology, College (1999)
23. Dey, A.K.: Understanding and using context. Pers. Ubiquitous Comput. 5, 4–7 (2001)
24. Henricksen, K., Indulska, J.: Developing Context-Aware Pervasive Computing Applications: Models and Approach. J. Pervasive Mob. Comput. 2, 37–64 (2006)
25. Thomas, S.: Pervasive, persuasive eLearning: modeling the pervasive learning space. In: 1st IEEE International Workshop on Pervasive eLearning (PerEL 2005), pp. 332–336 (2005)
26. Syvanen, A., Beale, R., Sharples, M., Ahonen, M., Lonsdale, P.: Supporting Pervasive Learning Environments: Adaptability and Context Awareness in Mobile Learning. In: Intl. Workshop on Wireless and Mobile Technologies in Education, pp. 251–253 (2005)
27. Patten, B., Arnedillo-Sanchez, I., Tangney, B.: Designing collaborative, constructionist and contextual applications for handheld devices. Comput. & Educ. 46, 294–308 (2006)
28. Mödritscher, F., Wild, F.: Sharing Good Practice through Mash-Up Personal Learning Environments. In: Spaniol, M., Li, Q., Klamma, R., Lau, R.W.H. (eds.) ICWL 2009. LNCS, vol. 5686, pp. 245–254. Springer, Heidelberg (2009)
29. Han, L., Jyri, S., Ma, J., Yu, K.: Research on Context-aware Mobile Computing. In: Advanced Information Networking Applications Workshops, pp. 24–30 (2008)
30. Sharples, M., Corlett, D., Westmancott, O.: The Design and implementation of Mobile Learning Resource. Pers. Ubiquitous Comput. 6, 220–234 (2002)
31. Dey, A.K., Mankoff, J.: Designing mediation for context-aware applications. ACM Trans. Comput.-Hum. Interact. 12, 53–89 (2005)
32. Korpipää, P., Hakkila, J., Kela, J., Ronkainen, S., Kansala, I.: Utilizing context ontology in mobile device application personalization. In: 3rd Intl. Conf. on Mobile and Ubiquitous Multimedia, pp. 133–140 (2004)
33. Hagras, H.: Embedding Computational Intelligence in Pervasive Spaces. IEEE Pervasive Comput. 6, 85–89 (2007)
34. Trifonova, A.: Mobile learning—Review of the literature. Technical Report (2003)

35. Banavar, G., Beck, J., Gluzberg, E., Munson, J., Sussman, J., Zukowski, D.: Challenges: an application model for pervasive computing. In: 6th ACM MobiCom Conf. (2000)
36. Perttunen, M., Riekki, J., Lassila, O.: Context Representation and Reasoning in Pervasive Computing: a Review. Intl. J. Multimed. Ubiquitous Eng. 4, 1–28 (2009)
37. Liu, Z., Liu, L., Kang, H., Zhong, S.: Ontology based User Modeling for Adaptive Educational Hypermedia System. In: 4th Int. Conf. on Computer Science and Education, pp. 1203–1207 (2009)
38. Gómez-Pérez, A., Fernández-López, M., Corcho, O.: Ontological Engineering (2003)
39. Soylu, A., De Causmaecker, P.: Merging Model Driven and Ontology Driven Development Approaches: Pervasive Computing Perspective. In: ISCIS 2009, pp. 730–735 (2009)
40. Meller, S.J., Clark, A.N., Futagami, T.: Model-Driven Development. IEEE Softw. 20, 14–18 (2003)
41. Ruiz, F., Hilera, J.R.: Using Ontologies in Software Engineering and Technology. In: Calero, C., Ruiz, F., Piattini, M. (eds.) Ontologies in Software Engineering and Software Technology, pp. 49–102. Springer, Heidelberg (2006)
42. Guarino, N.: Formal Ontology in Information Systems. In: FOIS 1998, Trento, Italy (1998)
43. Soylu, A., De Causmaecker, P., Wild, F.: Ubiquitous Web for Ubiquitous Computing Environments: The Role of Embedded Semantics. J. Mob. Multimed. 6, 26–48 (2010)
44. Diouf, M., Maabout, S., Musumbu, K.: Merging Model Driven Architecture and Semantic Web for Business Rules Generation. In: Marchiori, M., Pan, J.Z., de Sainte Marie, C. (eds.) RR 2007. LNCS, vol. 4524, pp. 118–132. Springer, Heidelberg (2007)
45. Hatala, M., Wakkary, R., Kalantari, L.: Rules and ontologies in support of real-time ubiquitous application. J. Web Semant. 3, 5–22 (2005)
46. Motik, B., Horrocks, I., Rosati, R., Sattler, U.: Can OWL and logic programming live together happily ever after? In: Cruz, I., Decker, S., Allemang, D., Preist, C., Schwabe, D., Mika, P., Uschold, M., Aroyo, L.M. (eds.) ISWC 2006. LNCS, vol. 4273, pp. 501–514. Springer, Heidelberg (2006)
47. Eiter, T., Ianni, G., Lukasiewicz, T., Schindlauer, R., Tompits, H.: Combining answer set programming with description logics for the semantic Web. Artif. Intell. 172, 1495–1539 (2008)
48. Kalyanpur, A., Pastor, D.J., Battle, S., Padget, J.: Automatic mapping of OWL ontologies into Java. In: SEKE 2004, Banff, Canada (2004)
49. Kazakov, Y., Sattler, U.: Zolin. E.: How many legs do I have? Non-simple roles in number restrictions revisited. In: Dershowitz, N., Voronkov, A. (eds.) LPAR 2007. LNCS (LNAI), vol. 4790, pp. 303–317. Springer, Heidelberg (2007)
50. Astrova, I., Korda, N., Kalja, A.: Storing OWL Ontologies in SQL Relational Databases. International J. Electr. Comput. Syst. Eng. 1, 242–247 (2007)
51. Vysniauskas, E., Nemuraite, L.: Transforming ontology representation from OWL to relational database. Inf. Technol. Control. 35, 335–345 (2006)
52. Knutov, E., De Bra, P., Pechenizkiy, M.: AH 12 years later: a comprehensive survey of adaptive hypermedia methods and techniques. New Rev. Hypermedia and Multimed. 15, 5–38 (2009)
53. Brusilovsky, P., Eklund, J., Schwarz, E.: Web-based education for all: A tool for developing adaptive courseware. In: WWW 1998, pp. 291–300 (1998)
54. Jovanovic, J., Gasevic, D., Knight, K., Richards, G.: Ontologies for Effective Use of Context in e-Learning Settings. Educ. Technol. Soc. 10, 47–59 (2007)
55. Chi, Y.-L.: Ontology-based curriculum content sequencing system with semantic rules. Expert Syst. Appl. 36, 7838–7847 (2009)

Extending an Educational Math Game with a Pedagogical Conversational Agent: Facing Design Challenges

Björn Sjödén[1], Annika Silvervarg[2], Magnus Haake[3], and Agneta Gulz[1]

[1] Lund University Cognitive Science
{Bjorn.Sjoden,Agneta.Gulz}@lucs.lu.se
[2] Department of Computer and Information Science, Linköping University
Annika.Silvervarg@liu.se
[3] Department of Design Sciences, Lund University
magnus.haake@design.lth.se

Abstract. We describe our work-in-progress of developing an educational game in mathematics for 12-14 year olds, by adding social and conversational abilities to an existing "teachable agent" (TA) in the game. The purpose of this extension is to affect cognitive, emotional and social constructs known to promote learning, such as self-efficacy and engagement, as well as enhancing students' experiences of interacting with the agent over an extended period of time. Drawing from the EnALI framework, which states practical design guidelines, we discuss specific design challenges and exemplify research considerations as to developing the agent's visual representation and conversational module. We present some initial findings from prototype testing with students from the target group. Promising developments seem to reside in pronouncing the agent's personality traits and expanding its knowledge database, particularly its range of conversational topics. Finally we propose some future studies and research directions.

Keywords: pedagogical agents, conversational agents, teachable agents, social learning, educational game, EnALI.

1 Introduction

Learning "in real life" is, arguably, always connected to some form of social interaction or communicative purpose with other human beings. Many educational researchers have noted that learning is an essentially social activity, and also that we are more likely to succeed in our efforts to educate if we recognize this principle [e.g. 1, 2, 18, 43]. But can we capture the social qualities of learning when students sit to learn on their own, in front of a computer?

In our on-going work of developing an educational game in mathematics for children, we have sought to address precisely that question. By including a *pedagogical conversational agent* in the game, we set out to create opportunities for social interaction between students and agents within the learning environment. We are presently

S. De Wannemacker, G. Clarebout, P. De Causmaecker (Eds.): ITEC 2010, CCIS 126, pp. 116–130, 2011.
© Springer-Verlag Berlin Heidelberg 2011

working on enriching the social dimension of the game by developing the agent's conversational capabilities as well as its visual embodiment.

The first and foremost motivation behind this extension is to make individual students who use the digital learning environment benefit from social interactions known to promote learning in natural environments, by increasing motivation, building self-efficacy and acknowledging new skills as they are building up. As to the effect of motivation on (reflective) cognition, Schank and Neaman [37] list three issues: the *participation issue*, as to whether students participate at all in a learning activity, the *indexing issue*, as to the way memories are organized, and the *attention issue*, as to the quality of attention to what should be remembered.

The pedagogical agent, then, should keep students engaged in the learning environment, without attracting too much attention to itself as an artifact (vis-à-vis the learning material). By elaborating the agent's social features, although it is clearly non-human, we capitalize on fundamental human tendencies for what makes a task engaging and cognitively worthwhile. For example, Chen and colleagues presented neurophysiological evidence that the very belief of a social experience activates the brain's reward circuitry, which helps cement newly learned associations [12, 13].

At the same time, one would like to utilize the possibilities of a designed digital environment to minimize detrimental social influences (such as distractors and negative feedback) that may also be at work in the real world. This goes hand-in-hand with an overall approach of presenting a subject domain (e.g. mathematics) in a generally more appealing and defusing context in order to attract a wider group of students. As will be exemplified below, the question of aesthetics must not go overlooked when designing a virtual learning environment: It has been demonstrated that visual appeal can influence both perceived usability [38] and user satisfaction, in terms of the perceived quality of interaction [29]. In the words of interaction designer and theorist Donald Norman, "attractive things work better" [32].

A second motivation for the extension is that we are looking to expand the target user group, from 7-12-year-olds, for whom a basic version of the game has been available, to 12-14 year-olds. Considering the greater computer and gaming experience of older students, they are likely to have higher expectations on both visual aesthetics and the complexity of interaction in the learning environment. With maturity comes also the ability to handle more complex interactions and (at least potentially) greater responsibility in their social role.

In particular, we focus on the development and social role of a *Teachable Agent* (TA) [8, 11], which is a form of AI-based educational technology that builds upon the pedagogy of "learning by teaching" [1, 3]. There are a number of reasons why students would learn more efficiently with a TA than without a TA in an otherwise identical game setup. A core factor is the so-called "protégé effect" [11]. That is, students tend to take more responsibility and put more effort into teaching someone else than into learning for themselves, while at the same time being able to ascribe failures and errors to the agent, rather than to personal shortcomings. In the following we describe how we design the TA as a social agent and how we conceive of the present challenges in working towards specific design decisions. We exemplify methods used and present some initial evaluations with target users.

2 Background

Previous research shows that pedagogical agents can be beneficial for learning, provided an appropriate – pedagogical and visual – design [5, 20, 23]. It is therefore imperative that one carefully considers the particular pedagogical and social role of a particular agent in a given environment, for example whether it be a mentor, a coach or a peer. Whereas visual appearance has not been a traditional focus of research on pedagogical agents, recent reviews have deemed agents' visual features important value for affecting motivation and engagement in the learning environment where it is employed [4, 22, 25]. Not the least, an appropriately designed agent may serve as a 'virtual role model', depending on how its represented social features (e.g. attractiveness, style, gender, age, etc) correspond to students' explicit and implicit preferences (e.g. stereotypes) [5, 23, 28, 35]. This idea is in line with Bandura's classical work on social modeling [1, 2] as well as research on stereotypes within social cognition, which suggests that one needs only perceive few, salient characteristics of a person to activate complex mental representations about him or her [10]. When having the opportunity of a prolonged interaction, the content and quality of conversation may add to or detract from this impression.

One major beneficial function of a purposefully designed pedagogical agent is then that students may assimilate a range of positive behaviors and attitudes in line with an attractive social model represented by the agent, for instance a "cool and successful peer in school" in the context of learning mathematics. Exploiting visual characteristics and conversation to communicate positive social stereotypes offer means of cueing model behavior in a way that is directly and effortlessly understood by the student. However, it is difficult to make straight-off comparisons between different learning environments due to the wide variety of contexts in which pedagogical agents are used [39]. We will therefore describe our learning environment in more detail, and elaborate on the visual and verbal aspects of what makes the "peer"-like social qualities of our TA in the game.

2.1 The Learning Environment: A Learning-by-Teaching Mathematics Game

Our work extends an educational math game named "The Squares Family", developed by Lena Pareto and Daniel Schwartz [33, 34]. The game specifically trains basic arithmetic skills, such as carry-overs and borrowings, with focus on grounding base-10 concepts in spatial representations. To do so, the game employs a board-game design with "playing cards" and a common game board, with a variety of game modes and levels of difficulty. All arithmetic operations are made visually explicit using graphical metaphors of colored squares and boxes that can be "packed" or "unpacked", in numbers of 10. The aim is to pick the card from a given set (visible to both players) that in combination with what is represented on the game board maximizes the number of carry-overs (in the addition games) or borrowings (in the subtraction games). See example screenshot in Fig. 1.

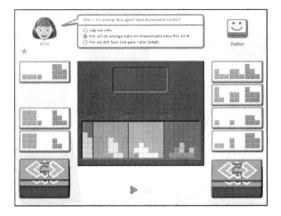

Fig. 1. Screenshot of an early version of the extended math game (actually in color). Here, the TA, called Kim, is set in a "Watch and learn"-mode against the computer (Swedish: "Dator"). Kim asks why the player received a point (star) for picking a particular card, the answer being "Because the orange squares together became more than 9".

The game includes a TA which can be put in different modes. In "Watch and learn"-mode, the TA picks up on game rules as the student responds to multiple-choice questions on particular tasks and game moves during game-play. A typical question from the TA would be "Why did you pick this card?". The student chooses between listed potential explanations (but only one correct answer), including a "don't know" option. Proper (or improper) choices of cards and answers promote corresponding skills in the TA throughout the game. In "Try and play"-mode, the agent can be set to suggest game cards, which the student can confirm by clicking "Ok" or deny by suggesting another card. Finally, in "Play Self"-mode, the agent is set to play a session of the game automatically (against the computer or another agent or human player), allowing the student to watch its performance.

In a recent study, we found empirical support for learning benefits of using a TA in this game: Compared to a control class of children the same age in the same school, which did not play the game, children who did play the game over an extended period of time improved both in performance on standardized math tests and in confidence in explaining math to a peer [24]. These findings have encouraged us to look further into ways of strengthening the student–agent bond, so as to be socially engaging, motivating and fun, in relation to the learning material.

2.2 Expanding on the Pedagogical Agent as a Social Being

Not much is needed for a human being to respond socially to an obviously non-human system. As evidenced by the much quoted and vastly demonstrated "media equation", formulated by Reeves and Nass [36], humans tend to treat computers as real social actors – for example, by responding rudely to a malfunctioning ("rude") computer, or praising a program which presents a positive evaluation of the user. This holds true even in the complete absence of a human-like representation (e.g. a photo or picture of a person, let alone a virtual agent). It is therefore not surprising that also the rudimentary agent (TA) of the original math game (depicted to the left in Fig. 2) elicits social responses, something we observed in our previous studies of students playing the math game in school [30].

Compared to human-human interaction, the original TA still leaves vast room for enriched social cueing, through elaborated visual features, animations, movement and verbal expressions. We maintain that expanding on the social dimension will affect not only the direct interaction with the agent, but how students approach the game as a whole, even affecting their decision (when free to decide) whether to play the game at all. The "media equation" is not limited to people's responses to a particular interaction with a computer, but tends to generalize to how they approach similar contexts and informational content [36]. We reason that students gaining a positive experience from engaging in the math game are more likely to play it again, and providing social interaction with the agent offers means to pick up on and respond to students' attitudes which otherwise remain unexpressed.

Elaborating the agent's social abilities both constrains and allows greater control of students' social responses: not only do we want to promote certain effects (such as affecting the student's mood) but also control the direction of effects (making the student happy). We will return to the challenges of actually meeting these criteria in subsequent paragraphs; first we want to present the tools we use for the purpose. In short, we conceive of elaborating the agent's social profile in a two-fold modular development, which consists of (1) Visual representation of the pedagogical agent, and (2) Conversational abilities of the pedagogical agent.

Visual representation of the pedagogical agent. Elaborating the visual design of the agent essentially targets two aspects of students' approach to the interaction: one is to provide visual cues for the constraints as to what students might expect from interacting with the agent (e.g. "will this be a cool or nerdy character to talk to?"); another is simply to increase likeability by pleasant looks and graphics, including a visual makeover of its original game environment.

A guiding question for our design considerations has been: "Judging by looks, whom would the students like to interact with?" An important choice in this regard was that of a cartoon-like character over naturalistic or semi-naturalistic looks. First, cartoon-like agents have been argued to make students accept limitations more readily [17]; second, they lend themselves better for animation of simple affective cues, such as smiles and head tilts. Fig. 2 depicts the development from the first rudiment of an agent via two iterations, involving students of the relevant age group.

Fig. 2. Visual representation of the pedagogical agent, revised following student input. The original, rudimentary agent image (left) was replaced by one female and one male alternative.

Conversational abilities of the pedagogical agent. The second main extension under development is a module for allowing free (not multiple-choice-steered) written conversation between the student and the TA. We make a primary distinction between *on-task* dialogue, which is constrained by the present math tasks and takes a multiple-choice format (see 2.1 for examples), and *off-task* dialogue, which takes the form of a chat window, open to freer conversation. The off-task dialogue content, in turn, can be distinguished into *on-domain* conversation related to school, math, the math game, etc., and *off-domain* conversation, related to any other topics. These distinctions are important for our design considerations, when it comes to the pedagogical functions of the social chat in relation to the learning content we want to communicate.

So, one might ask, what are the pedagogical benefits of dedicating a conversational module for topics *not* relating to mathematics in a math game? Again, the answer resides in what makes learning engaging and effective in real life. Our present developments of the math game strive to keep certain influence *within* rather than outside the educational game environment. Considering the agent's role as a type of co-learner and peer, it seems vital to promote the student's sense of factors such as trust in and rapport with the agent.

Bickmore [6], among others, has shown that including anecdotes and narrative storytelling can contribute to building rapport with a conversational agent, besides having a positive effect on people's general interest in interacting with it. Possibly connected to this, is the effect of "small talk" (irrespective of content) as offering some cognitive rest from arduous educational tasks. Finally, broad conversational abilities of the TA – particularly referring to the transitions between off-domain and on-domain topics – are hypothesized to help overcome another stumbling-block of math education in school, namely to make the subject of mathematics more attractive by reframing math tasks in a defusing and appealing context. This makes part of the strategy to have conversational content improve students' attitudes and self-efficacy for math. Besides enhancing the subjective learning experience, it has been demonstrated for a variety of learning material that such motivational constructs can have a vital impact on objective performance [2, 18, 31, 45].

3 Guiding Framework: Enhancing Agent-Learner Interaction (EnALI)

Turning to the questions of implementation, one might ask how one reaches a specific design decision among the myriad of possible alternatives. The research literature indicates a particular need for formulating guidelines as to how an effective communication can be achieved between a student and an agent, in order to cause as little frustration and conflict as possible. What should then *our* social, pedagogical and conversational agent look and behave like?

Whereas there is no theoretical framework to answer this question in detail, there are sufficient research-based and empirical findings not to leave all new design decisions to "designer's intuition" or other personal bias. The most comprehensive, recent and practical set of guidelines we have found to meet our present design needs, is the Enhancing Agent-Learner Interaction (EnALI) framework [41].

In short, the EnALI guidelines are divided into three design foci – user interaction, message, and agent characteristics – that the authors ground on socio-cultural notions of learning [43], cooperative learning [27], and conflict theory [15]. *User interaction* refers to the ways the agent and the student cooperate and relate to each other; *message* refers to the verbal information the agent sends to the student, and *agent characteristics* focuses on those variables that inherently define the agent. For the complete set of references to the empirical findings on which particular guidelines are based, we refer to the original EnALI article by Veletsianos, Miller and Doering [41]. An overview of the actual design guidelines is provided in Table 1.

Table 1. The Enhancing Agent-Learner Interaction framework, from Doering, Miller and Veletsianos [41]

	Design focus	Guidelines
1	User interaction	*Agents should be attentive and sensitive to the learner's needs and wants by:* - Being responsive and reactive to requests for additional and/or expanded information. - Being redundant. - Asking for formative and summative feedback. - Maintaining an appropriate balance between on- and off-task communications.
2	Message	*Agents should consider intricacies of the message by:* - Making the message appropriate to the receiver's abilities, experiences, and frame of reference. - Using congruent verbal and nonverbal messages. - Clearly owning the message. - Making messages complete and specific. - Using descriptive, non-evaluative comments. - Describing feelings by name, action, or figure of speech.
3	Agent characteristics	*Agents should display socially appropriate demeanor, posture, and representation by:* - Establishing credibility and trustworthiness. - Establishing role and relationship to user/task. - Being polite and positive (e.g., encouraging, motivating). - Being expressive (e.g. exhibiting verbal cues in speech). - Using a visual representation appropriate to content.

The challenges we face by adding the particular agent in the math game demonstrate how the EnALI guidelines sometimes overlap and influence one another when applied in practice. This is especially apparent in our overall challenge of designing a complex social character. For example, "Agent characteristics" can hardly be completely separated from the "Message" which the agent conveys in social (off-task) conversation, as regards expressing a certain personality. As to "User interaction", one must keep in mind that our pedagogical agent (especially considering the nature of a *teachable* agent; see 4.1 below) does not primarily serve for information retrieval and is not positioned in an "expert" or "guiding" role.

In the following section, we highlight three main design challenges that correspond to different aspects in the EnALI framework, before addressing the influence from actual students by empirical testing and observations. It should be made clear that these challenges and the approaches we take in meeting them, like the EnALI guidelines, are presented under separate headlines of expository reasons but must be viewed within the inter-related whole of the math game as a learning environment.

4   Implementation Challenges

4.1   The Agent's Knowledge Profile: What Should the Agent Know?

One of the first things students will ask themselves when being presented with the opportunity to chat with a pedagogical agent is what they can talk to the agent about. This poses a wide and conspicuous challenge of construing a knowledge database that can meet most student requests while keeping within the necessary limits of developers' time and resources. As such, this challenge applies to practically all conversational agents and similar systems, but there are certain aspects that both constrain and expand this challenge for the particular agent we aim to develop.

On the one hand, although students generally need to experience a pedagogical agent as being useful for information purposes for the learning task at hand [39], not all agents are equally important for obtaining specific information. In our case, because we employ a *teachable* agent, it is ostensibly "non-knowledgeable" in its subject domain (mathematics) from the beginning and can thus respond to information requests in this domain by referring to the fact that "you are supposed to teach me". This assumes, of course, that the agent's role as "teachable" is properly introduced to the student, and that there is a functional, underlying AI architecture that implicitly keeps track of what the agent learns throughout the game and reflects this in ensuing conversations. In other words, the agent is allowed to be perceived as un-knowledgeable, but not as unteachable.

On the other hand, the challenge of achieving a sufficiently comprehensive knowledge database becomes considerably more complex when making the agent more of a social actor, that is, when adding an off-task conversational module. According to the EnALI guidelines, messages should be "complete and specific" while being "appropriate to the receiver's abilities, experiences, and frame of reference". For an agent that supposedly should be able to converse about any topic, both the specificity and completeness of messages must be limited. In addition, there is an apparent risk of clashes as to the knowledge the agent exhibits in one area vis-à-vis another, for example, if it demonstrates good knowledge about school, but no knowledge about mathematics. Besides, the application does not contain any AI module for learning other domains than the math game. We conceive of this challenge as a need for carefully defining specific knowledge areas corresponding to students' interests, while balancing the complete knowledge profile of the agent over the on-task–off-task spectrum.

4.2 The Agent's Social Profile: How Should the Agent Communicate?

While the challenge of defining a knowledge profile corresponds to "what" the agent should know, the agent's social profile corresponds to "who" it should be and "how" it should communicate its knowledge. The EnALI guideline that the agent should be "polite and positive", in terms of being encouraging and motivating, refers to the demonstrated "politeness effect" of conversational agents [44]. However, an all-through polite and nice agent may be perceived as predictable and boring, especially if students are to interact with it repeatedly and over an extended period of time [cf. 40]. After all, we are used from everyday social interactions that people vary in exhibited moods and states of mind, but also that they have a consistent personality. A conflict might thus arise between predictability and consistency as regards the social behavior of the agent. Again, there are obvious limits to the complexity which can be construed for a digital character. At the same time, this challenge should be viewed in relation to students' expectations and experience of other non-human agents (e.g. characters in animated movies, computer games and other virtual agents), rather than to the full spectrum of a human personality.

In possible contrast to the expected politeness of the agent stands the potential (anti-)social behavior of the student. Previous studies have addressed the risk that, when students are assigned to freely converse with an agent, they sometimes engage in verbal abuse of the agent [9, 42]. In one (possibly extreme) case with a female conversational agent in a social science application, evaluations showed that only 5% of student comments were task-related and as much as 40% of comments were abusive (sexually explicit) [42]. Although a wide range of conversational subjects is wished for, there are clearly certain subjects one wishes to avoid from a social as well as from a pedagogical point of view. The risk of verbal abuse may be considered a sub-challenge to the social profile which is subject to the social affordances of the agent and the interaction situation.

4.3 Off-Task Engagement: Too Much or Too Little?

We propose one particular EnALI guideline as a separate challenge, concerning user interaction: "Maintaining an appropriate balance between on- and off-task communications". Due to the complexity of both knowledge and social features of our pedagogical agent, both the appeal and non-appeal of engaging in conversation with it may be problematic. It should be added, that in our game, students are not completely free to choose when to interact with the agent. A related challenge is then how to regulate the opportunities for agent-student off-task interaction from a system level.

First, the balance between on-task and off-task activities can be disturbed if off-task conversation becomes more engaging than the learning activities themselves. This has been noted to be the case for other agents allowing both on-task and off-task conversation, even to the point that students become completely immersed in the off-task conversation [40].

Second, there are studies which show that some students simply are not interested in off-task conversation, but prefer to treat the agent as exclusively a resource in working towards solving a task [21]. Then the potential pedagogical benefits of off-task conversation previously proposed will take no effect. Besides, under-engagement in off-task conversation makes it more difficult to capture students' attitudes and qualitative remarks during the game, including which tasks they find difficult, what they enjoy, when they become tired, etc.

5 Present Approaches and Initial Findings

We consider facing the challenges identified above – and reducing them to a manageable complexity – as largely a question of managing students' expectations on the agent's abilities. By that we mean to frame and guide the interaction with the student in such a way that, ideally, the shortcomings and knowledge gaps of the agent never become a critical issue for achieving an effective communication. As mentioned, one way of constraining expectations by visual means in the initial stage, was to opt for a cartoon-like character which carry less associations to the full capabilities of a "real" human being.

Similarly, carefully designed dialogue strategies may be used to frame expectations on what the agent is able to converse about, for example by using expressions and syntax corresponding to that of the target students' social group. Having the agent represent a member of a certain age group (say an 11-year-old for the interaction with 12-14-year-olds) is one approach to constraining the range of students' initiatives to likely conversational topics by both visual and conversational means [cf. 5]. In the case of a TA, it also makes sense to represent the agent as slightly younger and less advanced than the actual students, yet intelligent, in order to bring forward its "teachable" affordances [8, 11].

It seems clear that the EnALI guidelines we work from require further specification when it comes to actual implementation. Also "students' expectations" need to be clarified and concretized for different aspects of the interaction: What could students expect from an 11-year-old, virtual teachable peer? Can it share interesting views and comments? Does it appear outgoing, funny, natural, strange, cocky? To get a grip on these and related questions, we initiated an iterative design process involving representatives from the target user group in the following five steps:

1. The researchers compiled a preliminary sketch of the agent's personal profile, including a visual representation and an intentionally unspecific description of the agent's personality and interests (see 2.2 and Fig. 2).
2. The sketch was evaluated using focus groups of 4-5 target students (N=20), who were asked to review the profile, give feedback and suggest conversational topics with the agent. Importantly, the students expressed what they desired that a conversational agent of this type be like, in terms of exhibited "personality" traits.
3. Following student input, a testing procedure was conducted with a revised agent profile, such that students (N=7) worked in pairs on different computers, where one student acted as the agent in simulated off-task conversation. The dialogue logs were collected and used to identify conversational topics (e.g. "music", "school", "friends") as indicative of what an actual student–agent conversation would comprise.
4. Prototype 1 of the agent was developed, using AIML, focusing on off-domain topics and a simple mixed-initiative dialogue strategy. Students (N=38) tested the prototype in the context of playing the game by chatting with the agent on topics of their own

choice. As a follow-up, we used a questionnaire based upon the SASSI (Subjective Assessment of Speech System Interfaces) [26]. The questionnaire listed 25 statements relating to the subjective experience of using the system, for example "I rather play the game than talk to the agent" and "It felt natural to talk to the agent", rated on a 7-point Likert scale. The "personality" of the agent prototype was formally measured using a Swedish translation and adaptation of the TIPI (Ten Item Personality Inventory) test, which is based on the Big Five (or Five-Factor Model) personality dimensions [19].

5. Prototype 2 of the agent was developed on basis of corpus analysis of the dialogue logs and additional focus groups, expanding the agent's range of conversational topics and dialogue history. The prototype was tested on students (N=43) using the same procedure as in testing of the first prototype, using the same questionnaires.

5.1 Preliminary Conclusions Relating to the Agent's Knowledge Profile, Social Profile and Off-Task Engagement

From analysis of the SASSI questionnaires the most indicative item for students enjoying the conversation was "I had many things to talk to the agent about". This item strongly correlated to "I liked talking to the agent" ($r=0,84$, $p<0,01$) and "It was fun talking to the agent" ($r=0,77$, $p<0,01$). Still, the results indicated large individual differences that call for further investigation. The results from the TIPI test, which show the change in scores from prototype 1 to prototype 2 compared to the desired personality ratings proposed by the focus groups, are summarized in Table 2.

Table 2. Student mean ratings of how they desired and perceived the personality traits of the agent, including the difference between prototypes 1 and 2, as assessed on a 7-point Likert scale (1 = not at all pronounced, 7 = very pronounced)

Personality trait	Desired	Proto. 1	Proto. 2	Diff
Extraversion	6,00	4,33	4,99	+1,01
Agreeableness	6,04	4,39	4,98	+1,06
Emotional Stability	5,54	4,91	4,95	+0,59
Openness to Experience	5,29	4,16	4,42	+0,87
Conscientiousness	5,25	3,94	4,05	+1,20

Some clues as to what makes an engaging conversation with the agent were given by relating the agent's preferred knowledge areas (interests) to its desired personality. Expanding the agent's range of conversational topics seems a fruitful direction to take for achieving positive student experiences and engagement. In this respect, the developments point in the right direction, as the agent's personality is becoming more expressive and clear to the students. The initial findings from the iterative design-implementation-evaluation process referred above also point to some preliminary conclusions for meeting the implementation challenges of designing the agent's knowledge profile and social profile, as well as affecting students' engagement in off-task conversation.

The agent's knowledge profile. Some of the personal interests and possible off-task conversational topics listed by the researchers in the preliminary sketch (step 1 above) were confirmed, such as wanting to talk about friends and school in general. But there were also some presumed topics that students did not bring up, such as film and traveling. The focus groups consistently added topics of interest to the list: sports, music, and computer games. Following prototype 1 and analysis of this new corpus, revealed a number of additional common topics: food, animals and particular school subjects. Existing topics were also refined with subtopics, for example "music" with artists and songs and "school" with teachers. The following iteration (prototype 2) resulted in only one additional topic: television. A more detailed, qualitative analysis of the collected dialogue corpus remains to be done, including an analysis of possible gender differences as to preferred topics of conversation.

The agent's social profile. The focus groups confirmed that the agent should be friendly, curious, eager to learn, and like school, which aligns well with previous findings. However, it was added that the agent should not be too polite, but express some 'attitude'. This is one example of how a particular user group can differ from general design guidelines, and again emphasizes the importance of involving target students in the design. The specific design decision of age and gender in relation to the target group, we assume, would have particular effect on students' tendencies to abuse the agent (e.g. a cartoon-like agent representing an 11-year-old boy for male students would seem a less likely target of abuse than the attractive, adult female agent used in a previous study addressing this issue [42]). Naturally, there are more explicit means of setting students' expectations on the interaction, such as having the agent express that it is not interested in certain topics or has no knowledge about them.

Off-task engagement. A proper analysis of engagement in on-task versus off-task conversation (and the subdivision into off-domain and on-domain topics) will need to await further development of the conversational module. As to regulating the time spent on off-task interactions, we plan to have the agent take the initiative to conversation at particular intervals during game-play, and state that "now, the break is over, we need to return to the game" if too much time is devoted to social chatting (e.g., more than 5 minutes at a time). Besides, the student may deny an offer to chat with the agent. To our knowledge, such a mixed-initiative approach to student-agent interactions is unusual, and its effects on engagement in a game setting have not been previously evaluated in the literature.

6 Overall Conclusions and Future Work

One important lesson from the EnALI framework as a whole is that equal attention should be kept to the learner and the agent, implying that it would be fruitless to work on the agent out of context or lacking knowledge about the intended students (e.g. 12-14-year-olds) and the way they communicate. This makes a complexity of challenges that must also be taken into account for anyone in search for "straight" solutions to resolving agent-student conflicts of the types we discuss here. That is why we actively involve students from the target group at an early stage of the design process, and do not draw any definite conclusions by relying solely upon the framework as to the design decisions we make. At present, there appears a notable gap between what the students think the agent *should be* like and what they actually *perceive* it is like. This has led us to plan at least two more iterations and prototypes, targeting more advanced dialogue strategies and manipulation of verbally expressed personality traits.

Our approach of iteratively and continuously refining the design, until an effective and engaging learning environment is reached, corresponds to the explicit objectives stated by the EnALI for extending the framework. Student input, through questionnaires and observations, continuously serves as a basis for design decisions taken by the researchers and developers. Actual learning effects of selected implementations will be assessed using a research design with matched school classes playing the math game during math class (i.e. "experimental groups") compared to classes not playing the game, but following the regular educational curriculum (i.e. "control groups"). Theoretically, we aim at refining the ways in which specific, goal-relevant cognitive processes are triggered by social interventions.

We close this paper by proposing three planned studies into the effects on learning, attitudes and engagement in relation to the concerns we have raised. These are:

1. The value of off-task conversation. Evaluating effects of using the off-task conversational module in the game, compared to game-play without it.

2. Differential effects of gender representations. Evaluating differential effects for both sexes of students when using more or less pronounced masculine and feminine (including androgynous) agent looks. This will address the agent-student relation in terms of power (as reflected in dialogue) and the student's role as a teacher (as reflected in the agent's competence level).

3. Effects of types of conversational content. Exploring the effects from manipulating linguistic styles (e.g. the length of utterances, lexical and syntactical choices) and introducing, versus not introducing, content such as anecdotes and small talk relating to mathematics.

Acknowledgments. This research project was supported by the Knowledge Foundation (KK-stiftelsen). The authors would like to thank the two anonymous reviewers for constructive comments on a previous version of this paper.

References

1. Bandura, A.: Social foundations of thought and action: a social cognitive theory. Prentice-Hall, Englewood Cliffs (1986)
2. Bandura, A.: Self-efficacy: The foundation of agency. Lawrence Erlbaum Associates Publishers, Mahwah (2000)
3. Bargh, J.A., Schul, Y.: On the cognitive benefits of teaching. Journal of Educational Psychology 72, 593–604 (1980)
4. Baylor, A.L.: Promoting motivation with virtual agents and avatars: role of visual presence and appearance. Philosophical Transactions of the Royal Society B 364, 3559–3565 (2009)
5. Baylor, A., Rosenberg-Kima, R., Plant, E.: Interface agents as social models: The impact of appearance on females' attitude toward engineering. In: CHI 2006 Extended Abstracts on Human Factors in Computing Systems, pp. 526–531. ACM, New York (2006)
6. Bickmore, T.: Relational Agents: Effecting Change through Human-Computer Relationships. Ph.D Thesis, Media Arts & Sciences, Massachusetts Institute of Technology (2003)

7. Biswas, G., Katzlberger, T., Brandford, J., Schwartz, D.: TAG-V.: Extending intelligent learning environments with teachable agents to enhance learning. In: Moore, J.D., Redfield, C.L., Johnson, W.L. (eds.) Artificial Intelligence in Education, pp. 389–397. IOS Press, Amsterdam (2001)
8. Blair, K., Schwartz, D.L., Biswas, G., Leelawong, K.: Pedagogical agents for learning by teaching: Teachable Agents. Educational Technology Special Issue on Pedagogical Agents 47, 56–61 (2007)
9. Branham, S., De Angeli, A.: Special issue on the abuse and misuse of social agents. Interacting with Computers 20, 287–291 (2008)
10. Brewer, M.: A dual process model of impression formation. In: Wyer, R., Srull, T. (eds.) Advances in Social Cognition 1, pp. 1–36. Erlbaum, Hillsdale (1988)
11. Chase, C., Chin, D., Oppezzo, M., Schwartz, D.: Teachable Agents and the Protégé Effect: Increasing the Effort Towards Learning. J. Sci. Educ. Technol. 18, 334–352 (2009)
12. Chen, J., Shohamy, D., Ross, V., Reeves, B., Wagner, A.D.: The impact of social belief on the neurophysiology of learning and memory. In: Annual Meeting of the Society for Neuroscience, San Francisco, CA (2009)
13. Davachi, L., Mitchell, J.P., Wagner, A.D.: Multiple routes to memory: Distinct medial temporal lobe processes build item and source memories. Proceedings of the National Academy of Science 100(4), 2157–2162 (2003)
14. De Angeli, A., Brahnam: I hate you! Disinhibition with virtual partners. Interacting with Computers 20, 302–310 (2008)
15. Deutsch, M.: The resolution of conflict: Constructive and destructive processes. Yale University Press, New Haven (1973)
16. Doering, A., Veletsianos, G., Yerasimou, T.: Conversational Agents and their Longitudinal Affordances on Communication and Interaction. Journal of Interactive Learning Research 19, 251–270 (2008)
17. Dowling, C.: Intelligent agents: some ethical issues and dilemmas. In: Proceedings of AIC 2000, pp. 28–32. ACS, Canberra (2000)
18. Dweck, C.S.: Self-theories: Their Role in Motivation, Personality and Development. Psychology Press, Philadelphia (1999)
19. Gosling, S.D., Rentfrow, P.D., Swann Jr., W.B.: A very brief measure of the big five personality domains. Journal of Research in Personality 37, 504–528 (2003)
20. Gulz, A.: Benefits of virtual characters in computer based learning environments: claims and evidence. International Journal of Artificial Intelligence in Education 14, 313–334 (2004)
21. Gulz, A.: Social enrichment by virtual characters – differential benefits. Journal of Computer Assisted Learning 21, 405–418 (2005)
22. Gulz, A., Haake, M.: Design of animated pedagogical agents – a look at their look. International Journal of Human-Computer Studies 64, 322–339 (2006)
23. Gulz, A., Haake, M.: Challenging gender stereotypes using virtual pedagogical characters. In: Goodman, S., Booth, S., Kirkup, G. (eds.) Gender Issues in Learning and Working with Information Technology: Social Constructs and Cultural Contexts, pp. 113–132. IGI Global, Hershey (2010)
24. Gulz, A., Lindström, P., Haake, M., Pareto, L., Sjödén, B.: A Teachable Agent Based Game Affording Collaboration and Competition – Evaluating Math Comprehension and Motivation (2010) (submitted)
25. Haake, M., Gulz, A.: A look at the roles of look & roles in embodied pedagogical agents – a user preference perspective. International Journal of Artificial Intelligence in Education 19, 39–71 (2009)

26. Hone, K.S., Graham, R.: Towards a tool for the subjective assessment of speech system interfaces (sassi). Natural Language Engineering 6, 287–305 (2000)
27. Johnson, D., Johnson, R., Holubec, E.: Cooperation in the Classroom, 6th edn. Interaction Book Company, Edina (1993)
28. Kim, Y., Wei, Q., Xu, B., Ko, Y., Ilieva, V.: MathGirls: Increasing Girls' Positive Attitudes and Self-Efficacy through Pedagogical Agents. Paper presented at 13th International Conference on Artificial Intelligence in Education. AIED, Los Angeles (2007)
29. Lindegaard, G., Dudek, C.: What is this evasive beast we call user satisfaction? Interacting with Computers 15, 429–452 (2003)
30. Lindström, P., Gulz, A., Haake, M., Sjödén, B.: Matching and mismatching between the pedagogical design principles of a math game and the actual practices of play. Journal of Computer Assisted Learning (in press)
31. Maddux, J.: Self-Efficacy: The Power of Believing You Can. In: Snyder, C.R., Lopez, S.J. (eds.) Handbook of Positive Psychology, pp. 277–287. Oxford University Press, New York (2005)
32. Norman, D.: Emotion & design: attractive things work better. Interactions 9, 36–42 (2002)
33. Pareto, L.: The Squares Family: A Game and Story based Microworld for Understanding Arithmetic Concepts designed to attract girls. In: World Conference on Educational Multimedia, Hypermedia and Telecommunications 1, pp. 1567–1574 (2004)
34. Pareto, L., Schwartz, D., Svensson, L.: Learning by guiding a teachable agent to play an educational game. In: Proceeding of the International Conference on Artificial Intelligence in Education, pp. 662–664. IOS Press, Amsterdam (2009)
35. Plant, E.A., Baylor, A.L., Doerr, C., Rosenberg-Kima, R.: Changing middle-school students' attitudes and performance regarding engineering with computer-based social models. Computers & Education 53, 209–215 (2009)
36. Reeves, C., Nass, B.: The Media Equation. Cambridge University Press, New York (1996)
37. Schank, R., Neaman, A.: Motivation and failure in educational simulation design. In: Forbus, K., Feltovich, P. (eds.) Smart Machines in Education, pp. 37–69. AAAI/MITPress, Menlo Park, CA (2001)
38. Tractinsky, N., Katz, A., Ikar, D.: What is beautiful is usable. Interacting with Computers 13, 127–145 (2000)
39. Veletsianos, G.: Contextually relevant pedagogical agents: Visual appearance, stereotypes, and first impressions and their impact on learning. Computers & Education (in press)
40. Veletsianos, G., Miller, C.: Conversing with Pedagogical Agents: A Phenomenological Exploration of Interacting with Digital Entities. British Journal of Educational Technology 39, 969–986 (2008)
41. Veletsianos, G., Miller, C., Doering, A.: EnALI: A Research and Design Framework for Virtual Characters and Pedagogical Agents. Journal of Educational Computing Research 41, 171–194 (2009)
42. Veletsianos, G., Scharber, C., Doering, A.: When Sex, Drugs, and Violence Enter the Classroom: Conversations between Adolescent Social Studies Students and a Female Pedagogical Agent. Interacting with Computers 20, 292–302 (2008)
43. Vygotsky, L.S.: Mind in Society: The development of higher psychological processes. Harvard University Press, Cambridge (1978)
44. Wang, N., Johnson, W.L., Mayer, R.E., Rizzo, P., Shaw, E., Collins, H.: The politeness effect: Pedagogical agents and learning outcomes. International Journal of Human Computer Studies 66, 96–112 (2008)
45. Zimmerman, B.J., Schunk, D.H.: Self-regulated Learning and Academic Achievement. Lawrence Erlbaum Associates Publishers, Mahwah (2001)

Vocabulary Treatment in Adventure and Role-Playing Games: A Playground for Adaptation and Adaptivity

Frederik Cornillie, Igor Jacques, Stefan De Wannemacker,
Hans Paulussen, and Piet Desmet

Itec - Interdisciplinary research on Technology, Education and Communication,
K.U. Leuven Campus Kortrijk
E. Sabbelaan 53, B-8500, Kortrijk
{frederik.cornillie,igor.jacques,stefan.dewannemacker,hans.paulussen,
piet.desmet}@kuleuven-kortrijk.be
http://www.kuleuven-kortrijk.be/itec

Abstract. Although there is pedagogical support for using computer adventure and role-playing games in order to learn a second language (L2), commercial games often lack the instructional qualities for making their language comprehensible for learners. In an interdisciplinary approach, this paper proposes a technique for adapting in-game text in order to teach L2 vocabulary, grounded in research on second language acquisition and adaptive learning systems.

Keywords: adventure games, role-playing games, second language acquisition, vocabulary learning, input enhancement, adaptive learning systems, adaptivity.

1 Introduction

Computer adventure games, such as *(Colossal) Adventure*, *Zork* and *Hugo's House of Horrors*, and role-playing games (RPGs) such as *Finaly Fantasy* and *Divinity 2: Ego Draconis*, are genres of digital games in which the player assumes some kind of role in an interactive fictional story. The game unravels mainly through the player's interaction with a preprogrammed plot rather than through physical challenge. The game mechanism is centered around dialogues with computer-driven non-player characters (NPCs), often in the form of point-and-click dialogue trees or through (relatively) free text input, which is then parsed by the programme. RPGs differ from adventure games in that they generally also have episodes of physical action, and have rather complex internal economies and points management systems, but both genres share a focus on story and language, which makes them examples of interactive fiction.

Computer adventure games and RPGs may facilitate the acquisition of a second language (L2). Besides their presupposed effects on learner motivation, they have some characteristics that are interesting from an instructional point

S. De Wannemacker, G. Clarebout, P. De Causmaecker (Eds.): ITEC 2010, CCIS 126, pp. 131–146, 2011.

of view. Adventure games have for some time been associated with the development of communicative fluency [1]. First and foremost, they do not focus on language as such, i.e. they create immersive contexts in which language must be put to use, and in which grammar and vocabulary are subordinate to the functions, uses and pragmatics of language. Adventure games, in other words, entail a focus on meaning, rather than a focus on isolated linguistic forms, which creates possibilities for the incidental learning of a L2. This puts these games on a par with contemporary language teaching methodologies such as task-based language teaching [2]. Secondly, computer adventure games stimulate discovery learning, because rather than being confronted with the linguistic forms and functions as such, learners have to experiment with and unveil the underlying structures. Thirdly, adventure games generate opportunities for collaborative learning, either in physical spaces or on-line, as learners may discuss with peers the next or previous moves in the story. And finally, activities in and outside these games stimulate the integrative development of the four language skills of reading, listening, writing and speaking.

Despite generally enthusiastic accounts, commercially available adventure games and RPGs are being criticized from a pedagogical point of view (see e.g. [3]). Although these games undeniably contain the most language of all game genres, the kind of language and the way language is presented is not always favourable for second language learners. First, the language is often exotic, archaic or highly complex, making it only accessible to (highly) advanced learners. Secondly, learners have little control over the presentation of language in often long-winded conversations and cut-scenes, so that they cannot pause, go back, focus on linguistic specificities or request more information. This takes away many opportunities for *noticing*, one of the most fundamental requirements for language acquisition [4]. Thirdly, conversations and descriptions often refer to objects or events that are no longer present at the time of speaking or citing, which at least increases cognitive load, and may even counter the argument that games stimulate situated cognition. Next, many adventure games, and RPGs in particular, have a limited interface for language learning, often in the form of point-and-click dialogues, which requires little, if any, production from the learner. While this kind of interface may be perfect for beginning language learners, who require a lot of (comprehensible) input, this is limiting to more advanced learners. Moreover, the input-oriented reading and writing activities around which these games are centered are a mismatch with the alleged benefit for developing communicative fluency [5]. And finally, the choices which learners have to make in adventure games and RPGs often have little consequence on the narrative, which discredits to a great extent the statement that these games promote learning by discovery. If learners are to learn from (feedback on) the choices they make, e.g. in branched conversations, the choices presented have to be distinct and meaningful [6,7].

Most of these arguments against commercially available adventure games and RPGs, however, can be refuted if the technological frameworks within which these games are developed can be exploited and modified for creating explicitly educational games. In recent years, adapting existing games and creating new ones has become significantly more feasible. A number of commercially available games such as *The Sims* allow adaptation of the in-game language through third-party customization tools [7]. Further, some game developers, such as the makers of the RPG *Never Winter Nights 2* [8], *The Elder Scrolls* [9] or *Spore Galactic Adventures* [10], release simplified or even full-fledged development toolkits of commercial off-the-shelf games. This allows players to make their own versions (so-called *mods* or modifications) of favoured games, so as to create games with educational content. And, finally, some independent game engines (such as *Unity* [11]) are being released under open-source licenses. As a result, all aspects of game design may become subject to pedagogical requirements, including changes to the (graphical) user interface.

The purpose of this paper is to provide a rationale for treating L2 vocabulary in computer adventure games and RPGs in order to promote the incidental acquisition of vocabulary, and to propose a methodology, both conceptual and architectural, for the adaptation of in-game text on the basis of pedagogy-driven adaptivity. The focus is on incidental acquisition of vocabulary as part of the development of L2 skills, rather than on explicit teaching of L2 vocabulary.

We will first review empirical research on vocabulary acquisition in digital games, and discuss this in light of second language acquisition (SLA) theory. Then, we will look at the research concerning adaptive learning systems. In the next section, we will propose a method for treating vocabulary adaptively in point-and-click style RPGs and put forward a possible software architecture with which to realize the presented approach. We will also discuss some limitations and put forward some methods by which our approach can be evaluated.

2   L2 Vocabulary Acquisition in Digital Games

In adventure games and RPGs, vocabulary learning is incidental, as it inherently forms part of reading, listening or (to a more limited extent) writing practice. Vocabulary instruction in these games, then, is an example of a fully contextualizing technique [12]. Although the pace of vocabulary learning in adventure games and RPGs will be considerably lower than in semi- or decontextualizing techniques, such as rote memorization of word lists, it clearly has some advantages. First, unfamiliar words crop up in a context that might have already activated mental schemata for these new words, allowing for better entrenchment in the memory. Second, concrete lexical items can be presented in auditive and textual or graphical form simultaneously. This stimulates the auditive as well as the visual processing channel, and is hypothesized to improve learning [13]. For textually presented materials, moreover, words may be highlighted in the transcript, so that they may be noticed and become candidates for intake. And finally, the meaning of unknown lexical items can be given when the learner requests it, for instance by clicking on a word presented on the screen or by formulating in writing a request for clarification or simply by repeating the word followed by a question mark. This allows for negotiation of meaning, which is beneficial for vocabulary acquisition. Negotiation of meaning is not always practical in classroom situations, where large groups may inhibit individualized instruction, and where negotiation might interfere too much with the communication task at hand [14, pp. 64-66].

2.1   Empirical Research on Vocabulary Learning in Games

A handful of studies suggest that adventure games and RPGs may indeed be beneficial for L2 vocabulary acquisition. An experimental study investigated which target language structures in the text-based adventure game *Colossal Adventure* were more likely to be acquired by 84 Chinese-speaking students of English in their first year of higher education [15]. On the basis of the in-game text, three groups of linguistic structures were identified: programme-specific vocabulary (e.g. nouns and verbs which are highly relevant to the game's narrative and flow), prepositions of place, and conditional structures. The study found that learners only improved significantly on programme-specific lexical items. The researchers conjectured that these items were retained better because learners needed to master them in order to make progress in the game, while knowing prepositions of place and conditionals was less crucial, although they too were frequent.

In a second experimental study with 15 English-speaking students of German, a control group read a story in German, while students in the experimental group worked their way through the same story in an interactive text-based adventure format [16]. Students in both conditions of this design-based study were required to afterwards complete homework assignment based on the vocabulary presented in the story, and to write a short essay. Learners who were exposed to the game were found to have stronger established mental schemata of the lexical content and thus better vocabulary retention. Also, it is noteworthy that the students who worked with the print-based materials expressed more confidence in their instructional treatment than the students in the gaming condition.

A small-scale observational study found that 2 beginning Swedish learners of English (aged 9 and 11) improved their vocabulary knowledge by playing a computer adventure game accompanied by L1 translations of target words [17]. Interestingly, on a lexical posttest they restricted all possible meanings of a word that had occurred in the game to meanings that could be related to the game, even if other meanings were equally plausible. This may imply that they had established strong form-meaning links for the words encountered in the game.

Two consistent experimental studies in the simulation game *The Sims* observed that ESL learners who, while playing the game, could rely on supplementary materials such as vocabulary lists, exercises and cultural notes had significantly higher scores on post-treatment vocabulary tests than learners who only played the game [18,19]. Students also found the supplementary materials useful, in particular the vocabulary activities. These findings indicate that adaptation and elaboration of in-game language may facilitate vocabulary acquisition. Even though *The Sims* is not an adventure game or RPG *pur sang*, this observation seems to be applicable to all game genres.

Finally, one study demonstrated that video games may increase extraneous cognitive load, and as such impede vocabulary acquisition [20]. This experimental study examined the effect of interactivity on L2 vocabulary noticing and recall. 80 Japanese students of English were paired based on similar language and game playing proficiency. One student played an English language music video game, while the second student simultaneously watched the game and listened to the auditive cues. Students who only watched the game remembered significantly more vocabulary both on immediate and delayed posttests. The results imply that the kind of interactivity of this game, which was to a large extent based on speed and rhythm, increased extraneous cognitive load, which impedes vocabulary acquisition.

2.2   Discussion in Light of SLA Theory

A theoretical framework that is often quoted in connection with incidental vocabulary learning in games, but which is rarely discussed in detail, is the Involvement Load Hypothesis [21]. This hypothesis states that retention will be higher for vocabulary that is acquired incidentally if the involvement induced by the task is high. The construct of involvement is defined along three dimensions: need, search and evaluation. *Need* is the motivational factor in the construct of task-induced involvement load, and occurs when the learner is urged by some kind of future achievement, e.g. when comprehension of a specific word is required for task completion. *Search* is a cognitive dimension and signifies the attempt to find the meaning of an unknown L2 word or trying to find the L2 word form expressing a concept, e.g. by consulting a dictionary. *Evaluation*, finally, is another cognitive aspect of involvement and is the extent to which a learner has to compare a specific word or word meaning with other words or meanings. These three factors can be simultaneously present in a task and can promote retention. Hence, the challenge is to design tasks that have a high involvement load, and to simultaneously take into account the learner's profile. It makes little sense, for instance, to have a learner evaluate words which are way beyond his or her proficiency level.

The first study summarized above [15] provides some evidence that the involvement load factor *Need* influences L2 vocabulary acquisition in games. Words which are crucial for task (or quest) completion may thus be better retained than words which are not. The dimension *Search* may also be conducive to vocabulary learning in games. Tasks which urge the learner to focus on and query specific formal or semantic features of L2 vocabulary, e.g. by highlighting specific words, or by giving the learners the option to view hidden lexical explanations [18,19], stimulate *noticing* and exhibit a higher search factor than tasks which do not. Research makes it clear that not all kinds of game interactivity can stimulate noticing and search [20]. Finally, adventure games and RPGs can create contexts that display a high factor of *Evaluation*. Text-based adventure games often provide lengthy descriptions of physical objects or events, upon which players have to evaluate which word is appropriate in this context, so that the action may continue. It is plausible that the presence of this factor results in higher retention in games that stimulate learners to produce vocabulary through retrieval [16]. Also, games seem to stimulate learners to make strong form-meaning connections in the mental lexicon, so that they may exclude other equally plausible meanings for given word forms outside of the gaming context [17].

2.3 Challenges for Language Learning

A first problem with adventure games and RPGs is that they contain significant amounts of often fairly complex text, which players tend to skip. It is advisable that these texts are adapted, so that opportunities for noticing may be created. Secondly, a significant drawback of point-and-click style RPGs for vocabulary acquisition is their limited output practice. Simply clicking on a word and attending to the input does not guarantee that a word will be learned, and being able to guess the meaning from a context does not ensure that the word has been acquired. A measure for checking whether a word is productively known which can be employed in a game is that the learner has to produce it in meaningful contexts, which requires some form of input signal from the learner, either textual or in speech. Finally, games usually provide a certain amount of freedom to the learner, which reduces the chances that learners will encounter the words in the order which the instructional designer has foreseen, or sometimes a learner may even never be exposed to the words which the materials developer had in mind. This calls for careful planning in the development of the learning materials, or it requires run-time planning by an adaptive software component which makes sure that words are presented at the right time in the learning process.

3 Adaptive Learning Systems

Adaptive learning systems are designed to take into account individual differences between learners. At first researchers of artificial intelligence, education and psychology designed Intelligent Tutoring Systems (ITS), substituting a human teacher for an automated interactive tutor while still providing highly personalized instruction. Later it was noticed that tutors taking full control of the learning process somehow restrain the explorative behaviour of the learner, which gave rise to a new type of learning environments that puts more emphasis on learner control [22]. Educational Adaptive Hypermedia Systems (EAHS), named after the hypermedia paradigm of the nineties, stimulate learners to navigate through the learning content and manage their own learning process [23]. Personalization in this approach is mainly to be found in hyperlinks that are automatically personalized based on the learner's knowledge, behaviour and inferred intentions. Although ITS and EAHS inherently start from another point of view on learner control, they share a lot of characteristics. In the following overview, simularities and differences of both approaches are described. Next, a synopsis on existing software technologies for adaptive learning systems is given. In the final subsection, a number of challenges is listed.

3.1 ITS versus EAHS

ITS typically have a very specific focus in terms of knowledge domain and target group so as to allow to provide highly optimized one-to-one instruction. Based on close learning process monitoring, continuous assessment and sometimes even plan recognition they can adjust guidance, support and feedback, which results in highly interactive learning environments. While most ITS research focuses on guidance through and between problems, EAHS try to steer the selection of the next learning topic in the right direction. The learning material in EAHS often consists of standalone text or mediatized pages about a learning topic, which are connected through hyperlinks. In contrast to ITS, which tend to direct the learning process completely, EAHS facilitate learner control by giving navigation recommendations, which stimulates explorative learning behaviour. Some EAHS also adapt the page content to the learner, for instance with conditional text [23]. Adaptivity in both approaches is realized through often hardcoded rules which reflect the instructional strategy and operate on the content metadata as well as on a learner model. The latter holds individual characteristics such as knowledge, learning and cognitive style, affective state, (learning) goals, learning history, behaviour, preferences, and background. As especially knowledge is important, ITS also hold a representation of the target instructional domain (domain model) containing all knowledge elements and their interdependencies. This model together with the learner model serves as input for accurate knowledge tracing which is crucial to provide personalized instruction or learning control. To manage the learner model ITS mostly operate on sophisticated stochastic techniques such as Bayesian Networks [24,25] and Fuzzy Logic [26], while in EAHS implementations tend to be simpler [24] often estimating knowledge based on rules of thumb such as the number of times a topic was visited or the time spent interacting with a topic [27]. Note that this is just a stereotyped comparison. In reality, many systems adopt strengths from both approaches.

3.2   Existing Adaptive Learning Systems

In the last decades many adaptive learning systems have been designed. Especially ITS are plenty in number (e.g. [28,29,30]), but they tend to be focused on concrete cases in a specific instructional domain, which often results in standalone software that limits reusability and integration with other technologies. By contrast, EAHS implementations are often reusable and extendable because of their lower complexity and domain independent nature, such as AHA [27], which offers a versatile open source platform and INSPIRE [31], an adaptive hypermedia framework providing a customizable amount of learner control. Currently, a great deal of technological research in adaptive learning focuses on the design of generic adaptive learning system architectures, thereby trying to integrate and stimulate reuse of different technologies and educational methodologies. In the literature, a shift may be noticed from architectures focusing on once-only personalized retrieval and recommendations of educational content (e.g. [32,33]), towards more complex architectures combining ITS and EAHS principles for steering and guiding the learning process either from a more global level, e.g. the GRAPPLE project [34] or from more nearby, e.g. [35,36,37,38].

3.3   Challenges for Adaptive Learning Systems

The literature suggests that combining the strengths of both ITS and EAHS can result in very effective learning environments [35,39]. However, despite decades of inter-disciplinary research on adaptive learning systems, most implementations stayed in a prototype phase. We believe one of the reasons for this is the lack of clearly identified ready-to-use adaptivity strategies. Although for some content types possible adaptations have been identified (e.g. [23] for web based), educational content exists in many other different shapes (e.g. mini-games, plain text, ...) and each time targets a very specific instructional domain, resulting in many different potential adaptations and adaptivity strategies. Therefore, we think it is useful to formally look for and identify different types of adaptations of a particular content shape, to develop instructional strategies which steer these adaptations and to test these strategies by performing evaluation studies in the instructional context they are designed for.

4   A Method for Treating Vocabulary in Adventure Games and RPGs

The objective of this design proposal is to provide a mechanism for treating L2 vocabulary incidentally in point-and-click style adventure games and RPGs that contain an orthographic transcription of the game's conversations. The use case described below mainly focuses on the aspect of *noticing*. Even though it may be argued that a lot of L2 acquisition in games happens implicitly, it is generally accepted in the SLA literature that a certain amount of (explicit) attention to formal aspects of an L2 is required, so that new (word) forms may be noticed by learners, and become candidates for intake [40]. Still, it seems important that the player should not feel disturbed by information not asked for or by information that draws him away from playing the game. For this reason, we would like to inject into the game-playing experience short periods that allow (but don't compel) the learner to focus on formal aspects of an L2 while he or she attends to the meaning of the language that emerges from the game.

4.1   Use Case

In point-and-click adventure games and RPGs, the game typically consists of a number of quests which the player has to complete. In order to obtain information on these quests, the player('s) character (PC) has to engage in conversation with non-player characters (NPCs). The player is presented with a series of utterances spoken by the NPC, each of which is followed by a number of options which the player can click. When clicked, such an option becomes a response from the PC to the NPC. Each response leads to a reply from the NPC. In this way, a pre-programmed tree of PC and NPC utterances is translated into a linear dialogue with a reasonable amount of choice and freedom for the player.

We propose to exploit this mechanism of choice for having the L2 learner request more information on difficult, unknown or domain-specific words in the

NPC utterance. For each such a word in an NPC's utterance, an option is added to the list of PC options (e.g. "What do you mean by WORD X?") which, when clicked, leads to a short but natural explanation of that word, spoken by the NPC (e.g. "Well, WORD X is when you ...") (see Fig. 4.1). This way of explaining words is e.g. to be found in the COBUILD monolingual learner's dictionary [41].

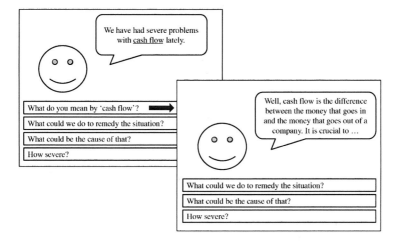

Fig. 1. Mockup showing help option for vocabulary in a conversation with an NPC, and subsequent elaborated input

The proposed technique is of course very similar to glossing words in a reading text, but it is interwoven with the game-playing experience. Moreover, by having an NPC give the explanation of a specific word, rather than a pop-up dictionary, these explanations are examples of what has become known as *elaboration*, i.e. the ways in which native speakers (NSs) modify their discourse in order to make it comprehensible for non-native speakers (NNSs). Elaborations also occur very frequently in teacher-learner and learner-learner talk, and are highly valued in communicative language teaching methods because they focus on the communicative task rather than on the L2. In natural communication, elaboration typically occurs during an interaction known as *negotiation of meaning*, when NSs and NNs (or L2 learners) are focused on achieving communication while working together on a task. An increasing number of studies suggest that negotiation of lexical content leads to more learning than learning without negotiation [14, pp. 64-65]. Evidently, for L2 learning, negotiated elaboration of L2 word forms is superior to lexical simplification, because the new words are not removed from authentic texts. Negotiated elaboration has become a central component in task-based approaches to language teaching, and pleas have been made for including them in e-learning contexts as well [42].

In addition to inserting an option for each word in a L2 dictionary, words which are assumed to be rather difficult for the learner given his or her current vocabulary proficiency level can be highlighted in the NPC utterance (e.g. in a bold font), in order to increase the chances of 'noticing', which is the starting point for language acquisition. A starting point for a reasonable estimation of lexical difficulty is word frequency. Frequency counts on the basis of large corpora can classify words in frequency bands. Normally the first band of most frequent words of a particular language consists of function words and a limited set of common content words, which allow to understand most of a text. Lower frequency bands contain less widely used words, and more specialised vocabulary. These frequency bands can then be related to learner proficiency on a probabilistic basis. If a learner knows most of the words in a certain frequency band, then he or she can be understood to have a vocabulary proficiency related to that frequency band.

Obviously, the limited nature of the learner's interaction with the game's text (i.e. through point and click) prevents measuring lexical knowledge reliably, because tracking clicks is a measure of learner behaviour and not knowledge, but this knowledge can be dynamically assessed in the game at least in a partial way. If a learner requests the meaning of a word which he or she is supposed to know (on the basis of probabilistic estimations of the learner's vocabulary proficiency), then the action of clicking might imply a lack of knowledge of that lexical level, and the level of the learner may be adjusted downwards. E.g. if the learner has proficiency level x, and he or she clicks on a vocabulary item in the frequency band x-3, then the probability of the learner having level x may be decreased, and the probability of him or her having level x-3 can be increased. The learner may then be redirected to educational activities outside of the game (e.g. in a learning management system) or inside the game (in the case of an educational game containing activities designed for learning). In a learning management system, this can be done through traditional vocabulary exercises which are assessed ; in an educational game, a meaningful side-quest can be presented in which the learner must decide in a conversation with an NPC upon the meaning of a word, or upon the specific form for a given word meaning. When the learner re-enters the main game quest, vocabulary items will be highlighted in accordance with his or her adjusted proficiency level.

4.2   System Architecture

In the following section, we will outline a high level system architecture for implementing the use case. Our technique of adapted utterances in conversation turns provides a personalized way of learning support, while still leaving full control to the learner. In this way, it bears a large resemblance with the individualized recommendations in EAHS, but we will use a specific methodology to construct the learner model. We will entrust the proposed technique to an external learning system service, which is dedicated to the adaptation of the clickable options in a conversation turn. This service will pass on the required educational adaptations to the game through an API provided by the game, and will rely on other services of the learning system (e.g. assessment service) in order to get information based on which it can tune the utterances of a conversation turn to the learner and the game situation. For the realization of our adaptive technique we will employ the architecture pictured in Fig. 2. The learning system on the right-hand side of the architecture contains a database and implements some services: a logging service, a conversation adaptation service, a vocabulary exercise service, and an assessment service. The game client is equipped with an API through which conversation turns can be adapted on the basis of content external to the game, an API through which additional vocabulary exercises can be sent to the game, and a logger which will inform the learning system logging service at run-time about what happens in the game (e.g. what support was asked for).

For the use case described above, the learning system database needs to keep four types of information. First of all, a representation of each conversation turn in the game is needed, in which all present words or linguistic expressions are described. We assume this information is generated beforehand, but the process of obtaining the conversation turns and preprocessing them could also be done at run-time. Secondly, it will contain information on the vocabulary domain to be learned. Next to the L2 dictionary, it will keep estimations on difficulty (based on frequency counts) for each lexical item. Thirdly, it contains a representation of the current knowledge of the learners. We will use knowledge estimations for each vocabulary domain complemented with reliability parameters, which can be interpreted through Item Response Theory (IRT [43], a Bayesian network like technique) by involving levels of difficulty for the words of the vocabulary domain. Additonally, we will also keep a collection of vocabulary exercises which can be launched in the game when there are indications that the learner's learning process gets stuck or when detailed assessment is required. When the player starts a specific conversation in the game, the Conversation Adaptation Service will adapt that conversation to the vocabulary proficiency level of the learner. This conversation will then be passed back to the game through the Conversation Adaptation API. The adaptivity strategy behind this personalization will be interchangeable and will decide on (1) which utterances will be added to each conversation turn, (2) which words in each utterance will be highlighted and how (e.g. italic, bold, coloured etc.), and (3) it will compose the exact elaborated input which the NPC should return in case the learner clicks on an utterance asking for support. The Assessment Service keeps a one-dimensional estimate of the learner's knowledge for each vocabulary domain (e.g. business English, nursing etc.) in a way conformable to IRT. Information on the frequency bands and the number of times help has been requested for each lexical item will be stored and will serve as input for heuristics which will adjust the estimations of knowledge (as explained in 4.1). As stated earlier, we don't expect interactions with the point-and-click dialogue system to lead to knowledge estimations, but only to contribute to them. Therefore, to keep an accurate account of a learner's knowledge level, the Vocabulary Exercise Service will be used which will once in a while redirect the learner to easily assessable vocabulary exercises in unobtrusive windows on top of the game scene. Hereby we assume there is a mechanism in the game to pop up a series of sequential vocabulary exercises (e.g. in Flash), which can be operated through an API of the game, here called Pop-up Excercise API.

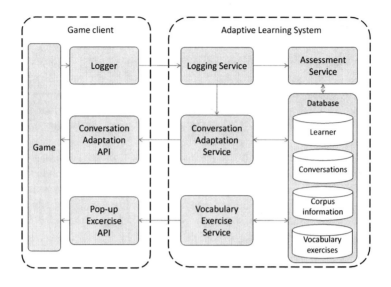

Fig. 2. System architecture realizing the adaptations

Our approach is in accordance with the generic architectures for centralized adaptive learning systems discussed in 3.2, and adopts their advantages. First, our service providing adapted conversation turns can easily make use of existing assessment and management services of the learning system thereby increasing quality, integration and maintainability, and facilitating the development of the service. Secondly, it enables the reuse of the service's implementation with renewed RPG versions or even with other RPGs, at least if the latter implement the required API. Alternatively, we could embed the adaptivity logic in the game by making use of game specific tools or frameworks (e.g. scripting code), but that would hinder the reuse of our implementation. Compromise solutions include automatic generation of scripting code based on game independent adaptivity logic, but this method increases development and maintenance costs as scripting languages often change and most games require different generators. Third, putting the decision making process on educational adaptations in a dedicated learning environment outside of the game allows new educational adaptive strategies to be tested and implemented very efficiently, and can ignore the specificities of implementation on the game client. Finally, our approach allows easy integration of existing educational services, such as the included Vocabulary Exercise Service, which could make use of existing software offering traditional (e.g. web-based) learning objects.

4.3   Limitations

A number of limitations to this approach must be noted. First, if it were to be applied to commercial games, this technique will probably only work with advanced learners. It is suggested that vocabulary can be treated incidentally if at least 95 % is known of the running words in the input a learner is focusing on [14]. Thus, a detailed lexical analysis of a commercial game's text is first of all required. Second, it is important to know that elaboration alone will most likely not account for all learning. A blend of several vocabulary instruction techniques is required, even if the focus is on meaningful communicative tasks [14, p. 65]. Third, this technique can only be applied to NPC utterances, as it would be awkward if a player requested the meaning of a word which his PC utters himself. However, it is to be expected that most of the new words are spoken by NPCs, since it is generally they who present the learner (the PC) with new contexts and assignments. Next, the presented approach assumes game conversation turns to be adaptable at run-time. This presupposes the presence of a game API, which may be hard to put in place since most commercial games do not offer such way of external control. Finally, until now, we have assumed elaborations of PCs and NPCs to consist only of transcriptions. However, if the utterances provided by the game are also spoken, then the elaborations require a corresponding auditive representation. To this end, one can fix all possible vocabulary elaborations and record them in advance, but this would take a lot of time and so would be a burden to the development of content. Alternatively, one can use text-to-speech software to dynamically create the speech.

4.4 Suggestions for Future Work

Several aspects of our proposal can be evaluated. First, we will optimize our initial implementation by some small-scale experiments. Thereby, we will fix what words will be highlighted and how, and we will optimize the presented assessment techniques especially ensuring that the heuristics which adjust the knowledge level converge well. Once the architecture is up and running, we can perform experimental studies to answer various research questions some of which are discussed below. The logging data resulting from these experiments can also be employed to fine-tune the assessment service afterwards.

If the objective is to evaluate whether the lexical elaborations provided by the NPCs lead to more vocabulary learning, a study can be set up with one experimental condition in which learners have the option to request lexical help, and a control condition in which the learners just play the game. Although it is likely that learners who get help will learn more vocabulary, as previous studies have demonstrated [18,19], topics such as the usage of in-game help options and their effect on vocabulary learning as well as on gaming experience warrant futher research.

One step further would be to compare two experimental conditions, one of which provides optional elaborations, while the other one forces learners to request the elaborations, e.g. by inserting a separate player turn containing only help options for the next turn, rather than showing the help options together with the other options for the PC. As one study has shown before, mandatory usage of lexical help will lead to more learning [18], but in the context of gaming this might compromise the playing experience.

What could also be evaluated is whether highlighting novel words in the NPC utterances leads to more requests for help, and whether this correlates with vocabulary learning. As a previous study in a hypertext environment has pointed out, language learners tend to demonstrate less conscious and less focused clicking (so-called 'happy clicking') when links are made more visible or salient [44]. Point-and-click conversations in games seem particularly apt to stimulate such a behaviour, especially in RPGs, where players might be eager to get to their next exploration or combat phase as quickly as possible.

5   Conclusion

In this paper, we introduced a mechanism for increasing the chances of noticing vocabulary in dialogue-based RPGs or adventure games. A game player who is not familiar with a word uttered by his virtual conversation partner can request an elaboration of that word which will subsequently be provided by the computer character. We reviewed the literature on vocabulary acquisition in digital games in the light of second language acquisition, and situated our technique in this context. We also outlined the relevant research concerning adaptive learning systems, and observed a trend towards centralized learning system architectures. For the realization of our proposal, we put forward and explained such an architecture. Finally, we pointed at some limitations, and proposed directions for empirical research after the system has been built.

Acknowledgments. The research activities that have been described here were funded by the Interdisciplinary Institute for Broadband Technology (IBBT) in the context of the LLINGO project: Language Learning in an Interactive Game Environment.

References

1. Baltra, A.: Language Learning through Computer Adventure Games. Simulation & Gaming 21(4), 445–452 (1990)
2. Ellis, R.: Task-based language learning and teaching. Oxford Applied Linguistics. Oxford University Press, Oxford (2003)
3. DeHaan, J.: Learning Language through Video Games: A Theoretical Framework, An Evaluation of Game Genres and Questions for Future Research, pp. 229–239. Inter-Disciplinary Press, Oxford (2005)
4. Schmidt, R.W.: The role of consciousness in second language learning. Applied Linguistics 11(2), 17–46 (1990)
5. Jordan, G.: Exploiting Computer-Based Simulations for Language-Learning Purposes. Simulation & Gaming 23(1), 88–98 (1992)
6. Hubbard, P.: Interactive Participatory Dramas for Language Learning. Simulation & Gaming 33(2), 210–216 (2002)
7. Purushotma, R.: Commentary: you're not studying, you're just.... Language Learning & Technology 9(1), 80–96 (2005)
8. Atari: Never winter nights 2 gold. [PC DVD-ROM], Obsidian Entertainment (2008)

9. The elder scrolls construction set wiki, http://cs.elderscrolls.com/constwiki/ (An open-content website)

10. Electronic Arts. Spore galactic adventures. [PC DVD-ROM] (2009)

11. Unity Technologies. Unity. A multiplatform game development tool, http://unity3d.com/

12. Oxford, R., Crookall, D.: Vocabulary learning: a critical analysis of techniques. TESL Canada Journal 7(2), 9–30 (1990)

13. Paivio, A.: Mental representations: a dual coding approach. Oxford University Press, Oxford (1986)

14. Nation, I.S.P.: Learning Vocabulary in Another Language, 2009 edn. Cambrige Univeristy Press, Cambridge (2001)

15. Cheung, A., Harrison, C.: Microcomputer Adventure Games and Second Language Acquisition: A Study of Hong Kong Tertiary Students, pp. 155–178. Multilingual Matters, Clevedon (1992)

16. Neville, D.O., Shelton, B.E., McInnis, B.: Cybertext redux: Using digital game-based learning to teach L2 vocabulary, reading, and culture. Computer Assisted Language Learning 22(5), 409–424 (2009)

17. Palmberg, R.: Computer games and foreign-language vocabulary learning. English Language Teaching Journal 42(4), 247–252 (1988)

18. Miller, M., Hegelheimer, V.: The SIMs meet ESL. Incorporating authentic computer simulation games into the language classroom. Interactive Technology and Smart Education 3(4), 311–328 (2006)

19. Ranalli, J.: Learning English with "The Sims": Exploiting Authentic Computer Simulation Games for L2 Learning. Computer-Assisted Language Learning 21(5), 441–455 (2008)

20. DeHaan, J., Michael Reed, W., Kuwada, K.: The effect of interactivity with a music video game on second language vocabulary recall. Language Learning & Technology 14(2), 74–94 (2010)

21. Laufer, B., Hulstijn, J.H.: Incidental vocabulary acquisition in a second language: the construct of task-induced involvement. Applied Linguistics 22(1), 1–26 (2001)

22. Kay, J.: Learner control. User Modeling and User-Adapted Interaction 11(1-2), 111–127 (2001)

23. Brusilovsky, P.: Methods and techniques of adaptive hypermedia. User Model. User-Adapt. Interact. 6(2-3), 87–129 (1996)

24. Brusilovsky, P.: Adaptive hypermedia. User Modeling and User-Adapted Interaction 11(1-2), 87–110 (2001)

25. Conati, C., Gertner, A., Vanlehn, K.: Using bayesian networks to manage uncertainty in student modeling. User Modeling and User-Adapted Interaction 12(4), 371–417 (2002)

26. Kavcic, A.: Fuzzy user modeling for adaptation in educational hypermedia. IEEE Transactions on Automatic Control 34(4), 439–449 (2004)

27. De Bra, P., Aerts, A., Berden, B., de Lange, B., Rousseau, B., Santic, T., Smits, D., Stash, N.: Aha! the adaptive hypermedia architecture. In: HYPERTEXT 2003: Proceedings of the Fourteenth ACM Conference on Hypertext and Hypermedia, pp. 81–84. ACM, New York (2003)

28. Eskenazi, M., Heilman, M.: Language learning: Challenges for intelligent tutoring systems. In: Proc. Workshop on Intelligent Tutoring Systems for Ill-Defined Domains, Proc. 8th Int. Conf. Intelligent Tutoring Systems (2006)

29. Mitrovic, A.: An intelligent sql tutor on the web. Int. J. Artif. Intell. Ed. 13(2-4), 173–197 (2003)

30. Chipman, P., Olney, A., Graesser, A.C.: The autotutor 3 architecture: A software architecture for an expandable, high-availability ITS. In: WEBIST 2009, pp. 466–473 (2005)
31. Papanikolaou, K.A., Grigoriadou, M., Kornilakis, H., Magoulas, G.D.: Personalizing the interaction in a web-based educational hypermedia system: the case of inspire. User Modeling and User-Adapted Interaction 13(3), 213–267 (2003)
32. Tsai, K.H., Chiu, T.K., Lee, M.C., Wang, T.I.: A learning objects recommendation model based on the preference and ontological approaches. In: Proc. Sixth Int Advanced Learning Technologies Conf., pp. 36–40 (2006)
33. Costello, R., Mundy, D.P.: The adaptive intelligent personalised learning environment. In: Proc. Ninth IEEE Int. Conf. Advanced Learning Technologies, ICALT 2009, pp. 606–610 (2009)
34. Grapple, a generic responsive adaptive personalized learning environment (June 2010), http://www.grapple-project.org
35. Nicholas, A., Martin, B.: Merging adaptive hypermedia and intelligent tutoring systems using knowledge spaces. In: Nejdl, W., Kay, J., Pu, P., Herder, E. (eds.) AH 2008. LNCS, vol. 5149, pp. 426–430. Springer, Heidelberg (2008)
36. Chen, S., Zhang, J.: The adaptive learning system based on learning style and cognitive state. In: KAM 2008: Proceedings of the 2008 International Symposium on Knowledge Acquisition and Modeling, Washington, DC, USA, pp. 302–306. IEEE Computer Society Press, Los Alamitos (2008)
37. Rani, S.J., Ashok, M.S., Palanivel, K.: Adaptive content for personalized e-learning using web service and semantic web. In: Proc. Int. Conf. Intelligent Agent & Multi-Agent Systems, IAMA 2009, pp. 1–4 (2009)
38. Khalid, S.U., Basharat, A., Shahid, A.A., Hassan, S.: An adaptive e-learning framework to supporting new ways of teaching and learning. In: Proc. Int. Conf. Information and Communication Technologies, ICICT 2009, pp. 300–306 (2009)
39. Conati, C.: Intelligent tutoring systems: new challenges and directions. In: IJCAI 2009: Proceedings of the 21st International Joint Conference on Artifical Intelligence, pp. 2–7. Morgan Kaufmann Publisers Inc., San Francisco (2009)
40. DeKeyser, R.: Implicit and explicit learning, ch. 11, pp. 313–348. Blackwell Publishing Ltd, Oxford (2005)
41. Sinclair, J., Knight, L.S., Clari, M., Macaulay, A., Saeton, M. (eds.): Collins COBUILD advanced learner's English dictionary, 5th edn. Collins, London (2006)
42. Doughty, C.J., Long, M.H.: Optimal psycholinguistic environments for distance foreign language learning. Language Learning & Technology 7(3), 50–75 (2003)
43. Kim, S.-H., Baker, F.B. (eds.): Item Response Theory: Parameter Estimation Techniques, 2nd edn. Statistics: A Series of Textbooks and Monographs. CRC Press, Boca Raton (2004)
44. De Ridder, I.: Visible Or Invisible Links: Does the Highlighting of Hyperlinks Affect Incidental Vocabulary Learning, Text Comprehension, and the Reading Process? Language Learning and Technology 6, 123–146 (2002)

Author Index